THE GREEK TRAGEDY
IN NEW TRANSLATIONS

GENERAL EDITORS
Peter Burian and Alan Shapiro

EURIPIDES: Herakles

EURIPIDES

Herakles

Translated by
TOM SLEIGH
With Introduction and Notes by
CHRISTIAN WOLFF

OXFORD
UNIVERSITY PRESS

2001

OXFORD
UNIVERSITY PRESS

Oxford   New York
Athens   Auckland   Bangkok   Bogotá   Buenos Aires   Calcutta
Cape Town   Chennai   Dar es Salaam   Delhi   Florence   Hong Kong   Istanbul
Karachi   Kuala Lumpur   Madrid   Melbourne   Mexico City   Mumbai
Nairobi   Paris   São Paulo   Shanghai   Singapore   Taipei   Tokyo   Toronto   Warsaw

and associated companies in
Berlin   Ibadan

Copyright © 2001 by Oxford University Press, Inc.

Published by Oxford University Press, Inc.
198 Madison Avenue, New York, New York 10016

Oxford is a registered trademark of Oxford University Press

Library of Congress Cataloging-in-Publication Data
Euripides.
[Hercules. English]
Herakles / Euripides / translated by Tom Sleigh, with introduction and notes by
Christian Wolff.
p.   cm. — (The Greek tragedy in new translations)
Includes bibliographical references.
ISBN 0-19-513116-9
1. Hercules (Greek mythology) — Drama.   I. Sleigh, Tom.   II. Wolff,
Christian, 1934–   III. Title.   IV. Series.
PA3975.H5 S58   2000
882'.01 — dc21

00-020348

9 8 7 6 5 4 3 2 1
Printed in the United States of America

EDITORS' FOREWORD

"*The Greek Tragedy in New Translations* is based on the conviction that poets like Aeschylus, Sophocles, and Euripides can only be properly rendered by translators who are themselves poets. Scholars may, it is true, produce useful and perceptive versions. But our most urgent present need is for a *re-creation* of these plays — as though they had been written, freshly and greatly, by masters fully at home in the English of our own times."

With these words, the late William Arrowsmith announced the purpose of this series, and we intend to honor that purpose. As was true of most of the volumes that began to appear in the 1970s — first under Arrowsmith's editorship, later in association with Herbert Golder — those for which we bear editorial responsibility are products of close collaboration between poets and scholars. We believe (as Arrowsmith did) that the skills of both are required for the difficult and delicate task of transplanting these magnificent specimens of another culture into the soil of our own place and time, to do justice both to their deep differences from our patterns of thought and expression and to their palpable closeness to our most intimate concerns. Above all, we are eager to offer contemporary readers dramatic poems that convey as vividly and directly as possible the splendor of language, the complexity of image and idea, and the intensity of emotion of the originals. This entails, among much else, the recognition that the tragedies were meant for performance — as scripts for actors — to be sung and danced as well as spoken. It demands writing of inventiveness, clarity, musicality, and dramatic power. By such standards we ask that these translations be judged.

This series is also distinguished by its recognition of the need of nonspecialist readers for a critical introduction informed by the best recent scholarship, but written clearly and without condescension.

Each play is followed by notes designed not only to elucidate obscure references but also to mediate the conventions of the Athenian stage as well as those features of the Greek text that might otherwise go unnoticed. The notes are supplemented by a glossary of mythical and geographical terms that should make it possible to read the play without turning elsewhere for basic information. Stage directions are sufficiently ample to aid readers in imagining the action as they read. Our fondest hope, of course, is that these versions will be staged not only in the minds of their readers but also in the theaters to which, after so many centuries, they still belong.

A NOTE ON THE SERIES FORMAT

A series such as this requires a consistent format. Different translators, with individual voices and approaches to the material in hand, cannot be expected to develop a single coherent style for each of the three tragedians, much less make clear to modern readers that, despite the differences among the tragedians themselves, the plays share many conventions and a generic, or period, style. But they can at least share a common format and provide similar forms of guidance to the reader.

1. *Spelling of Greek names*

Orthography is one area of difference among the translations that requires a brief explanation. Historically, it has been the common practice to use Latinized forms of Greek names when bringing them into English. Thus, for example, Oedipus (not Oidipous) and Clytemnestra (not Klutaimestra) are customary in English. Recently, however, many translators have moved toward more precise transliteration, which has the advantage of presenting the names as both Greek and new, instead of Roman and neoclassical importations into English. In the case of so familiar a name as Oedipus, however, transliteration risks the appearance of pedantry or affectation. And in any case, perfect consistency cannot be expected in such matters. Readers will feel the same discomfort with "Athenai" as the chief city of Greece as they would with "Platon" as the author of the *Republic*.

The earlier volumes in this series adopted as a rule a "mixed" orthography in accordance with the considerations outlined above. The most familiar names retain their Latinate forms, the rest are transliterated; -*os* rather than Latin—*us* is adopted for the termination of masculine names, and Greek diphthongs (such as Iphigen*eia* for Latin Iphigenia) are retained. Some of the later volumes continue this practice, but where translators have preferred to use a more consistent practice of transliteration or Latinization, we have honored their wishes.

2. *Stage directions*

The ancient manuscripts of the Greek plays do not supply stage directions (though the ancient commentators often provide information relevant to staging, delivery, "blocking," etc.). Hence stage directions must be inferred from words and situations and our knowledge of Greek theatrical conventions. At best this is a ticklish and uncertain procedure. But it is surely preferable that good stage directions should be provided by the translator than that readers should be left to their own devices in visualizing action, gesture, and spectacle. Ancient tragedy was austere and "distanced" by means of masks, which means that the reader must not expect the detailed intimacy ("He shrugs and turns wearily away," "She speaks with deliberate slowness, as though to emphasize the point," etc.) that characterizes stage directions in modern naturalistic drama.

3. *Numbering of lines*

For the convenience of the reader who may wish to check the English against the Greek text or vice versa, the lines have been numbered according to both the Greek text and the translation. The lines of the English translation have been numbered in multiples of ten, and these numbers have been set in the right-hand margin. The notes that follow the text have been keyed to the line numbers of the translation. The (inclusive) Greek numeration will be found bracketed at the top of the page. Readers will doubtless note that in many plays the English lines outnumber the Greek, but they should not therefore conclude that the translator has been unduly prolix. In most cases the reason is simply that the translator has adopted the free-flowing norms of modern Anglo-American prosody, with its brief-breath- and emphasis-determined lines, and its habit of indicating cadence and caesuras by line length and setting rather than by conventional punctuation. Other translators have preferred to cast dialogue in more regular five-beat or six-beat lines, and in these cases Greek and English numerations will tend to converge.

Durham, N.C.   PETER BURIAN
Chapel Hill, N.C.   ALAN SHAPIRO
2000

CONTENTS

HERAKLES

INTRODUCTION

Herakles is a figure rarely found in Athenian drama playing a tragic role. Darker aspects of his life appear briefly in Homer. In the *Iliad* Achilles evokes him as prototypical of a hero's tragic mortality (18.117–18). Odysseus, visiting the world of the dead, meets Herakles' ghostly double who is haunted by his former life of misery (*Odyssey* 11.601–26). More commonly Herakles is characterized by his fantastic exploits, by his geniality and by an immense capacity for endurance capped by final successes. This most famous and ubiquitous hero appears in the worlds of fairy tale and legend, close to the gods in the ancient time of the heroes, but also in the aristocratic world of the wellborn who achieve successes in their competitive life; and, as one can see in religious cult and dramatic comedy, he can be found to be a comfortably familiar figure of everyday life. Euripides' play brings something of all these facets of the hero together to tragic effect, which may well be something like a dramatic experiment, bold and risky. This introduction will look at the play's structure; how the hero is characterized by his deeds and by his family relations, human and divine; at the role of the gods and the place of religious practice in the play's action; and, emerging out of all these, the role of poetic performance as the play itself draws our attention to it.

I

The play, while centrally focused on a single heroic figure (as rarely in Euripides[1]), is marked by an apparently irregular and sometimes

---

1. Medea and possibly Hecuba, in the plays named after them, are comparable. The single male heroic figure of Herakles is quite unusual among Euripides' surviving plays (the youths Hippolytos and Ion, in the plays named after them, and Pentheus in *Bakkhai* come closest).

violently surprising dramatic movement. This movement or structure, as in all Attic tragedies, is made out of a number of plot elements or actions, variously combined and transformed. At the start both hero and his family are in mortal danger. The family—old stepfather, wife and three boy children—are on stage, huddled around an altar of Zeus the Savior, a spectacle that signals the familiar plot element of supplication. The helplessness of Herakles' family is occasioned by his absence on the last of his famous Twelve Labors (the descent to Hades to bring back its monstrous guardian dog Cerberus), that is, Herakles' confrontation with death. The supplication plot involves the helpless and weak—often women, children, the old—taking refuge at an altar, putting themselves under a god's protection. Religious and political issues are at stake: Will the deity of the altar provide efficacious protection? Will the human community where the altar is located protect and enforce the altar's sanction? In this instance the human community of Thebes has been at war with itself.[2] A tyrannical usurper, Lykos, has emerged after assassinating the city's legitimate ruler, Kreon, father of Megara, Herakles' wife, as well as her brothers. In a spirit recalling contemporary political realities,[3] Lykos will not put religious scruple above his political self-interest. He means to destroy what remains of his enemies; the children represent future avengers and legitimate claimants to his power. In response to Lykos' threat to remove them violently from the altar's protection, Herakles' wife persuades her reluctant, determinedly hopeful father-in-law, Amphitryon, that the family should give itself up voluntarily for execution and so maintain a semblance of dignity. She also gets from Lykos a concession, to be allowed to dress the children for death. This briefly delays the execution, gets Lykos temporarily off stage and makes possible Herakles' all but too late arrival. The suppliant action, ending in apparent failure, is followed by another set of actions, whose outlines are again drawn

I would like to acknowledge here my debts to many scholars who have written about this play. A particular debt is owed to Helene Foley's *Ritual Irony: Poetry and Sacrifice in Euripides* (Ithaca 1985). My sense of the play's ending is close to Pietro Pucci's strong reading in "Survival in the *Herakles*," an appendix in his *The Violence of Pity in Euripides' Medea* (Ithaca 1980). Anne Michelini's chapter on *Herakles* in her *Euripides and the Tragic Tradition* (Madison 1987) is also valuable.

2. The civil war in the background of the play's action is a contemporary realistic, not mythic, feature of the play. Intense internal political conflict was endemic to a number of Greek city-states, not least among them Athens where there was a bloody, though short-lived, oligarchic coup in 411 B.C.E. We have no firm date for *Herakles*, but there are grounds for putting it close to the time just preceding that coup, somewhere between 417 and 414.

3. The breakdown of traditional, religiously sanctioned values is vividly expressed by Thucydides, famously at 3.82–84. The great majority of supplications reported by the historian were ineffective or violated.

from a standard repertoire: return (*nostos*) of the hero, rescue or recovery (*sôteria*) and a revenge.[4] The suppliant story and the rescue dovetail, but the efficacy of the altar's divine sanction is left in doubt. The savior Herakles arrives after the altar is abandoned; Megara says, "He'll be more help to us than Zeus" (680). As for the communal, political support normally expected for the altar's sanction, it has been notably absent.

The rescue is quickly sealed with the revenge killing of Lykos, a double reversal (what Aristotle in the *Poetics* calls *peripeteia*) in which the lives of the helplessly endangered noble family of Herakles are saved, and the dominating criminal usurper Lykos is overthrown and killed. The initial plot structures are played out and the drama might be finished.[5] This halting of the dramatic movement—not yet half the time of the play has elapsed—is unsettling and might cause what has happened to feel, in retrospect, rather sketchy and perfunctory (though much of importance has been said that remains to be addressed). In parallel with these actions the chorus of old men, citizens of Thebes and supporters of the legitimate royal household, sing and dance their songs, about old age and its weaknesses—their utter helplessness, which links them to Herakles' family, about Herakles' great past achievements, the Twelve Labors—manifestations of extraordinary endurance and victorious strength; and, as rescue and vengeance are done, about the power of youth and the vindication of the gods' justice. Their weakness is offset by the power of their poetic performance and their declaration of enduring dedication to it.

Their last triumphant song is instantly followed by the appearance above the house roof[6] of two divine figures, and they are abjectly terrified by these unexpected presences looming over them. Divine appearances are normal at the beginning of a play, where they serve as prologue, explaining and foretelling; and at a play's conclusion, where they mark part of a resolution and complement it with prophecy. This abrupt appearance of deities in the middle of the play is a very unusual

4. These patterns are found, for example, in the *Odyssey*, Aeschylus' *Libation Bearers* and the *Electra* plays of Euripides and Sophocles. In each of these there is also a recognition scene, perhaps suggested in this play by Megara's momentary hesitation in recognizing Herakles (669–70). Revenge in these works involves some kind of deception and ambush, not Herakles' usual mode of action: his initial impulse to use outright force is modified, fitting the pattern (727–37, 750–69).
5. As it is after the sequence of these patterns in, for example, Sophocles' *Electra*.
6. A not uncommon but still striking theatrical effect. Since Iris is said to be coming from and returning to Olympos, that is, on high, the actor playing her part is most likely to have been suspended from the "machine" or crane and swung up and in and out of view above the roof of the stage building representing Herakles' house. Lyssa will enter the house as Iris swings away. She is thus more likely to have stepped out on the roof (from behind the building) and gone off the same way, as if down into the building.

structural feature, an enactment of disruption. Instead of a divine epilogue we get a prologue for a new sequence of events. The dissonances of this moment are underscored by the nature of the deities themselves: two maiden figures, one, Iris (which means rainbow), familiar messenger of the Olympian gods, the other, Lyssa (which means frenzy, raging madness), belonging to a more ancient pre-Olympian world; the first complacently vindictive, the other paradoxically restrained and judicious: two maiden goddesses representing and acting for the mature, enraged and wronged wife of Zeus, Hera. The divine incursion foretells and sets in motion a new action—divine punishment,[7] the gods' version of a revenge action.

A further, more astonishing *peripeteia* is set in motion. Herakles in his madness becomes the agent of what he had come to prevent. What he had for a moment achieved, a return, a rescue and a revenge, is just as quickly, in the case of the first two, reversed, and, in the case of the latter, revenge, is made to recoil on himself. The initial action of suppliancy too, first elided by Herakles' initial rescue, is dreadfully replayed. The children when prepared for execution are presented, with bitter irony, as sacrificial victims: "Where's the priest and his knife?" (594) This marked the apparent failure of the play's opening suppliant action. Now the undoing of the rescue is marked by Herakles' going mad in the process of performing a sacrificial ritual, a formal, technical procedure that involves the slaughtering of animals, intended to purify him after the revenge killing of Lykos and his men. Both the earlier supplication and now the madness-inducing sacrifice take place at an altar of Zeus (59–60, 1269). In the face of Herakles' madness Amphitryon supplicates (1269) and the third, last surviving child assumes the traditional suppliant posture (1292–93) only to become Herakles' final sacrificial victim (1302).

However, the divine "prologue" does not quite prepare us for two further actions. The first is recognition (what Aristotle called *anagnôrisis*), a learning of what is really the case and who one really is.[8] Herakles, with Amphitryon's help, comes to realize what he has done; he makes an initial recovery from mad delusion and self-alienation. But the process of coming to understanding continues as Herakles wrestles with an identity now threatened after extreme disaster, in desperate

---

7. Other examples are found in Aeschylus' *Prometheus Bound*, Sophocles' *Oedipus the King* and Euripides' *Hippolytus* and *Bakkhai*.

8. Sophocles' *Oedipus the King* dramatizes an outstanding example. This recognition has behind it the traditional notion of knowing oneself as a human being, as mortal and subordinate vis-à-vis the gods. This may be what is meant when Iris says, "It's time he [Herakles] learnt the depths of Hera's rage" (1087).

need of recovery or perhaps redefinition. He first intends to commit suicide to salvage his honor. Then, as the play moves to its conclusion, that decision is reversed (a kind of *peripeteia*, again). Linked with this process is a second action of rescue. Herakles' arrival to rescue his family came for them unexpectedly, in the face of utter despair. Now the Athenian hero Theseus appears unexpectedly, though his recent rescue by Herakles in Hades had been reported—as the cause of Herakles' near-fatal delay in coming to rescue his family (784–85). Herakles' rescue came just in time, only to be utterly negated. Theseus, supposing he was coming to offer help against Lykos, is too late for that, and so perhaps too late to have forestalled the occasion for Herakles' madness. This second rescue, like the process of *anagnôrisis*, is complex. Theseus will offer a refuge in Athens for the hero who is now a polluted killer of his own family and thus forbidden to live in Thebes. But first Herakles must be persuaded to live. Again there is a structural replay: Herakles' wife Megara had persuaded the family to give up hope of rescue and accept death nobly as, she says, Herakles would have wished it. So now Herakles argues for suicide as the honorable response to the condition of his life, which he regards as beyond all hope of redemption. Megara and the family were rescued, as it were, in spite of themselves, and then destroyed. Herakles—and here the story pattern shifts[9]—changes his mind. With Theseus' help he persuades himself to go on living. (Megara had persuaded Amphitryon to give up hope, and he had changed his mind in doing so.) Herakles decides to accept the saving help of Theseus, and by making that decision he becomes again, with Theseus, a rescuing figure—now of himself.

These transmuted actions of recognition and rescue finally conclude with yet one more *peripeteia*, which frames the whole play. The plot was set in motion because of Herakles' absence. His return brings a victory, saving his family and home, and perhaps the city of Thebes. This is followed by defeat and destruction of family and (literally) his house. Coming home Herakles makes himself homeless; his return brings about his departure in exile. The powerful, victorious hero finally leaves the stage defeated and broken, so weak he has to be held up by Theseus. Yet Theseus *is* there to hold him up and take him to another, adopted home in Athens, which is also the home of Euripides' dramatic production.

---

9. In Sophocles' *Aias* the great warrior hero, like Herakles, is made mad and humiliated by the gods. Aias, adhering to an older, individualistically sustained heroic code, resists the appeals of those closest to him and commits suicide. On the issues involved see Sumio Yoshitake, "Disgrace, Grief and Other Ills: Heracles' Rejection of Suicide," *Journal of Hellenic Studies* 114 (1994): 135–53.

Euripides' play has often been considered structurally flawed, lacking in coherence and unity. In fact it has underlying it a powerful, almost relentlessly repeating and transforming structural procedure. It is not the play's structure that lacks cohesion, it is the whole story, generating the destabilizing transformations and reversals, contained within the play's structure, that threatens a larger coherence of meaning.

II

Herakles is the central figure around whom questions of meaning are raised. One can trace them along two interconnected lines throughout the play: Herakles' traditional, heroic achievements, principally his famous Twelve Labors, and, what may well be a distinctively Euripidean innovation, a various—both mythic and realistically intimate—representation of Herakles' family relationships.

Herakles undertakes the labors traditionally[10] as expiation for killing his children in a fit of madness. But at the start of our play we hear that the labors are performed as payment to Eurystheus, Herakles' cousin and ruler of the region around Argos, so that Amphitryon, once native there and now in exile, might be able to return.[11] This arrangement is said to have been instigated by Hera or brought about by necessity, a doubled motivation, both mythic and abstract, that introduces us from the start to the play's characteristically multilayered perspectives on its action: mythic or legendary, abstract and rationalistic, contemporaneous—historical and political, and personal or psychological. It is, then, Herakles' own individual choice to undertake the labors on behalf of his human foster father.

The first labors we hear about are two of the best known, killing the Nemean Lion and destroying the many-headed Hydra. But we hear about them from Herakles' enemy Lykos who debunks and trivializes them as mythic exaggerations irrelevant to the uses of the human community, the city-state (*polis*). Lykos also goes on to attack Herakles' iconic weapon, the bow, as a coward's, good only on one's individual behalf, in contrast to the shield and spear of those fighting with true

10. The traditions are fluid. The majority of the labors are essentially folktale material where motivations are a mix of the mysteriously necessary and arbitrary. Tasks are imposed on the (young) hero so that he may prove himself. Herakles' exploits extend into his maturity, which gives him more weight as an individualized heroic figure. On Herakles' traditional story material and its development see, for example, Walter Burkert, *Structure and History in Greek Mythology and Ritual* (Berkeley 1979).

11. The cause of Amphitryon's exile is his killing of Alkmene's father Elektryon who is his uncle as well as his father-in-law. This exile for kin-killing prefigures Herakles' killing of his own family and his subsequent exile. Herakles' labors, which will end in his madness, are contingent on Amphitryon's crime (1562–64).

courage in the close, interdependent combat of hoplite formation. Having the politically and morally villainous Lykos argue effectively for a positive, communal ideology is a characteristically disconcerting Euripidean move. One might tentatively see it as pre-emptive. From a realistic, contemporary point of view the exaggerations of mythic stories are acknowledged, yet, because this realism is articulated by an otherwise negative figure, symbolic weight and space for the myth's expressive fantasy is still allowed. In defending Herakles' reputation and his use of the bow Amphitryon briefly refers to an association of Herakles with the gods' mythic world, but then, as though admitting the irrelevance of such a world, he adopts the rationalizing terms of Lykos' argument. Amphitryon's arguments, though, thus make Herakles' use of his fabulous bow seem no more than a calculated stance. And, more pointedly, the play's subsequent events will show the drastic inadequacy of such rationalism. Herakles' madness will be the terrible refutation of Amphitryon's claim, at the center of his argument, that the bow makes the hero's autonomy possible. Focus on the bow in this debate also evokes for a moment a facet of Herakles' traditional and archaic character as heroic hunter,[12] a role played at the margins of human communities, in the wild, among threatening, often monstrous animals, in a realm of initiatory activities and stories. Early in the play, however, Herakles' image is drawn into a contemporary political and intellectual world at odds with his older, traditional heroic character. Euripides is asking what can such a hero mean to us [Athenians] now?

After the exchange between Lykos and Amphitryon Herakles' family give up all hope of the hero's return. They despair at what they have been persuaded are the limits of his mythic prowess. In contrast a long choral ode follows, amply filling the mythic space, sung and danced by the old Theban citizens who are deeply loyal to the hero and his family. But they too assume Herakles' death. Their ode is a poetic memorial and a dirge, finely wrought and archaically stylized. The effect is of distancing or at least a retrospective view. The splendor of the labors debunked by Lykos is reasserted. Herakles' exploits are often those of a culture hero who has made the world safer from the forces of a violent wildness—including the alternative community of Amazons against whom he has led an expedition, asserting an ideological hierarchy of differences between Greek male and "barbarian" female warriors. In several labors the hero does the gods service (though

---

12. Archaic examples are Orion and Actaeon. Odysseus in the *Odyssey*, as master of the bow, has assimilated this role, among his others. In his madness Herakles will become hunter again, of his own family (see 1270–72). On the background and implications of Herakles as bowman see Helene Foley, *Ritual Irony*, 169–75.

Athena, often his patron deity, is notably absent: she will appear later in the play). Other labors, the quest for the golden apples and for "the triple-bodied herdsman," called Geryon, as well as for Hades' dog Cerberus, touch on themes of transcendence—immortality and the afterlife. Herakles' involvement with wild forces also leads to their appropriation. He brings them back from his journeys, or a part of them. The lion provides his distinguishing dress, its skin on his back, its head covering his own. The Hydra supplies the poison for his arrows.

The celebration of the labors stops short of the last, the descent to Hades to get Cerberus. The chorus assumes that Herakles has at last failed. But he does return, though, as it turns out, bringing Hades— death—back with him. This last labor is the fulcrum of the play's action. It also makes the intersection of a mythic world, celebrated in the choral song, with the more immediate, realistic world of family and politics visible to the audience on stage. Herakles' absence during the Hades journey triggers the play's initial crisis, his family's dilemma. When he actually appears on stage, Megara has to reassure herself that he's not a ghost, not a "dream flickering in the sun" (674). Amphitryon will even ask if Herakles *really* went to Hades (776). But the final requirement of this labor, that Cerberus be brought to Eurystheus, is not yet fulfilled. This delay in finishing the labor, motivated by Herakles' desire to learn first about his family's condition (783), makes possible his being just in time to save them from Lykos (balancing his being almost too late because of taking the time to rescue his friend Theseus in Hades).

Herakles' first response to what he finds at home also links the traditional, heroic mode, in all its violence—he proposes singlehandedly to tear down Lykos' palace, kill and decapitate him and slaughter all Thebans who had owed him support but failed to provide it—to more familiar realities. Strikingly too the hero measures what he owes his own family against his great mythic achievements. His enemy Lykos had scathingly contrasted the fabulous labors of lion and hydra with the exercise of civic military values. Herakles now contrasts these same two labors (just previously celebrated without qualification by the chorus) with his ability to save his family and his willingness to share the risk of death they have endured on his account. Euripides draws his great hero, unusually, into an intimate domestic family orbit. Herakles asserts an equality among human beings, irrespective of status or wealth, on the basis of a universal human affection for children (799–804).

After Lykos is killed the chorus blend Herakles' older and immediate achievements into a continuing series. Lykos, so far a purely secular figure, joins the company of conquered dangerous beasts (his name, meaning wolf, is, so to speak, activated). But they do not sing about the saving of Herakles' family, insisting instead on the justice done with the downfall of Lykos and the restoration of the city's legitimate authority.[13] They appear to be bracketing the exceptional character of Herakles' assertions about his labors and his love for his children. Perhaps too they are made to anticipate in this way the oncoming demonstration of a highly problematic gap between heroic and domestic values.

In the divine prologue to Herakles' killing of his children Iris links the hero's labors, now called bitter contests, to the infanticide. The labors appear now as a precondition of Herakles' downfall, a heroic achievement allowed so that it can be crushed by greater powers. This prologue indicates, perhaps irreconcilably, both a greater backdrop for Herakles' destiny and his destiny's peculiarly specific conditions. A kind of cosmic or natural hierarchy and balance may be suggested, which the pre-Socratic philosopher Anaximander had called *dikê* (justice or the way of things). Mixed with this, and more explicit, is an archaistic religious perspective in which Herakles is made into an example of the impossibility of human autonomy where divine powers are active. Cosmic nature is suggested by Iris as rainbow and Lyssa as raging turbulence, daughter of Night and Heaven who invokes the Sun (1107). Lyssa uses the language of natural cataclysm, ocean storms, earthquake and thunderbolt (1112–14, see also 1195) to describe what will happen to Herakles. On the other hand, Iris says that the basic distinction of divine and human will disappear if Herakles "doesn't pay the penalty" or "render justice (*dikê*)." Yet Lyssa protests on Herakles' behalf in the name of a normative, social principle of justice based (as was Anaximander's cosmic justice) on the notion of reciprocity. Why is Herakles paying a penalty when he has "brought the wild powers of the earth to heel / And leveled the waves of the storming sea" and "raised up the honors of the gods / That the arrogance of human beings knocked aside" (1099–1102)? She recalls in summary both what the labors achieved and the recent killing of the impious Lykos. No answer is forthcoming to the question she raises. We have instead a raw, unresolved clash of human and divine spheres. Herakles will succumb to what is both cosmic justice and a malevolent power represented in

13. The chorus seem overenthusiastic in this. They call Herakles "our king" (951, cf. 982 and 1049–50). But he says nothing about any claim to rule in Thebes, nor do his traditional stories. The play indicates that Lykos had a substantial following in the city. As the play progresses Thebes' political problems fall into the background; one assumes they remain unresolved. The fortunes of the city and of Herakles' family are kept apart (770–71, 1067–68).

grossly anthropomorphic terms that are also family terms. The high religious law of retribution is embodied in the jealous rage of the offended wife of Zeus.

A divine father is a way of accounting for the extraordinary capacities of heroic figures. But the mix of human and divine is problematic and ambivalent. Herakles' actual, so to speak, biological father is the divine Zeus. His human mother is Alkmene. He has a human foster father in Amphitryon and a divine stepmother in Zeus' wife Hera. Herakles himself is a bastard with no fixed origin in one or another community.[14] There is in this family configuration a pattern of crossing categories: human and divine; male and female; "real," or according to nature and what one might call functional or socially legitimated. At issue too are absence and presence and differing modes of perception and knowing: what is imagined and what is visible, that is, what is represented by language and reported myth and what is dramatically present and witnessed on stage. Thus the "real" father, Zeus, is notably absent, invisible and uninvolved; though much called on he never shows any signs of himself. Alkmene, the biological, human mother, is simply absent.[15] Those who are effectively present are the human substitute father and the divine stepmother. For the events of the drama they are the functional figures, and contrast sharply. Amphitryon (on stage more than any one else in the play) is old and physically helpless, yet in

14. In Athens, starting in the latter part of the fifth century B.C.E., one could only be a citizen with full legal and political rights if both parents were Athenian citizens. From an Athenian viewpoint Herakles is illegitimate not only as the issue of an adulterous union but also because he has one parent from Olympos the other from Thebes. One of his best known cults, in the Attic district of Kynosarges, was reserved exclusively for illegitimately born sons.

15. She must be presumed dead. Usually, as for example in Euripides' *Children of Herakles*, she survives her son. Her absence, on the one hand, highlights and isolates Hera's relationship to Herakles. On the other hand, Alkmene as a potentially supporting female figure is replaced in the earlier part of the play by the strongly independent figure of Megara. References to Alkmene in the play are very few: Lykos and Iris are scornful of her; Herakles refers to her in despair on account of her adultery with Zeus; the chorus invoke her positively only once, as granddaughter of the hero Perseus and mother of Zeus's son.

The configurations of Herakles' family make an interesting comparison with those in Euripides' *Ion*, a play probably produced within a few years after *Herakles*. The young Ion, hero to be, is presumed an illegitimate orphan child. He turns out to be the son of the god Apollo and a human mother, the Athenian queen Kreousa. As in Herakles' case these roles are doubled, but with significant differences. Ion gets a surrogate human father, Xouthos, and has had a foster mother (or stepmother) who is human, though a virgin priestess of Apollo (and as such outside of the normal structures of family and marriage). The human father is deceived into believing that he is the real father (thus averting social and political scandal and disadvantage). The stepmother is a benign and rescuing figure. Apollo, the divine father, though distant, still manages — through others and with some hitches, but in the end successfully — to set things right. In this story of the Athenian ruling house, the female and mother figures are integrated into a final action of rescue and return, even though Kreousa had twice misguidedly tried to kill the child she once did and then did not know was hers.

words and feeling, however imperfectly, an untiring source of support for the hero and his family, sustaining hope at the start, defending Herakles' reputation in argument and, after the catastrophe, helping to guide Herakles gently out of his madness. Herakles will consider him as "true father . . . more than this Zeus!" (1570). Hera, though never visible on stage, is represented by deities who, even if in an archaizing poetic and dramaturgical style that might suggest some ironic distance, make a theatrically indelible impression. Everyone on stage will attribute what they set in motion directly and feelingly to Hera. The human, old, weak, all but helpless yet emotionally supportive figure is countered by a divine, mature, powerful and malevolently destructive one. Each also crosses gender stereotypes. Amphitryon's part suggests a concerned mother's, Hera's a competitive and punishing father's. Herakles himself is represented movingly as father and husband, then both roles are destroyed. Though his descendants, the Herakleidai, are notable in myth and ideological history, here he survives only as a son. He will try to cast himself as father to Theseus after he has lost his own children (1759), but he leaves the stage finally like "a little boat in tow" after Theseus, as his own children had been "the smaller boats" in tow after him (1784, 798).

These confusions and subversions of normal roles are part of the ambivalent fabric of tragedy. The anomalous family structure as well as the relation of hero as hero to family are involved. Herakles' heroic identity requires deeds of force and violence, carried out usually far from home. When he comes home to save his family and be with them, looking forward to passing on his fame, his heroic example, to his sons, the heroic identity, with its divine baggage, will not adapt; it self-destructs. One might suppose that Herakles brings home the craziness that makes great warriors and that his madness, a caricature of his heroic behavior, is psychologically plausible. But the play does not encourage this view. It insists on a more traditional, and more opaque, connection between the gods' power and the hero's identity. What happens to that identity when its victorious course has come to an end, one could say when the gods are done with Herakles, is the burden of the play's last phase.

After the catastrophic killing of his family Herakles determines to kill himself, then he is moved to reconsider and chooses to go on living. This change of mind evolves through a debate with Theseus. In making his argument for suicide Herakles looks back over his life and declares it to have been no life at all, "a botch." (1561) The basis of his family line, irregular from the start, led only to trouble. His famed achievements—he mentions his infant feat of strangling serpents put into his cradle by Hera, four labors (again lion and hydra, also centaurs and Hades) and his battle on the side of the Olympian gods against the monster Typhon and the Giants—are no more than instances of his life's wretchedness. "Labor" (the Greek word is *ponos*[16]) refers to what is achieved by hard, determined effort as well as to the pain and misery such effort may bring with it. In the first case labor is bound up with producing social values and is rewarded by fame; in the second case it is only abject suffering and a potential source of ignominy. Herakles now only sees, and feels, the latter. He joins child-killing to the sequence of his traditionally celebrated labors, calling it his last labor, his culminating misery. Iris, with fierce irony, had forecast the infanticide calling it "the crown of all his [Herakles'] labors" (1086). Herakles acknowledges this subversion of his heroic life's meaning. Suicide seems the only logical response. It also implies an autonomous action dictated by no outside force.

But it will not happen. One could say that Herakles' traditional stories, known to everyone, will not allow the figure on stage to do what he has argued is his only choice. The focus and emotional force of the drama on stage must allow the audience to suspend their fuller knowledge of those stories. But the play does draw specific attention to a kind of framing around the dramatic figure of Herakles: the hero's familiar presence in actual Athenian cult activities, his association with shrines and his representation on monuments. In trying to persuade Herakles to go on living Theseus offers to take him to Athens to be purified of the pollution from the bloodshed of his kin. In addition Theseus offers a share of his property, including sacred precincts, and he promises, after Herakles' death, sacrificial honors and monuments. This is etiology, a common Euripidean practice, linking figures in a drama to a contemporary cult and thus anchoring the fluid, onetime only dramatic material of a play to permanent or ever repeating real-life, social-religious practices. This usually takes place at a play's end as part of an epilogue. Herakles' etiology here, though, is closely bound up with the play's ongoing action and the hero's confrontation with his identity.

The etiology is a reminder of a Herakles familiar to Athenians as a strong, protective and victorious figure whose cults are sites of genial festivity—a figure similar to the one celebrated by the chorus after Lykos' defeat. This consolatory perspective, however, is in strong ten-

---

16. On *ponos* and its relation to Herakles see Nicole Loraux, *The Experiences of Tiresias* (Princeton 1995): 44–58. This book is also to be recommended for its account of the figure of Herakles in classical Greek culture.

sion with the drama before us. If Herakles' heroic life is shown to have no meaning, to be helplessly subject to uncontrollable forces, whether called gods or chance, what might this say about the hero whom Athens celebrates? Or what might it say about the coherence and viability of Athenian cult and the wider social fabric of which it was part?[17] Giving Herakles asylum in Athens may also be seen as belonging to an ideologically colored, yet also strongly ambivalent, pattern found in other tragedies. Taking in Herakles Athens displays her openness, her enlightened and generous support of heroes who have been driven into exile because of deeply polluting crimes: the matricide Orestes, the incestuous parricide Oedipus, the infanticide Medea. These figures bring their ambiguous fame to the city and enhance hers, and their pollution may work as a kind of inoculation for its host community as well as a source of the religious power inherent in the ambivalence of accursed and sacred. Like the etiology this is a perspective on the play's horizon, put to the city's service, while still suggesting the mysterious opacity of divine involvement in heroic life.

On stage Athens' representative is Theseus, but he acts more on his own account than the city's. He is moved by personal friendship and a debt due for the saving of his life. He is also shown as weak and ordinary. He is generous and devoted toward Herakles, but we also know that he signally failed on a private adventure in Hades from which he had to be rescued. His arguments are conventional: misfortune is universal, one must endure it; Herakles should live up to his reputation as the great hero of Greece. Herakles responds to the friendship and generosity but not to the arguments: "My troubles . . . what have they got to do with all your talk?" (1673). The hero changes his mind on as near to his own terms as he can manage. He decides to go on living because he thinks of his reputation as a warrior who, because of his human mortality,[18] must not give way even in extreme adversity. Concern for a soldier's reputation, for a civic role, outweighs living with the infamy of having killed one's own family. But the pull between asserting a warrior's identity and the intense grief felt at its private cost is strong. Herakles, as he says, succumbs for the first time in his life to tears (1693–94, and see 1752). In his long speech of decision

17. I raise these questions hypothetically. We have no sure way of addressing them, but they do suggest themselves.
18. The theme of mortality is part of the play's movement toward a kind of humanistic realism, a sense of life apart from divine and heroic myth. But that movement is only partial, and here there may also be an allusion to an older, epic heroic code in which human mortality is the basis of life-risking action for the sake of immortal fame. This is Achilles' story in the *Iliad* (see also *Iliad* 12.322–28).

the central portion is taken up by lament for his family and instructions to his father for their funeral. He invokes, then, in one breath the "bitter sweetness" of last kisses for his dead wife and children and the "bitter companionship" of the weapons that are both the mark of his warrior identity and, vividly personified as physical and speaking presences, the killers of his sons. His bow, arrows and club have been lying on the ground beside him from the time he emerged from his madness (1402–3). Now he hesitates between leaving them and picking them up. In a theatrically marked gesture he does the latter. Herakles states that with these weapons he achieved glory in Greece and that without them he would risk ignominious death at his enemies' hands. He suggests a kind of blend of a civic, military model of behavior (what Lykos had invoked in his attack on Herakles' reputation) and his traditional identity as the Panhellenic hero of the labors, the identity he had just drastically devalued. The weapons tie him more firmly to the latter, though. The issue of fame or reputation and of disgrace joins the two. The possibility of Herakles' enduring fame is derived from his mythic and heroic status, his disgrace from his domestic catastrophe. The former exists as poetic tradition in imagination and song, the latter is witnessed dramatically on stage. The heroic deeds are Herakles' independent achievement, it would appear; the killing of his family was beyond his control. Yet the goddess Hera is an inextricable thread between the deeds and the killing. Herakles' speech of decision ends with her (1751). Embedded in his name she is always part of him. That name means Hera's fame. That is, he is both famous and infamous on her account. Or, to put it another way, the contradictions inherent in the hero's being must be attributable to a divine source.

Herakles' reference to Hera is the last time a deity is mentioned in the play. The play ends entirely within a human sphere, which also is ambivalent (and thus the more affecting). Theseus tries to strengthen Herakles' resolve by recalling the heroic labors (and this is the last time they are mentioned), only to have Herakles revert to his despair of their worth in the face of what he now suffers (1768–69). Herakles then calls up the memory of the Athenian hero's wretchedness in Hades, which causes Theseus to admit that there he himself was "Less than the meanest soul" (1774). Both heroes are brought close to an ordinary humanity. The play's concluding theme is friendship. Herakles extols it above wealth and power. But this oversimplifies. It is Theseus' wealth, won by service to his city (1655–57), and Athens' power that makes this friendship viable. Yet a look back will recall that friendship has also been shown as helpless (the chorus, Amphitryon, Lyssa), unreliable (the citizens of Thebes, the Greek world) or simply absent where expected (Zeus). Friendship, *philia* in Greek, is a wide-ranging notion, comprising social and political alignments as well as the mutual ties and obligations of kin and personal relations of feeling. This last is, as the play implies, hazardously contingent on the rest.

The play's concluding action, departure for the haven of Athens, is also hedged by a detour. At the start we were waiting for Herakles to complete his last labor, bringing the monster dog Cerberus back from Hades to Eurystheus in Argos. At the end that task has still to be completed. Because of the loss of his children Herakles does not trust himself emotionally to carry it out alone; he asks for Theseus' help (1741–45). The shadow of Hades, of things having to do with death, is cast over the length of the play. There are, from beginning to end, journeys to and from Hades, impending death, dirges and laments, dressing for death, killings, corpses, funeral and burial arrangements, contemplation of suicide. The horizon of Herakles' future seems also to include little else. No further heroic achievements are so much as hinted at. The cult honors he is to receive in Athens are predicated on his death, when he descends "to Hades" (1662–63),[19] one last time. The final lines of the play chanted by the chorus are a lament for the *loss* of Herakles, the greatest of friends. The audience may remind itself that this is Thebes' loss. It should be Athens' gain, but only as foretold, to be realized outside of the drama that has been witnessed.

III

At the heart of the tragedy there is subversion. Presumed norms of order are called into question: the coherence of mythic and heroic values, political order, the relationship of public and private life. Religion and poetry are part of this too. The first through the gods of myth, as recounted and dramatized, especially where questions are raised about justice or theodicy, and through reference to the relationship of gods and humans in the actual religious practices of cult ritual. The issue of poetry is acutely involved because Euripides' drama and its language are the means by which all these subversions are represented, and this poetry is itself part of a normative tradition.

19. Notice too the imagery of Hades in the account of Herakles' madness, and his supposing himself to be back in Hades when he awakes from his madness (1406–10). Hades is also mentioned as a realm, connected to the goddesses Persephone and Demeter, where the salvation of the Eleusinian Mysteries is available. At line 779 Herakles refers to his being initiated. Reference to these mysteries, though made in passing and eclipsed by the action that follows, constitutes another link to Athenian cult life.

Among the gods two link Herakles' story to Athens. Athena, offstage, brings Herakles' madness to an end, with a violence appropriate to it, hurling a rock at his chest. (This rock, "inducing a sane mind," was reportedly shown as a sacred relic in a sanctuary of Herakles in Thebes.) Amphitryon confusedly sees her action as a hellish earthquake (1195–97), but it saves Herakles from killing him (1309–15) and so could be seen as forecasting Athens' role in providing a refuge for the hero and a way to support his decision to go on living. The goddess does again recall Herakles' ambivalent relationship to the gods. She is called "child of Zeus" (1189–90)—as he had been (192, 890–91)—just when his human vulnerability is ineluctably demonstrated.

Another connection to Athens is through Dionysos (again, a child of Zeus). Like the Herakles of the Athenian cult Dionysos is associated in the city with joyous festivity. The chorus set the two side by side in their song, "for Herakles / To crown his victor's brow. / As long as Bakkhos keeps on / Splashing out wine . . ." (870–71). But god and hero are subject to tragic inversion. Herakles' madness is represented as Dionysiac. Madness [Lyssa] dances like a Dionysian celebrant through Herakles' house (1179–81). Dionysiac imagery runs through the account of Herakles' frenzied actions (1266–67, 1388–89, 1430, 1450). He is called a Bakkhic celebrant from Hades, "drunk—on death" (1427). The Dionysiac power linked to madness, that destroys his family and, in some sense, himself, manifests itself in Thebes.[20] But as god of the theater Dionysos is connected to Athens in the city's great festival for him, the Dionysia, an essential part of which included the performance of this play. A kind of self-referencing points to this connection. Herakles' madness is represented as alienated mimetic action. He is described miming a journey from Thebes to Argos, and then he casts his own family in the role of his enemy Eurystheus'. His family and the household slaves are at first spectators, the latter not knowing whether to laugh or be afraid. Then this play within a play goes badly wrong. The boundaries between actor and on-stage audience are erased. Illusion, of which Dionysos is a master, becomes ruinous delusion. Herakles' Dionysiac madness is also an image of subverted theater.

Hera is the last named deity in the play, Zeus the first. He is immediately introduced as Herakles' father and then in a cult function:

20. As commonly in Attic tragedy Thebes and Athens are antithetical mythical constructs, Thebes being the tragically subverted city serving as a foil to an idealized Athens. On this see Froma I. Zeitlin, "Thebes: Theater of Self and Society in Athenian Drama," in John J. Winkler and Froma I. Zeitlin, eds., *Nothing to Do with Dionysus?* (Princeton 1990): 130–167; and Froma I. Zeitlin, "Staging Dionysus between Thebes and Athens," in Thomas H. Carpenter and Christopher A. Faraone, eds., *Masks of Dionysus* (Ithaca 1993): 147–182.

the theater altar is identified as belonging to Zeus the Rescuer.[21] It was dedicated by his son. But the altar proves to be useless; Herakles was the rescuer. We later learn about another altar to Zeus inside the house (1211), where Herakles attempts a purification ceremony only to be struck down by the madness ordered by Hera. Zeus' role as father is addressed by Amphitryon. The god, having "borrowed" Amphitryon's wife and thus made himself closest kin to Herakles' family, is doubly indebted. He should be a friend (*philos*), especially in time of need. If he is not, Amphitryon says in an unusual indictment, his heart is "hard," failing in moral feeling or "Without justice." Amphitryon, human and mortal, claims a higher moral status than the "great" god's (381–92). Zeus falls outside the reach of humanly conceived morality (compare also 830–31). This asymmetry between divine power and human moral expectations, expectations that the gods are traditionally meant to enforce, is especially pointed because Zeus is regarded as most particularly concerned with justice. That justice is understood at least as having to do with a larger structure of order, among gods and between gods and human beings. Divine justice is celebrated by the chorus after the defeat of Lykos. It is attributed to the gods in general and its manifestation is taken to confirm that Zeus is the true father of Herakles. The god seems somehow to be a *philos* after all and is proved to be the divine source of the hero's noble greatness. This realignment of the claims of human morality with a turn of events that the chorus attributes to the gods turns out to be as temporary as can be. The word *just* has barely been sung (1058) when Iris and Lyssa appear. The gods may have something to do with punishing the wicked, but this says nothing about rewards for the good. Herakles, who carries out Lykos' punishment, is made mad. That Lykos is punished could be attributed simply to Herakles' superiority as a warrior and the lucky timing of his arrival back in Thebes. What Iris calls his punishment is attributed to Hera, and the meaning or justice of it, as noted earlier, is obscure. Iris does explain that Zeus and Necessity (or Destiny; compare lines 30–31) had protected Herakles from Hera until the labors were finished. Now Zeus can do nothing. He himself is subject to a higher, more abstract force that for the moment allows Hera to have her way. The unfolding of Zeus' uselessness runs parallel with the fading and transforming of the traditional heroic figure of Herakles.

Zeus provides an initial condition of the play's story. Herakles finally

---

21. This is imagined for the play in Thebes. There was in fact a building and statue in Athens dedicated to Zeus the Rescuer. See Jon D. Mikalson, "Zeus the Father and Heracles the Son," *Transactions of the American Philological Association* 116 (1986) 89–98, esp. 90 n. 2.

reduces him, alluding ironically perhaps to a standard prayer formula, to a "whoever" (1567) and holds Amphitryon to be his father (1569–70). The immediate driving force of the story is Hera. Her involvement is vivid and direct. No one questions it or who she is. Herakles cannot shake her off. He can only cry out in outrage and disgust: "Who would stoop so low as / To pray to such a goddess?" (1630–31) Zeus perhaps represents the inscrutability of divine power intellectually, Hera unquestionably represents it emotionally. We recall too how each deity is cast in family and gender roles: the remote, inaccessible father and the angry, resentful, all too involved stepmother.

The most direct discussion of the gods occurs between the speeches of Theseus and Herakles when the latter decides to go on with his broken life. Theseus uses the same anthropomorphic terms that Amphitryon had in his challenge to Zeus. The gods, he says, do and suffer bad things—lawless sexual unions and repressive violence against fathers, yet their life on Olympos goes on. So should Herakles, only a mortal, endure his life. The form of the argument as consolation is conventional enough and as a kind of rationalizing it has a contemporary resonance.[22] But it is awkward, creating something like a cognitive dissonance. The underlying point is that misfortune comes to all beings and there is no choice but to submit. To this Herakles essentially agrees (1695, 1750–51). The gods too are subject to a greater and indeterminate power, the uncontrollable turn of events called tukhê, (what happens). But surely we notice that the argument's examples do not fit. Misfortune comes to Herakles against his will while the gods chose to inflict theirs on each other. Within this play too there is no hint of sexual irregularity on Herakles' part, and he has devoted his life to serving both his fathers. One might think of Zeus' adultery with Herakles' human mother (but Theseus' example refers only to gods) and violence in the family to assert power (but by Hera against the human Herakles). Theseus' argument could imply that sexual drives and the forceful pursuit of power are universal, apart from any distinction of human and divine. Herakles, at any rate, responds first with a cry of anguish and then a dismissal of what Theseus has proposed. But he cannot let the argument go. He asserts a belief that the gods have nothing to do with illicit sex and power relations; true deity is free of such constraints, "Needing nothing" (1678). Euripides here draws on pre-Socratic (the philosopher-poet Xenophanes) and more recent (the

22. There is a particularly harsh instance in the argument Thucydides represents the Athenians making for their takeover of the island of Melos: they cite the example of the gods to justify their unrestricted exercise of military power for the sake of political domination (Thucydides, 5.105.2). See also Godfrey W. Bond, ed., Euripides, *Heracles* (Oxford 1981): 393.

Sophist Antiphon) speculative thinking—which will be taken up by Plato and Epicurus. But what Herakles asserts would undercut his whole story by denying the mythic configurations that shape it. And that story will not go away. His speculative challenge to myth is emotionally and dramatically overcome or bypassed. A vision of deity untainted by human characteristics is given striking expression and then left suspended. Herakles himself will end his speech with a cry against Hera, a goddess who could not have existed as a goddess in his theology.

Myth and its gods are indispensable to tragic drama. They provide both some sense of coherence through a story line, the causation of narrative, and are a kind of emblem of the human psyche as it is irreducible to rational accounting. Herakles' theology is a challenge to the drama itself, a challenge met at least by the fact that the drama continues. Euripides has folded into this deeply dramatic moment of his play a metadrama about his function as dramatic poet. Both Theseus and Herakles, the one using myth, the other denying it, refer questioningly to poets: they might be lying (1642); their accounts are "wretched," that is, responsible for false representations of the gods (1680). This suggests a competition between poetry and speculative thought in which poetry subsumes the latter while maintaining its own power of fictional creation, a power, though, acknowledged to be ambivalent.

In Herakles one may also see that his view of the divine here could refer to himself. Where Theseus calls up an image of heroic submission and endurance, Herakles attributes to true divinity an autonomy and self-sufficiency that might have defined his own heroism, but that is now utterly lost to him.

Herakles' theology isolates the gods and thereby undermines two working assumptions of Greek ritual practice, that the gods are involved in human affairs, for good or ill (ritual seeks to encourage the one and abate the other), and that there is some reciprocity between gods and humans; both notions are basic to sacrifice, for example (they were also presupposed by Amphitryon's earlier indictment of Zeus).[23] But ritual is a substantial part of the play's dramatic fabric. As noted, it is mostly shown as failed or perverted: supplication doesn't work, sacrifice goes very wrong, Bakkhic celebration turns murderous. Though this might appear to risk a subversion of actual religious practice, the dramatically enacted subversion can give richer definition to what is represented as

23. See Harvey Yunis, A New Creed: Fundamental Religious Beliefs in the Athenian Polis and Euripidean Drama (Göttingen 1988).

subverted. The representation of ritual gone awry is a generally familiar feature of Greek tragedy. That in addition the drama is itself part of a ritual and civic occasion (Dionysos' festival) suggests that actual ritual is not so much challenged as dramatized in its ambivalent power, and may in fact in this way be reinforced.

In the play poetry is also represented as intrinsic to ritual performance, especially in the singing and dancing of the chorus who regularly signal self-referentially what they are doing: for example, performing a dirge to music modeled on Apollo's (399–406, compare 132–33); invoking to celebrate victory the Muses, Dionysos and the music of lyre and pipe (856–87); performing a paean, a song of thanksgiving and victory, like the maidens at Delos worshiping Apollo (878–91); and calling for ritual dance and festivity in Thebes (971–78). All this is before Herakles' catastrophe. After it is forecast by Iris and Lyssa the chorus' vision sees their dance and music taken over and perverted by the mad hero: "The dances are beginning . . . not the dances / Of the god of wine . . . The pipe keeps shrieking / Notes of ruin" (1163–78). The chorus sing only one more formal song, although nearly a third of the play is still to come. This song is their shortest, disturbed and rhythmically irregular (there is no usual balance of corresponding stanzas). It is a shocked response that compares the greater enormity of Herakles' mad crime to the daughters of Danaos' killing their forty-nine bridegrooms and the Athenian princess Prokne's killing of her one son (1329–33). These mythic parallels (like the ones Theseus uses in trying to persuade Herakles to live) are suggestively and unsettlingly oblique. The crimes cited apply to Herakles insofar as they concern spouse and child killing respectively. But they are committed by women who have deliberately plotted them, if under great duress. Herakles, the man, is declared simply doomed to madness (1336–37) and acts for no cause of his own, unwittingly. Prokne's slaughter of her child, quite remarkably, is called sacrificing to the Muses (1334–35). There is here a tragic nexus of ritual and poetry (in the context of an Athenian story too). As with Herakles, intrafamilial killing is represented as perverted ritual. The reference to the Muses may recall that because of her crime Prokne was turned into the beautifully singing nightingale. In the myth this was an act of the gods; in effect it is a poetic invention, a kind of rescue operation for a hideous crime whereby the crime is powerfully registered while poetry asserts its power, and indeed draws it from the very horror of the crime. Euripides' play as a whole does something like this with the tragedy of Herakles, but, one might say, more realistically. Herakles occasions the beautiful songs of the chorus, then the hero's devastating ruin puts an end to them. Just after their short formal song the chorus refer one last time to their ritual activity, asking what lament or dirge they might sing or what dance of Hades they might perform (1338–41). There is no hope of an answer. They and their poetry, traditional and close to ritual, are overtaken by the story's events. For what remains of the play they are almost completely silent and motionless.

Yet the play goes on, moving through an extended conclusion in which its hero, with his companion's help, wrestles with how after utter catastrophe one can go on. Herakles tries to put the greatest distance possible between himself and the mythic, divine forces who seem to be the cause of his unjust downfall. Theseus tries to recall the hero to his previous greatness and, not without contradiction, to his human mortality, so that the two might be joined in the strength for endurance. What we see on stage allows neither effort easily to be regarded as a success. Divine power is overwhelming and unaccountable, undeniable in its effects, and necessary for the whole story to be told. Herakles' strength at the end is disturbingly fragile and completely dependent. We are left with the emotional impact of that. Out of this bleakness some balancing — consoling is perhaps too much to say — factors remain. To the extent that the gods are distanced, humanity emerges in sharper relief and definition. The figures on stage at the end have been drawn — forced — to a greater self-reliance, at the ideal center of which is friendship. The gods of myth are both devastating and yet also distanced. They could be seen as extreme cases in both their violence and lack of care. Yet their power may also be partly channeled and regularized in ritual that, though perverted within the play, outside of it is still glimpsed as part of a civic community's ordered life. The humane Theseus makes an unusual personal disavowal of the effects of pollution from Herakles' hands stained by the blood of his kin (1521–25, 1537–39, 1758). But the play allows no question about the religious and civic law requiring the hero's exile from Thebes and his ritual purification for the pollution he has unintentionally incurred (see 1652). Though they can hardly be forgotten, at the end of the play there is no more talk of gods. We are left with the work of Euripides' dramatic poetry, which has included and then moved past the traditional singing and dancing of his chorus. This poetry, like the figure of Herakles, is shown to be part of a tradition that has become unsettlingly fragile and in need of readaptation. Euripides has somehow, perhaps just barely, held the threads of the drama together, has made the play possible, and sent its action home to Athens.

ON THE TRANSLATION

I wanted a line that could embody swift shifts in mood and thought, whose nimbleness and speed kept pace with the play's sudden reversals and disasters. In the speeches, I generally used a pentameter-based line frequently broken up into smaller units and a trimeter-based line for the choruses. When the original or my English demanded it, I've broken with this scheme, particularly in the alternating, single lines of dialogue known as *stichomythia*. (In the case of turnover lines, short turnover lines are aligned flush right. To avoid long turnover lines, I've indented the entire line to the left so that the line can fit within the bounds of the right margin.)

I've benefited from Christian Wolff's literal version of the play and his corrections and suggestions. I've also consulted many other versions and/or commentaries, especially those of Godfrey Bond, Michael Halleran, William Arrowsmith, and Shirley Barlow.

My hope is that this translation will live on both the page and the contemporary stage. What I've attempted to do is reimagine Euripides' play from the inside, to get the feel and timbre of the characters' voices, and to embody those voices in a way that doesn't violate the spirit of Euripides' Greek. At the same time, I've tried to make those voices over into contemporary English full of the nuances and subtleties, the intimate qualities of morals and mind, of each character's individual habits of speech.

Tom Sleigh

HERAKLES

CHARACTERS

AMPHITRYON Herakles' foster father

MEGARA Herakles' wife

CHORUS of Theban Elders

LYKOS the usurping power in Thebes

HERAKLES son of Zeus and Alkmene, foster son of Amphitryon

IRIS messenger of the gods

MADNESS

MESSENGER

THESEUS ruler of Athens

HERAKLES' THREE SONS

Followers of Lykos and of Theseus

Line numbers in the right-hand margin of the text refer to the English translation only, and the Notes on the text at p. 93 are keyed to these lines. The bracketed line numbers in the running head lines refer to the Greek text.

HERAKLES

Outside of HERAKLES' *house. Seated at the altar of* ZEUS *the* RESCUER, AMPHITRYON, MEGARA, *and her* THREE SONS *by* HERAKLES.

AMPHITRYON   Say the name Amphitryon of Argos
    And the whole world snaps to. I'm the very man—
    That same Amphitryon who shared his wife with Zeus.
    You'll recognize my father, Alkaios,
    And Perseus, my grandfather—another household name.
    And as for my son, can there be anyone
    Alive who hasn't heard of Herakles?
    I've settled here in Thebes.
           Thebes, where dragonteeth
    Were broadcast and sprouted full-grown fighters
    Berserk to kill each other.
          Ares kept a few back   10
    From the slaughter and they put down roots—their
              children's
    Children grew up here in this city Kadmos
    Built from the ground up. And from them
    Sprung Kreon, the son of Menoikeus—
    Kreon, who *was* our king;
           and the father

Of Megara here . . .
                              Once the whole city
Turned out to celebrate her wedding,
Singing and playing pipes as Herakles
Led her through the streets—home to his father's house.
But my son left home. Left me and Megara   20
And all his in-laws here in Thebes. He wanted
To take back dear old Argos, a city so huge
You'd think the Cyclopes planned it—
                              those high-built walls
Shadowed me when I had to flee to Thebes
For striking down Elektryon. Well—for me,
To brighten an exile's grief, and take back
Home ground, he had to make a deal.
He struck a tough bargain with Eurystheus:
Tame the old powers, make the whole world safe—
And Eurystheus would let him and me go home.
                              Who knows   30
If Hera's hatred or Necessity itself
Made him shake hands on such a price?
He pushed through to the end—now, one labor's left:
To force his way through the jaws of Tainaron
And bring back from the underworld
Its three-headed watchdog.
                              But Hades
Swallowed him like light.
                              He still hasn't come back . . .
There's an old story among the Thebans:
Old King Lykos, who was married to our Queen Dirke,
Once held power here. This was before Zethus   40
And Amphion controlled the city's seven gates.
Twins sired by Zeus, they were nicknamed the white
                              colts.
But Lykos' son, who was named after his father
—Kadmos didn't breed him; he came from Euboea—
Ambushed the city. Civil war had broken out.
But I'll cut the story short: Lykos killed Kreon.
And killing made Lykos boss.
                              Now our blood ties
To Kreon have become a noose.
                              Because my son is
Down in the dark depths of the earth, Lykos—

That hero, new strongman of Thebes—plans to murder

us: 50

Herakles' little boys. His father. His wife—
Murder on top of murder, like using
Fire to put out fire: Me, I'm just a blathering
Old nuisance. I scarcely count. But these boys—
If they grow to men, they'll pay back blood with blood.

When Herakles went down to the blackness
Underground, he left me behind—to play nursemaid
To these boys. Now all I can do is kneel
With their mother before this altar—
And pray to Zeus the Rescuer . . . this altar,   60
A reminder of what my son's spear can do;
That he set up to celebrate his great victory
Over the Minyans.

                    But us, we're worse than beggars—
No food; nothing to drink; no clothes. We're camped
Out here on the bare hard ground. Locked out
Of our own house. Destitute. Doomed.

                              And as for friends—
Well, most won't lift a finger. And those that will
Have no power. When bad luck catches up to you,
You learn that friendship won't stand up to misfortune.
No matter how two-faced my worst friends' smiles,   70
I wouldn't wish on them this trial of friendship.

MEGARA So, old man—remember when you commanded
         Our Theban spearmen? You razed the city
         Of the Taphians. But the gods work out our fates
         In ways too crooked and devious for human eyes.
         My father was acclaimed great. His greatness
         Was my luck—I wasn't brought up wanting.
         My father was rich and had the power
         To protect us from his rivals' spears;
         But power and wealth make for greed;

                              and spear   80
         Lifted against spear is the way to power.

                              My father
         Had us children as a further blessing—
         And as for me—my luck, and his will, granted me

Your Herakles.
　　　　　　　But now that's over. Dead. Flown.
And you and I, old man—we're done for;
And along with us, these three chicks of ours,
Huddling and nestling under their mother's wing.
They can't help themselves, they keep asking
After him: "Mother, where's our father gone?
What's he doing? When will he come home?"   90
They don't understand, they're just too young . . .
The way lost children stumble blind at night,
They call out, "Father? Father?"
　　　　　　　　　　　　　　I keep
Putting them off. Distracting them with chatter.
But when they'd hear the door latch creak, they'd all
　　　　　　　　　　　　　　　　　scramble up
And run to hug their father's knees.
　　　　　　　　　　　　So, old man—
What are our chances? I'm counting on you
To rescue us. The borders are sealed tight,
Guards everywhere, patrols bottling up
Every road. Our friends have let us down.   100
If you've got a plan, let's hear it.
　　　　　　　　　　　　We all know
What will happen if we keep on standing here.

AMPHITRYON My girl, I don't know what to say. Our troubles
Call for hard thought, not casual chatter.
When you're weak, what can you do but wait?

MEGARA Wait for something worse? Do you love your life that
　　　　　　　　　　　　　　　　　　　much?

AMPHITRYON I'm still alive, aren't I? Even that gives me hope.

MEGARA I love being alive too. But it's hopeless to hope for what
　　　　　　　　　　　　　　　　　　　can't be.

AMPHITRYON By playing for time, hard times can be cured.

MEGARA The time spent waiting is worse than being tortured.   110

AMPHITRYON Look. The wind can change course. The storm
Blows over, and our troubles melt like mist.

Trust to Herakles. He still may come
To rescue us—me, his old father, you, his wife.
Try to stay calm. The tears welling up
In your boys' eyes, brush them away;
Tell them a story that will make their crying stop,
No matter how much a lie the story seems to you.
The wind blowing against us, that makes us
Desperate now, won't always be this strong—   120
It'll blow itself out. Good luck too
Blows hot and cold. Everything changes;
Things look as if they'll never end and then—
Before we know it—they too are swept away.
We have to keep on. That's what courage is.
Only if we lose heart can they call us cowards.

Enter CHORUS.

CHORUS To this high-roofed house
We come like ghosts,
Apparitions leaning on our staffs,
Our voices ghost-voices   130
Whispering round an old man's bed.
The dying swan whose song is sad
Can't match ours for misery.
What good is our good will
When things go from bad to worse?
You boys have lost your father.
Old man, you've lost your son.
And you, unhappy wife,
Our words can't touch your grief:
Your man is locked away   140
Down in the house of death.

Keep moving. Heavy step
By step lift your tired feet
The way a horse pulls the weight
Of a chariot up a rocky slope.
If anyone needs your help,
Give him a steadying hand
The way when we were younger,
Fighting with our spears,

We drove off the enemy   150
For the glory of our country.

Look at those boys' eyes
Gleaming like their father's:
Fierce. Stony. A stare
That hardens one to stone.
Yes. And they've inherited
Their father's rotten luck.
Along with his good looks.

Greece, what defenders you lose
If you lose these boys!   160

Look—it's the headman, Lykos,
Strutting toward the house.

                    Enter LYKOS, *with* FOLLOWERS.

LYKOS   You, who claim you're Herakles' father,
        And you, his wife—allow me a few questions,
        Won't you? I thought you might. Let's face it:
        I'm in charge here. I'll ask whatever I want.

        Still nursing your hopes? A snap of my fingers—
        And you're done.
                        Or are you cracked
        Enough to think that these boys' father,
        Who's dead—will suddenly show his face?   170
        Aren't you ashamed of your stupid blubbering?
        And all because you're about to die . . .
                                        you,
        Who bragged all over Greece about pimping
        Your wife to Zeus—and you, who boasted
        That your husband was a hero. What's so glorious
        About killing some slimy marsh snake?
                                Or that Nemean Lion—
        He claimed he strangled it with his bare hands . . .
        But everybody knows he trapped it in a net.
        Your case has more holes than a net,
        If that's all the evidence you've got.
                                He's a nobody—   180

He made his reputation by slaughtering
Dumb beasts. Let's see him with a shield
On that brawny left arm, parrying a spearthrust.
But he uses a bow—handy for retreat.
A bow's for cowards. A man with real guts
Stands his ground, face to face, when a spear
Comes hurtling through the ranks.

                       So—killing
His sons isn't cruelty, but shrewd policy.
We all know who killed Kreon. We all know
Who took away his throne. I'm not about   190
To let these cubs grow up and bare their fangs.

AMPHITRYON Zeus, Herakles is your son, too. Use your power
To defend him!

                 My part's to speak out
Against such stinking lies—

                      with the Gods
As my witnesses, Son, I'll make him eat his words;
I'll show him up for the liar that he is:

You're unspeakable, to call my son coward!
But maybe Zeus' thunderbolts don't impress you?
Or Zeus' chariot that my son drove into battle
When the gods fought against those giants,   200
The monstrous children of the earth?

                         Stuck between their ribs,
The arrows of Herakles taught that gang a thing or two.
And afterwards, my son took his place among
The other gods to sing the victory song!
Or go to Pholoe, you dirty tyrant,
And ask the Centaurs—those four-legged savages—
Who they think is the bravest man on earth:
Herakles. My son. That's how they'll answer.

                           Herakles,
Whose courage you talk down—

                     but since you think
He's such a phony, why don't you go back   210
To your hometown, Dirphys in Euboea—
And ask what your own people think of you?
Who calls you brave—let alone a hero?

There's no place in all Euboea
That could talk up one brave deed you've done.

And as for sneering at that thinking-man's invention,
The bow—
          let me put you straight.
                              Your infantryman
Is a slave, hauling around his spear and shield.
He's at the mercy of his fellow soldiers
In the ranks. If the man next to him   220
Holds back or breaks rank because he's scared,
He's dead—
          and because someone else turned coward.
And if your spear shaft breaks—your sole weapon
Against death—you might as well be standing naked.
But let's say you've got a bow—and you're a good shot.
First, you can shoot arrows all day, as many arrows
As you want: you can *always* defend yourself.
And second—you can fight at long range.
                              Your enemy
Can't spot you. While their taking heavy
Casualties, the wounds from your arrows   230
Are all the enemy can see. And you—you're snug
As a baby. They can't strike back.
                              In war,
That's the best strategy. To train your firepower
On whoever's in range while you keep
Your own head down.
                    So that's that. I've put
The record straight. For every claim you made,
The truth is really just the opposite.

And these boys—why murder them? What have
They done to you?
                  Of course, you're smart in one thing:
Since you're a coward, you fear a real man's children.   240
But that *we* should have to die to prove your cowardice—
That's the worst. Our swords would be at your throat—
We, who are your betters—
                          if Zeus' mind were just.
But if power over Thebes is your game,

Send us into exile. You leave us unharmed,
No one will harm you. Just like that—
God can turn the wind against you.

And you, city of Kadmos! Don't think you'll get off
Without my curses.
                        Is this how you show gratitude
To Herakles and his sons? Herakles, who   250
Single-handedly routed the whole Minyan army,
And made you Thebans free to hold up your heads again?
In fact, all Greece ought to be ashamed:
I can't keep quiet!
                        Greece should be on the march,
Campaigning with all she's got to protect these boys!
She owes it to Herakles! His labors cleared the earth and
                                                        seas
Of monsters: For us, he made things safe.
But look at them, boys—these Thebans don't lift a finger.
Nor do the other Greeks.
                        And me, what can I do?
I'm useless as the rattling of my tongue.   260
I'm winded. Utterly spent. Just look at me,
I'm trembling!
                        If only I were young and strong again,
My spear would bloody those blond curls of his.
I'd drive the coward beyond the bounds of Atlas—
Past land's end—trying to dodge my spear!

CHORUS Whether his words come easily or not
        An honest man always can find inside
        Himself a reservoir of authentic speech.

LYKOS Go on, keep babbling! Pile up and up your tower
       Of words.
                        But to pay you back, I'll do more than talk.   270
       You there, go to Helikon—and you, to Parnassos.
       Tell the crews there to cut down a stand of oak
       And bring the logs here.
                        To keep our friends
       Cozy and warm, we'll pile wood around the altar,
       And once the flames get roaring, we'll have

A roast—
            the whole lot of them—
                                    that should teach you
The dead have no power here. From now on,
I'm the one who calls the shots.
                            (*To Chorus.*) You
                            burned-out old fools!
For taking their part, you'll weep for more
Than Herakles' sons.
                        I'll give you something real   280
To cry about: Your own houses torn down
Around your ears. That should teach you
Who's in charge here. And who's a slave.

CHORUS Ares tore the teeth from the dragon's jaws
        And planted them like seeds. We sprouted up,
        Earth's sons, Thebans who don't scrape or bow
        To murderers like you.
                                These staffs we lean on
        Make good clubs. You control the young men,
        But watch out! You're a stranger here—
        I'll hand you your head. You can't push us around.   290
        I've worked myself to the bone. But all I've worked for
        Won't go to you—you, an outsider!
                                        Go back where
        You came from. Do your dirty work there.
        As long as I'm alive, you won't harm a hair
        On these boys' heads. Herakles left his sons—
        But he hasn't gone so far under the earth
        That we forget what we owe him.
                                        He saved
        Our country.
                        You destroyed it. Took over.
        Cheated him of the honor that he's due.
        Call me an agitator,
                                but friendship commands   300
        That I help Herakles—now, when he needs it most.
        If only my right hand was strong enough
        To grip my spear again.
                                But I'm spent.
        If I were younger, you wouldn't get away

38

With calling me slave!

                  Instead of your filthy pleasures,
We'd live honorably here in Thebes.
But our city was torn apart by civil war.
Thebes went mad and took bad counsel.
Otherwise, you'd never have come to power.

MEGARA Thank you for standing up for us. Old friends   310
        Are the truest friends. But be careful your anger
        Doesn't put you in danger too.

                      Amphitryon,
        For what it's worth, hear me out.

                            I love these boys—
        How could I not? *My* labors gave them breath
        And nurture.

                I'm afraid of dying. Of death.
        But it's hopeless to fight against our fate.
        We have to face the fact: We die.

                        But to be burned
        Alive—the butt of our enemy's jokes:
        To me, that's worse than death.
        We have a code to live up to, our family honor   320
        Must be preserved. You made your name
        As a great soldier. It's unthinkable
        For you to die a coward's death.

                      And no one
        Needs to remind me that these boys' father
        Wouldn't lift a finger to save his sons
        If it meant disgracing our family name.
        I'm like him in that:

                      If your heart is good
        And true, when you see your sons disgraced,
        It breaks you.

             So think about it—
        What are you pinning your hopes on?   330
        Do you really believe that your son will return
        From the earth's depths?

                  Who, of all the dead,
        Has ever come home from Hades?
        Or do you imagine all our talk will persuade

Lykos to feel sorry for us?
                                    Maybe
If your enemy's a man of conscience
And honor, you can touch his heart
And he'll show you mercy.
                                    But this man
Is a savage.
                        It even occurred to me,
What if we begged to have these children   340
Sent into exile? But isn't that worse?
To save their lives, only to make them
Beggars?
                        And when it comes to exiles,
You know the old saying: "Your host's smile
Turns to a frown in a single day."
We have to face up to death—it's coming anyway.
Old friend, I challenge you: Face it with us.
I know how brave you are at heart.
When the gods trap you in their schemes,
To fight against them shows spirit—   350
But it's hopeless.
                        Fate itself nets us in.
What must happen happens. We can't escape.

CHORUS If only I had my old fighting strength back,
        I'd shove his threats back down his throat.
        But I'm old. Done in. Good for nothing.
                                            Amphitryon,

        It's up to you to fight clear of this trap.

AMPHITRYON I'm no coward. It's not longing for life
            That keeps me from facing death.
                                    But these boys—
            They're the sons of my son.
                                    I want
            To save them. But what I want can't be.   360

            Go ahead. Cut my throat. Stab me.
            Or throw me off a cliff.
                                    But do us one favor:
            Murder us before you murder these boys.

Spare us the sight of that—

                 their last breath
Gasping, "Mama!" "Grandpa!"

                     For the rest,
Since you're so eager, go ahead. No one
Gets off death. We have to die.

MEGARA Grant me a last wish too—I'm begging you.
One favor from you will oblige us both.
Let me dress up my children for their deaths.   370
Unlock the door to our house.

                  Give these boys
At least this much of their inheritance.

LYKOS I can give that much. Men, unlock the doors.
Go on. Take what you need. I don't begrudge you
Funeral robes. And when you're finished dressing,
I'll be back—

            and give you away

                  to the world below.

Exit LYKOS, *with* FOLLOWERS.

MEGARA Boys, let's go in. Follow your poor mother
Into your father's house. Everything
He had has been taken away from him.
But no one can take away from us his name.   380

Exit MEGARA *and* CHILDREN *into* HERAKLES' *house.*

AMPHITRYON So, Zeus. You slip into my bed, you take
What you want—

              and you pay me back like this?
You were one of us . . . I thought of you as my friend—
You and I the father of Herakles!

                 But Zeus,
Now, all that means nothing. And I'm nothing
But a weak old man.

             But I'm better than you—
Who call yourself a god. I have my principles,
I haven't betrayed the sons of Herakles. But you—

                       you've

Abandoned us, your own people. You don't
Lift a hand to help. Either you're blind   390
To the troubles of human beings.
Or you're heart's hard. Without justice.

Exit AMPHITRYON *into house.*

CHORUS When victory's all we know,
Our songs are full of joy.
But then they turn to grief:
We know hatred.
Strife. Death.
And both our joy and grief
Blend in Apollo's notes
So pure they break our hearts . . .   400
With his golden pick he plucks
Taut strings that quaver
Deep in the inner ear
Hearing beneath that sound
The deads' toneless music
Welling from underground.

I've learned to sing in praise
Of my friend lost
In darkness. My song
A wreath for his labors—   410
For everything he suffered.

A life lived in all our faculties
Is happiness; and the glory
Of the dead. Like Herakles, whether
We're children of gods or men,
Each moment takes our measure:
We live the best way we can.

First, he killed the lion prowling
In Zeus' wood. He cloaked
Himself in its tough hide,   420
Used its jaws as a hood.
Golden hair, tawny mane,
Who could tell beast from man?

Next he drew his bow,
Arrow after arrow killing
A centaur in its mountain pasture.
They trampled down furrows
Until crops wouldn't grow,
Tore up pines and brandished
Them like spears, or set
The pitch on fire: Whole towns   430
Torched, driven into hiding!
Peneios, the river god, who
Peered up from his swirling waters,
Mount Pelion's valleys
And Homole's grassy slopes
Witnessed the devastation:
Backs and rumps of horses,
Sharp hooves, swift runners,
Appetites of wild creatures—
Faces just like ours.   440
Look: They were monsters,
Half animal, half human,
Rampaging over
Thessaly, instinct
At war with reason.
So Herakles took aim:
His bow shot straight.

He had to hunt down
The stag with golden horns
And dappled hide that drove   450
The farmers from their fields
And battered the countryside.
Killer on impulse. Beast mind.
High on the mountain shrine
Its blood stained his hand
When he slit its throat
In sacrifice to Artemis, cruel
Goddess of the hunt.

Unbridled in the barn
Diomede's mares neighed for more   460
Than oats. Their teeth snapped
And tore, devouring

43

Their master's guests.
Herakles had his work cut out
To curb such appetites.
To the bit and chariot
He broke their spirits,
Teeth champing iron
Instead of human guts.   470

Like a man obsessed
He kept on going, under orders
From Mycenae's king
Who set him labor
After labor. So Herakles
Pushed past all common
Human limit, crossing
Silver-flowing Hebros
Whirlpooling toward the sea.
He reached the tall   480
Headland near a river
Called Anauros where
Springs from underground
Lured travelers to rest:
Pure water. Pure pleasure.
But the place hid a monster:
Kyknos, who loved slaughter,
And beheaded his own guests.
Herakles took aim:
The springs boiled and gushed.   490

Then he traveled to where
The horses of the Sun,
Panting, lathered, end
Their daylong run,
Sky turning bloody when
Light sinks in the West.
There in the garden
Of Singing Maidens
Pure as their song,
He plucked the golden apples   500
From the flashing bough.
But the apples cost blood.
He had to shoot the coiling

Dragon whose scales, flaming red,
Smouldered round the tree.

In hidden coves and cays
He hunted pirates down
And made the open sea safe
For sailors at their oars.

He came to Atlas' mansion,   510
And stretching out his arms, balanced
Heaven on his back: His strength
Was more than human to bear
Up under the weight
Of the gods' immaculate
Halls glittering with starlight.

He recruited troops
From every town in Greece
And crossed the black sea's
Storming waves, mind fraught   520
As the great rivers that
Pour into a delta marsh
Teeming with birds and fish.
But the abundance in his head
Was his own violence
Trained on the Amazons
Fierce as the god of war,
Ready to fight fire with fire.
Their cavalry went down
Before Herakles' club, blood   530
Staining their shining robes.
The Greeks stripped their corpses
Knocked sprawling in the dirt—
And back in Mycenae,
As if it were the pelt
Of a wild beast, Herakles
Hung up for all to see
The dead queen's golden belt.

He faced down Lerna's hydra
Barking and howling,   540
Its murderous teeth snapping

45

In all its thousand heads
That he chopped off and seared
To ash. And on the tips
Of his arrows he smeared
Her slobber so lethal
He brought down Geryon,
The triple-bodied herdsman,
With a single shaft.

He ran whatever course   550
Fate set him—and he won.
But the crown of all his labors
Is common to everyone:
The end of endeavor,
Of all we hold most dear.
He sailed into the harbor
Of sighs and tears, of airless
Hades where our sails go slack.
Hero, slave, everyone
But the gods disembark.   560
And no one crosses back.

His house is ruined.
He's been abandoned
By his friends. His children
Are queued up for Charon's boat
That ferries us one way.
Don't talk to me of gods;
Or Justice; Wrong or Right.
Only your strong hands,
Herakles, can set   570
Things straight. You alone
Can rescue them. But you're gone.

When I was young and strong
I knew what a spear was for!
All of us when we were young
And fighting in the ranks
Would have stood by these children.
But I'm useless. Broken down.
The old days' glory is done—

And I'm done with them.   580
Only those who are young
And strong can be truly happy.

           Enter MEGARA, AMPHITRYON, *and the* THREE BOYS.

There they are, dressed in funeral robes,
The sons of Herakles who once dazzled
The whole world with his strength.
                              See his wife
Dragging her boys by the hand,
Balking like colts against their traces.
And here comes Herakles' poor
Father, as broken down as we are.
It's true that as we get older   590
Our spirits get heavier from the weight
Of all we suffer: My eyes are blurry.
I can't keep blinking these tears away.

MEGARA Where's the priest and his knife? We're ready
To be butchered—though the butcher calls it sacrifice.
Here the victims are—now lead us off to Hades.
We make a mismatched team under one yoke:
Old and young, children and their mother—
All pulling together toward our deaths.

I gave you boys life, nursed you, reared you.   600
And for what? So that those who hate us
Can humiliate us for their pleasure
Before they cut us down?
                        Now I'm looking
At your faces for the last time . . .
                              I had high hopes
For you—
              but those are done. Hopes I built
On your father's promises.
                        Your father.
Who's now dead . . .

                        He planned to give you
Argos and all her rich farmland. Eurystheus' palace

And his power were to be yours. Remember
How your father draped the lion skin   610
He wore as armor over your shoulders?

And you were to rule Thebes and all her chariots—
The plains round the city that my father
Passed on to me were your inheritance:
                                        You behaved
Like your father's son when you asked for Thebes
The way other children ask for toys:
And he gave it to you. Remember the huge
Carved club he used to carry? He'd put it
In your right hand and pretend that it was yours.

And he promised you Oechalia   620
That he took with his well-aimed arrows.

Your father's care for you boys was as great
As his strength: For three sons, he intended
To raise up three kingdoms.
                                        And I was to choose
For each of you a wife from Athens, Thebes or Sparta—
To moor you the way a ship's stern hawsers do
So you'd ride out all storms safe and happy.
But the winds have shifted round on us:
Fortune's given you your own deaths for brides.
And my tears have become the lustral water   630
For the ritual bath . . .
                                        more pain to bear.
Your old grandfather gives the marriage feast
For Hades—which makes death your bitter in-law.
If I hug you first,
                                        which should I hug last?
Do I kiss this one?
                                        Or hold you close?
You've seen how a bee goes flower to flower
And gathers nectar for the hive—
                                        if only I could gather
All the sorrow that we suffer
And condense it into a single drop
That I could weep for us all . . .
                                        Herakles,   640

Love, if any words from here
Ever make their way below, listen to me now:
Your father and your boys are about to die—
And I'm to die too. All Greece once called me
Blessed because of you.

                         So help us. Come.
Even if it's just your shadow.

                               Or come
As a dream. That's all you need to do—
These men are such cowards—to stop them
From slaughtering your sons.

AMPHITRYON   My girl, keep praying
To the gods below while I raise up my hands   650
To the sky:

                Zeus, help these children now!
If you intend to help at all. One moment more—
And it will be over.

                     But I'm wasting my breath.
I've prayed and prayed—

                     and nothing happens.
We can't avoid death. We have to die.
And as for life, old friends, what does it amount to?
The best we can hope for is to fend off pain
Between dawn and dark.

                   Time could care less
About our hopes. It rushes off on its
Own business—and it's gone.

                   Just look at me,   660
The prime example: Who didn't sing
My praises or call me famous or applaud me
For accomplishing great things?

                 Wealth. Reputation—
The wind blows them away just like a feather:
All you've worked for is wrecked in a single day.
The wind keeps shifting. Nobody's secure . . .
We were all boys together, grew up with one another.
So take a long, last look at your old friend.

              HERAKLES *appears in the wings.*

MEGARA It can't be. Who could believe it? Father,
Is that Herakles? My own dear husband?   670

AMPHITRYON My girl, I can't say. I'm speechless.

MEGARA It *is* Herakles. They told us he'd gone down
Forever under the earth—
                            unless he's come back
As a dream flickering in the sun.
But I'm not dreaming—
                        or seeing things
My aching mind makes more real than day:
It's Herakles, your son!
                        Boys, run to him!
Hold tight to his coat. Never let him loose!
Hurry now! He's come to rescue us:
He'll be more help to us than Zeus!   680

                        HERAKLES *moves on stage.*

HERAKLES   There it is—
My own roof—and the gate before my house!
Just sunlight on my face and hands
Gives me such pleasure—
                        I made it back home. Alive.
Bless these old walls!
                    There my boys are—
Before the gate.
            What?
                    What's all this?
They look to be dressed—for their own funerals.
Heads crowned with wreaths.
                            And my wife—
Out of doors?—surrounded by that crowd of men!
And there's my father—
                    in tears!
                        Tell me what's happened here?   690
What's come over this house?

MEGARA   My love, my husband . . .

AMPHITRYON My boy, welcome as sunlight to these old eyes!

MEGARA   You're alive—and now you've come—in time to rescue
                                                             us!

HERAKLES   Will someone tell me what's happened here?
           Father? What is all this?

MEGARA   Murder, that's what.
           They want to murder us!
                             Forgive me, old man,
           For speaking out before you. A woman
           Feels her troubles more readily than a man.
           They were about to kill my boys. And me.

HERAKLES   Great God Apollo! What will you tell me next?   700

MEGARA   My brothers and my old father—they're all dead!

HERAKLES   How? What happened? Or was it someone's spear?

MEGARA   Lykos killed them. He's the power now in Thebes.

HERAKLES   Was it a fair fight, spear against spear? Or the waste of
                                                            civil war?

MEGARA   Civil war. He lords it over us, the upstart, and our seven
                                                                gates.

HERAKLES   But what frightened you and the old man so?

MEGARA   He planned to murder us: Me, your father, and your
                                                            boys.

HERAKLES   Kill them? What made him fear my orphaned sons?

MEGARA   That one day they'd revenge my father's death.

HERAKLES   Why are my children dressed up like the dead?   710

MEGARA   We put on funeral robes . . . to get ready for our own
                                                            deaths.

HERAKLES   He was about to murder you? That breaks me!

MEGARA Our friends abandoned us. We were told that you were
                                                         dead.

HERAKLES But why did you lose heart that I'd come back?

MEGARA Eurystheus' heralds kept telling us you were dead.

HERAKLES Why did you leave our home? Locked out of our own
                                                         gates?

MEGARA He forced us. Dragged your father out of his bed.

HERAKLES No respect for age? Where's his sense of shame?

MEGARA Lykos feel shame? The only goddess he knows is force.

HERAKLES My friends while I was gone—were they so scarce?   720

MEGARA Friends? If your luck goes bad, you have no friends.

HERAKLES All I suffered in the Minyan wars, they shrug that off?

MEGARA I'll say it again: bad fortune has no friends.

HERAKLES Those wreaths of death—
                                   tear them off your heads!
            Look up into the sunlight—look!
                                        After death's
            Darkness, feel how the sun comes back to warm us!

            My work's cut out. Now let me go about it.
            With this hand I'll tear down around his ears
            The pillars of this upstart tyrant's house.
                                             Then chop off
            His perverted head and throw it to the dogs   730
            To gnaw.
                     This victorious club
            Will make the rounds of Thebes and pay its respects
            To the ones who turned traitors—
                                      despite all I suffered
            For them!
                     Or I'll fill the air with arrows

52

Raining like a cloudburst round their heads
Until Ismenos overflows with corpses
And Dirke's pure waters boil with blood.

A man's first obligation is to defend
His wife and children, his old father.
My labors and all I suffered—
                              the madness of it!   740
I let down those whom I ought to die for—
After all, they were about to die for me.
Killing lions and hydras for Eurystheus
And not toiling for my own sons' threatened
Lives—
            that's honor and glory for you!
Had *that* been the outcome of all my labors,
Who now would call me Herakles the Conqueror?

CHORUS   It's only right that a man should stand up for his sons,
            His old father, and his wife who's his faithful mate.

AMPHITRYON   Son, it's always been your way to love your friends   750
            And hate your enemies. But don't move too fast.

HERAKLES   Am I rushing into something, Father?

AMPHITRYON   Lykos and his gang—a bunch of lazy,
            Big-spending climbers, who went bankrupt
            While trying to pass themselves off as wealthy—
            Raised the riots that brought Thebes down:
            They wanted to rob their neighbors
            And fill their pockets.
                              You were seen
            Entering the city, so don't be caught offguard:
            Your enemies will come swarming soon enough.   760

HERAKLES   I could care less if the whole city saw me!
            But a bird settled on an ill-omened perch—
            I knew right then there was trouble,
            So I slipped undetected into Thebes.

AMPHITRYON   Well done. Now go in and greet your household gods—
            Let your fathers' house welcome you face to face.

53

Soon Lykos will arrive to haul us off
To slaughter—your wife, your sons, and me.
If you wait inside, he'll fall into your hands—
And no risks.
                    Don't stir up things in Thebes   770
Until you set things straight in your own house.

HERAKLES I'll do as you say—I'll go inside.
Just feel that warmth. After all I went through
In the earth's sunless depths, I won't forget
To thank the gods who protect our home.

AMPHITRYON Son, I'm eager to hear—did you really go down to
                                                        Hades?

HERAKLES Yes: I dragged up to the light his three-headed watchdog.

AMPHITRYON Did you fight? Or was he a gift from the goddess?

HERAKLES I had to fight. The Mysteries I witnessed gave me
                                                        strength.

AMPHITRYON Where's the monster now? At Eurystheus' house?   780

HERAKLES At Hermione. In the earth goddess's sacred grove.

AMPHITRYON Does Eurystheus know you've returned from the earth's
                                                        depths?

HERAKLES No. I came here first to see how things stood.

AMPHITRYON What kept you such a long time underground?

HERAKLES I stayed to rescue Theseus from Hades.

AMPHITRYON Where's he now? Returned to his homeland?

HERAKLES In Athens, glad to have escaped the underworld.

Boys, let's go in. Go with your father
Into our house. You're happier, aren't you,
Going in than when you were coming out.   790

Don't be frightened any longer. Dry your tears.
And you, my wife, take heart—stop trembling.
You can stop clutching my coat—

                              I don't have wings;
I'm not going to run from those I love.
Well!

                    They won't let me loose—

                                        they cling
To my coat tighter. How close you came
To the razor's edge.

                        Here, take my hands—
I'll be the ship that tows the smaller boats
Into harbor.

                    How could I not want
To take care of these boys? Human beings   800
Are alike in this:

                        Whether we're powerful
Or not, whether our luck is good or bad,
We love our children—

                              some of us are rich,
Some poor—

                    but all of us love our children.

          Exit HERAKLES, AMPHITRYON, MEGARA, *and the* BOYS.

CHORUS Old age weighs me
        Down worse than Etna's
        Stones. It's drawn like a curtain
        Between me and the sun.
        Gold bars that fill palaces,
        An Eastern king's wealth,   810
        Won't buy me back my youth.
        What I long for most—
        To come again full flower
        In body, heart and soul—
        All the spoils of power
        And privilege can't restore.
        This side of the grave,
        Whether we lock our gate
        Or sleep out in the street,
        Youth is what we crave.   820
        I hate old age, its feet

That stink of death creeping
Closer every hour.
Whirl it off like trash
Spinning in the storm.
Let the waves capsize it,
Drown it in the deep.
Banish it from the city.
Keep it far from my home.

The gods' ways aren't our ways: 830
Who knows what they think
Of what we think is wise?
But if they thought as
We do, they'd grant a second
Youth to a life of virtue.
Having run their race
To death, the good would catch
Their breath and double
Back to sunlight while
The wicked and mean 840
Live out their single span.
We could tell good from bad
As clearly as when a cloud
Shifts to reveal the stars
To sharp-eyed sailors.
But the gods' ways aren't ours:
Between good and bad action,
They don't draw a clear line.
And time, as the years roll on,
Does not lay things bare 850
Or blind us with the truth.
A bad man rakes it in
While a good man stays poor.
Age walks on their faces.
Wealth outlives them both.

Song is what I live for.
Song that joins together
The Graces and the Muses,
Each interwoven gesture
The currents of a river. 860
To me, music is water

I couldn't live without.
Even though I'm old
And my muse is Memory,
What life is left to me
I'll use to sing her praise—
She taught me to weave
A song for Herakles
To crown his victor's brow.
As long as Bakkhos keeps on   870
Splashing out wine
And my hands stay strong
To pluck the lyre's strings
Or play the shrilling pipe,
I'll keep on with my song:
The Muses who set me dancing
Still guide my crippled feet.

The girls of Delos sing
Their victory song
At the temple gate   880
Of bright-voiced Apollo,
Son of Leto.
They dance in a circle,
White feet so beautiful
That an old graybeard like me
Feels rising in his throat,
Here before your gate,
A song the dying swan
Might sing—but still a song
Of praise for the son   890
Of Zeus: Though his birth
Was divine, his deeds
Surpass that high beginning:
As he strove to rid the earth
Of monsters, wild beasts,
Of shapes that glide and prowl
When the house goes still,
Through fear and struggle
He became our double—
His labors made him   900
Human, open to it all;
But he also had to kill,

Rage like a wild animal.
That we mortals have the chance
To lead a tranquil life
We owe to his violence.

Enter LYKOS, *with* FOLLOWERS. *Reenter* AMPHITRYON.

LYKOS   So Amphitryon—you aren't a moment
Too soon. You took your own sweet time
In getting dressed for death.
                               Go on:
Tell the wife and sons of Herakles   910
To come here too—and without any fuss—
That's the deal we struck when you agreed to die.

AMPHITRYON   You drive me hard in my misery.
My son is dead—isn't that grief enough?
You're the power here; we all bow to you.
Why press us so hard? You command us
To die:
        Now.
                And so we will die:
What you order us to do, we must obey.

LYKOS   Where's Megara—and those cubs of Alkmene's dead son?

AMPHITRYON   As near as I can make out—I suppose—   920

LYKOS   What do you mean, you "suppose"? Tell me what you
                                                know.

AMPHITRYON   She's kneeling before the hearth-goddess's altar to pray—

LYKOS   For what? Praying won't save her life . . .

AMPHITRYON   A hopeless prayer. For her dead husband to return.

LYKOS   He's not here now. And he'll never come.

AMPHITRYON   Never . . . unless some god raises him from the dead.

LYKOS   Go inside the house and bring her out.

AMPHITRYON That would make me an accomplice to her murder.

LYKOS Well, well . . . such scruples!
                                        But no fears hold me back
         From dragging out this mother and her sons.   930
         Guards, follow me in.
                            The pleasure
         Of ending this "labor" will be all mine.

                                        Exit LYKOS *and* FOLLOWERS.

AMPHITRYON Well, go ahead—when fate commands, you too obey.
         Someone else will bring your labor to an end.
         What you did was evil—expect evil in return.
         Justice, my friends, this is justice—
                                        a net thrown
         Over his head, swords hidden in the mesh . . .
         There he goes, the coward—
                                        itching to murder us
         While he's the one being led to slaughter.
         I'll go in and watch him bleed.
                                        Nothing could be sweeter.   940
         He'll pay the just price—blood for blood.

                                        Exit AMPHITRYON.

CHORUS The gods demand reprisal: Evil
         Turns back on the man who commits evil.
         The river of Lykos' life flows backwards
         To death.
                            You'll pay with your own blood
         For all the blood you shed.
                                        For lording it
         Over your betters, your time comes to suffer.
         Each step brings you closer to the fate
         You planned for others.

                                        I'd lost all hope
         That he'd return—my eyes smart with tears,   950
         I'm so glad to see our king.
                                        Come on, old friends,
         Let's look inside the house—
                                        I want to see
         If it all happens the way we'd hoped.

59

LYKOS (from inside Herakles' house)   Help! Help!

CHORUS From inside the house the first note sounds sweet.
Another note, another—and the tune's soon over.

LYKOS (as before)   Country of Kadmos! They've laid an
ambush!
They're murdering me!

CHORUS   Yes, blood for blood,
Murder for murder. For what you owe,
You're paying the full price.

                              Who was the liar
Who claimed the gods have no power?   960
It had to be a human being. Only flesh and blood
Could spread such a senseless story.
A lawless man. A scoffer.

                    Old friends,
Our enemy—and all his evil—is wiped away.
The house has gone silent. Joy makes me want to dance.
Our friends won out! Just as I'd hoped!

After grief and pain, when
Good fortune starts to shine,
Every rut in every street
Brims over with light.   970
The dancers' flashing feet
Make us join their dancing
And tears that flowed down
Inspire in us new songs.
Take to the streets, celebrate
This change of fortune!
Dancing, singing, feasting—
The whole town seems divine!
The upstart eats dirt—
And power flashes   980
From the brow
Of our rightful king
Who set sail over Acheron.
I'd given up all hope
That he'd return

From death's chill harbor.
But hope reversed despair.

The gods watch over
The races that we run,
The unjust and the just   990
In breakneck competition—
Gold and Good Fortune,
Power and Lawlessness
Are the horses we lash
Into a lather to pull
Our chariot faster
Than Law gaining on us hard,
Coming up on the outside.
Yoked to his ambitions,
What driver looks ahead   1000
To the homeward stretch?
Whipped on by his own will,
He hurtles forward
In the black chariot
Of worldly success:
Spoke and axle snap—
He's thrown head over heels
Into drifting dust.

River Ismenos, put on
Your whirlpooling crowns!   1010
All the gleaming streets
Flowing out like rivers
To our city's seven gates
Join in the dancing
Of Dirke's rippling flow
And of Asopos' daughters
Whose heads toss like waves
Above their father's waters
Running cool, bright fingers
Through their streaming hair.   1020
Join in the victory song
Of our own Herakles!
Rocky woods of Delphi,
Muses on Mount Helikon,
Make your voices echo off

These walls of stone
Where our ancestors sown
From dragon teeth sprang up
Armored in bronze and hand on
Our country to their children's   1030
Children whose eyes burn
With the saving light of dawn.

Think of the bed that a god
And a human being shared,
The divine and mortal
Both longing to embrace
The same bride, Alkmene,
Granddaughter of Perseus.
I doubted at first that Zeus
Took part—but the years   1040
Don't lie: They shine down,
Zeus, on Herakles your son,
And reveal his strength
To be superhuman.
In Pluto's prison
He broke the chains of death
And came back to the sun
From the depths underground.
Power that settles
On the chosen man   1050
Proves that Herakles
Is worthier than
That low-class climber.
Put a sword in his hand,
Make him stand and fight—
And you'll find out fast
Whether the gods still favor
A cause they think is just.

IRIS *and* MADNESS *appear above the roof.*

Up there! Look!
                    Do you feel the same stroke
Of terror?
                    Old friends—are those phantoms   1060
Hovering above the house?
                    Let's get clear of this!

Come on, old bones! Move it! On the double!
Healing Apollo, don't let them near us! Keep them off!

IRIS   Don't be spooked by us, old men. This is Lyssa—
Her nickname's Madness—the child of Night.
And I—I am Iris. I serve the gods.
We don't mean to hurt you or the city.
Just one man's house is lined up in our sights:
The one known as the son of Zeus . . . and Alkmene.
As long as his labors made his life bitter,   1070
Necessity shielded him;

                  and Zeus himself
Held Hera and me off.

                     But he's carried out
Eurystheus' orders, so Hera's dreamed up
Another labor;

             and I'm in on it:

                     To stain
Herakles' hands with the blood of his own kin
And weigh him down under the guilt of murdering
His sons.

          Virgin daughter of black-shrouded Night,
Madness, you have no children:

                   Don't let your heart
Go out to him.

           Wind it up tighter
And tighter in your breast until it lets loose   1080
Such fits of madness the soles of his feet
Burn and tingle to leap after his sons!
Let the sails of murder swell so full
He jams the tiller with his bloody hands
And ferries his own children over Acheron—
His children, the crown of all his labors.
It's time he learnt the depths of Hera's rage.
And my rage, too.

            We gods are done for,
And human beings might as well take over
If he gets off without paying our price.   1090

MADNESS   The gods wince at the sight of me
For the office I perform—

              but I'm noble at heart:
My mother is Night, my father Heaven.

I take no pleasure in afflicting human beings
I count as friends.
                        And I don't want to see
You and Hera stumble—so hear me out:
Herakles' fame reaches from here to the gods
—It's *his* house you're sending me against.
He brought the wild powers of the earth to heel
And leveled the waves of the storming sea.   1100
Single-handedly, he raised up the honors of the gods
That the arrogance of human beings knocked aside.
Take my advice and give up this plan: It's monstrous!

IRIS   Spare us. Hera's and my schemes don't need your
                                              counsel.

MADNESS   I'm trying to set you on the straight road: You've gone
                                                    astray.

IRIS   The wife of Zeus didn't send you to show how temperate
                                                  you are.

MADNESS   As the Sun is my witness, I'm doing what I don't wish to
                                                    do.
                  But if that's how it has to be, if necessity binds me
To do what you and Hera ask, I'll plunge ahead
The way a pack of hunting dogs bark and snap
To be unleashed:
                        When I enter Herakles' heart   1110
And make it beat louder and louder in his ears,
Breakers pounding on a reef, or the ground
Shaking and cracking wide, or lightning slashing
Through gasping clouds, won't match my rage:
I'll smash through his roof and rampage room to room,
Slaughtering his sons.
                        And the murderer won't know
That his hands are stained by the blood of children
He bred from his own flesh—until in his breast the storm
Of my frenzy blows itself out.
                        Look there: Like a runner jumping
The starting line, he's off—
                              then stops, starts, head   1120

Tossing, pupils bulging while the whites of his eyes
Roll up;
            his breath pants hard, his head lowers
Like a bull about to charge:
                              Hear his snorts
And bellows, as if he called to the demons
Howling among screeching spirits of the dead—
I'll make you dance even faster to my notes
Of terror!
            Run along now, Iris. Your path of honor
Takes you soaring back to Olympos.
                              My job
Is to slip unseen into Herakles' house.

                                        Exit IRIS *and* MADNESS.

CHORUS   City of Thebes, grieve: 1130
         Can't you hear those notes
         Piercing as arrows,
         Venemous as snakes?
         Such music makes me weep
         For the son of Zeus, Greece's
         Best defender, the flower
         Of all manhood cut down
         By the ache in his mind.
         Lost to himself, we lose
         Him too, his spirit rent   1140
         By those crazing notes.
         Or else he hears a chariot
         Gaining from behind:
         The daughter of Night
         Whips her horses on,
         Hair writhing and hissing
         Like a hundred snakes,
         Gorgon-gaze turning
         Human beings to stone.

         The god blinks—
                          and the wind   1150
         Of fortune swings around.

The god blinks—
                              and a man
Massacres his sons.

AMPHITRYON (within the house)   Oh, unbearable!

CHORUS Zeus, your son
         Is being trampled down
         As though he weren't your child.
         And Herakles' sons, too,
         Will be lost to him.
                              Vengeance
         Slashes his mind to bits;   1160
         Madness breathes in his face
         And makes him wild . . .

AMPHITRYON (within)   Wretched house!

CHORUS The dances are beginning—
         Listen—not the dances
         Of the god of wine
         Joyously brandishing
         His ivy-covered staff;
         But pulsing in the mind
         A silent drumming . . .

AMPHITRYON (within)   The walls, the roof!

CHORUS What is that throbbing?   1170
         Not the pleasant ache
         Of grapes crushed to wine
         For the wine god's oblations—
         But a pounding in the head
         That drives us to the edge . . .

AMPHITRYON (within)   Children! Stay away! Run!

CHORUS The pipe keeps shrieking
         Notes of ruin. Driven
         Wild by the chase, he hunts
         You down. Madness dancing

                    Drunken through the house   1180
                    Won't dance for nothing . . .

AMPHITRYON (within)   Stop! Don't . . . such suffering!

       CHORUS Poor old man, your troubles
               Break my heart—grief won't stop
               Howling! Weep for Herakles' father
               And the wife and mother
               Who bore him sons for this!
               Look! A whirlwind shakes the house!
               The roof is caving in!

AMPHITRYON (within)   Wise Athena, child of Zeus
                      Who sprung full-blown from his head,   1190
                      Why are you doing this?
                      You've smashed this man's house
                      The way you smashed the giant
                      Who attacked Mount Olympos.
                      You've sent a shockwave
                      Shuddering from heaven down
                      To Hades' darkest pit!

                                              Enter MESSENGER.

MESSENGER White-haired old men—.

       CHORUS   Why do you cry out
               Like that?

MESSENGER   Inside the house . . . horrible.

       CHORUS   No need
               For an oracle. I can guess . . .

MESSENGER   The boys—they're dead.   1200

       CHORUS Ahh . . . AHHHH . . .

MESSENGER Grieve for them. Believe me—there's reason to grieve.

       CHORUS Murdered—by the hands of their own father!
               Could a man be that savage?

MESSENGER   I'm tongue-tied:
The words won't come—
                        for what we've suffered here . . .

CHORUS Tell us however you can—
                        about his boys—
Cut down by his own hands . . .
                        Come on, now. Speak.
What happened when the gods smashed the house?
And the poor madman's sons—
                        how did they die?

MESSENGER The victims . . . to be sacrificed . . . had been placed   1210
Before Zeus' altar. Herakles had thrown
The body of the king out of doors.
The house was ready to be purified.
There stood his boys—fine-looking youngsters—
And Megara and the old man.

                                    The basket,
With the sacrificial knife and barley,
Had already been carried round the altar.
We kept silent, observing the holy hush.
And then . . .
                reaching out his hand . . .
                                    to take the torch
And plunge it in the lustral water—   1220
Herakles stood frozen in his tracks:

Dead silent. Suspended. Not there.

                                    His boys
Kept staring at him—
                        his face contorts:
He looks . . . deranged. The whites of his eyeballs
Rolling up. Veins gorged and bloodshot.
Foaming at the mouth, slobber dripping down
His beard.
                His laughter was twisted,
Out of control:
                "So father," he says, "why waste time
With sacrifices and cleansing fire?

I might as well kill Eurystheus first   1230
And save the trouble of doing it all again.
When I cut off Eurystheus' head
And bring it back here, then I'll wipe
My hands of blood.
                         Pour out that water!
Throw down those baskets!
                                 My bow—
Bring it here! And my club!
                                 I'm off to storm Mycenae.
We need crowbars and pickaxes. Those Cyclopes
Are good builders, every stone squared to
The red chalk line and tamped down by masons'
                                              hammers!
But iron will pry up the cornerstones   1240
And smash those high-built walls to bits!"
Then he was off, talking like he had a chariot:
He jumps up into it, his fingers gripping air
The way a charioteer grips the rail,
His free hand lashing down to whip his horses on.
We didn't know whether to laugh . . . or shy away
In fear.
              Finally, someone whispers:
"Is the chief fooling around—

                                 or off his head?"
He was pacing wildly back and forth
All through the house—
                         he rushes into the main hall   1250
And shouts, "I'm here in Nisus' city!—"
                                        Right there
In his own home!
                    He lies down on the floor, still dressed
For sacrifice, and begins to make a feast.
He was at that only a moment before
He shouts, "I'm nearing the woods of Corinth!"
Like an athlete at the games there, he stripped down
And began a wrestling match—
                                 only he wrestles
With the air or with clouds of dust as he
Tumbles in the ring.
                         Acting as his own herald,
He quiets the crowd and calls out: 1260

69

"The winner of the crown—glorious Herakles!"
Next, he was in Mycenae, cursing out
Eurystheus; his father clings to his massive hand
And says, "Son, what's got into you?
All this make-believe traveling . . .

                                  Surely,
The blood of these upstarts hasn't made you come
Unglued?"

                     By now the old man was trembling,
But Herakles thought Eurystheus' father
Clung to his hand and begged his mercy.
He shoves the old man off, strings his bow   1270
And nocks an arrow, ready to shoot down
His three little boys:

                            He thought they were
Eurystheus' sons!

                    The children got so scared
They rushed around this way and that,
One ducking under his mother's skirt,
One crouching down in the shadow of a pillar,
The last huddling like a bird beneath the altar.
Their mother cries out: "You're their father—
Are you going to kill your own flesh and blood?"
The old man and the whole crowd of us   1280
Started shouting—

                  he chased his son around
The pillar, spins the boy about, and shoots him
Through the heart. The arrow knocks him backwards
Against the pillar where he gasps and collapses,
Staining the stone with blood.

                             Herakles
Crows his own triumph: "One down, Eurystheus!
Your fledgling here has paid the price for all your hate."
The next boy was cowering down by the altar's
Lowest step, hoping he was hidden.
But when he sees his father swing round   1290
With his bow to take aim, he throws himself down
Before his father's knees. He lifts up his hand
In appeal to his father's beard and neck
And cries out: "I'm your son, Father—yours—
Not Eurystheus'!

                 Herakles' eyes

Like a Gorgon's are rolling in his head —
And when he sees that the boy is too close
For him to draw his fatal bow, he raises
His club . . .

        and the way a blacksmith hammers
Red-hot iron, he swings it down on his boy's   1300
Blond head, smashing in the skull —

           his second son lay dead.
So he moves on to slaughter his third victim.
The mother was wild now with all she'd seen —
She swooped down in front of him and snatched
Her boy away into the house and locked the door.
He starts prying at the door frame and digging up
The posts —

        as if he really were tearing down
The Cyclopes' walls! —

        and with one arrow, shoots dead
His wife and son.

        His father's next — he charged
The old man — but something —

        a shimmering   1310
That firmed up into Athena's shape
(At least that's how it looked) shook her spear
Above her helmet's crest —

        she hurled a boulder
Against Herakles' chest —

        it knocked him senseless
And stopped his bloody rampaging.

        His back
Struck a pillar that had snapped in two when the roof
Collapsed —

        and he lies there now, sprawled against its base.
We all crept out from where we were hiding
And helped the old man tie him to the pillar
With good strong rope, double and triple knots —   1320
So when he wakes, he won't add more blood
To blood already shed . . .

        A man who's murdered
His wife and sons —

        and there he sleeps! . . .
Oblivious. Not knowing what he's done.

There's nothing you'd call blessed about such sleep:
No human being could be more miserable.

Exit MESSENGER.

CHORUS The memory of bloodshed stains the mind.
        It's like a film blurring everything we see.
        Greece can't forget the blood Danaos' daughters
        Shed at Argos: Infamous slaughter.   1330
        But this latest labor of Zeus' son surpasses
        That butchery . . .
                          Or I could tell you
        How Prokne murdered her only son—
        Poets try to blot the blood with song
        But such violence stains even the Muses' minds.
        Prokne had only the one boy—
                          while you, Herakles,
        Driven on by Madness
                          —father, destroyer—
        Murdered all three.
                          I can't find the tune
        To grieve for what you've done. The steps of the dance,
        The words of the song that would placate   1340
        The dead,
                  and help us bear our grief,
                          just won't come . . .

        Look: They've thrown back the bolts. The great doors
        Are creaking open . . .

          The doors open and reveal the bodies of MEGARA *and the*
          CHILDREN, *with* AMPHITRYON *mourning them;* HERAKLES,
          asleep, is tied to a broken pillar.

                          And there . . . are the children.
        Only look at them!
                          They lie at their father's feet;
                                      their father—
        Asleep . . . resting from the labor of slaughtering
        His sons:
                  A terrible sleep so heavy headed
        He can't feel the rope's knots tying down his body
        To the broken pillar of his home.

72

And here comes the old man—each step heavier,
More bitter than the last . . .

                              his soft moaning   1350
Like a bird mourning her unfledged young.

AMPHITRYON Old men, let him sleep. Keep still. Give him
This moment of forgetfulness before
He wakes to what he's done.

CHORUS   Old friend,
I can't keep back my tears:

                              For you. The children.
And for him—who wore the victor's crown.

AMPHITRYON Move back. Don't cry out! Make no noise
That will rouse him from his sleep so deep and calm.

CHORUS It's terrible . . . so much blood . . .

AMPHITRYON   Keep quiet!
You'll get us all killed!

CHORUS   . . . rises to engulf him.   1360

AMPHITRYON Can't you grieve in silence, old friends?

                                             If he wakes,
He'll break free of these ropes and go rampaging again.
He'll destroy us all:

                              The city. His father.
His own home.

CHORUS   I can't . . . I can't keep from crying.

AMPHITRYON Quiet! I need to lean down to hear his breathing.

CHORUS Is he sleeping?

AMPHITRYON   He's asleep, all right.
If you can call this heavy-bodied slackness
Sleep . . . for a man who's killed his wife and children
With his bowstring's deadly hum.

CHORUS   Go on, then—grieve.

AMPHITRYON I'm grieving with you.

CHORUS   Grieve for these dead boys.   1370

AMPHITRYON This tears my heart out.

CHORUS   Grieve for your stricken son.

AMPHITRYON Ahh . . .

CHORUS Old friend.

AMPHITRYON   Hush. Don't make a sound. He's stirring now,
He's turning. There—
                    he's awake! I'd better hide
Inside the house.

CHORUS   Don't be afraid. Darkness still weighs
His eyelids down.

AMPHITRYON   Be careful there! Watch out!
After all this—it's not dying I'm afraid of.
To lose my light would ease this misery.
But if he wakes and murders me—
                              he'll add
The guilt of his father's blood to the blood   1380
He already owes the Furies.

CHORUS   That day you took
Vengeance on the Taphians for the blood
Of your wife's kinsmen, storming their fortress
Surrounded by the sea—
                    that would have been
A glorious day for you to die.

AMPHITRYON   Run, old men!
Get clear of this house! Run as far as you can
From his rage!
              There—he's awake!
                              Soon, he'll be drunk
On killing again, murder on top of murder:
He's set to go rampaging through the city!   1390

CHORUS   Zeus, why should you hate Herakles so fiercely
         When he's your own son?

                              He'll drown in such rough seas
         Of suffering and pain.

                                        HERAKLES *wakes.*

HERAKLES   Huhhhh . . .
         I'm still alive. I'm seeing—what I should see.
         Clear sky. The ground. These shafts of sun.
         Like arrows. My head's aswim . . .

                              and my mind's
         All choppy like the sea after a storm.
         My breath swells high and hard into my aching lungs.
         Not flowing easy, the way it should.
                              What?
         Moored like a ship? Ropes around my chest and arms—

                              me?—   1400
         Herakles?

                   Anchored fast to this cracked stonework—
         And next to me:
                   Bodies. All dead.

                        There's my bow . . . and arrows
         Scattered on the ground . . .

                        which have always stood by me . . .
         The way a fellow soldier would . . .

                              Weapons that have
         Protected me the way I've protected them.
         Have I gone back down to the underworld?
         Run that race for Eurystheus over again?
         But I don't see Sisyphus hunched at his boulder.
         Or the god of death. Or the scepter of
         Demeter's child . . . Persephone . . . the god's wife.   1410
         I'm out to sea with all this—
                              I'm lying here,
         Helpless . . . at a loss to say where I am.
         Where could Herakles be helpless?
                              Hey! Friends!
         Where are you? Is there anyone around
         Who can cure me of this murkiness in my brain?
         Everything's a jumble. Nothing's the way it should be.

AMPHITRYON This cuts me to the heart . . . Old friends, should I go to
                                                            him?

CHORUS You won't go alone—I'll stand by you in your trouble.

HERAKLES Father—why are you hiding your eyes? You're crying!
         Don't stand so far off—I'm your son, Father—yours.   1420

AMPHITRYON Yes. No matter how desperate things are—you're still my
                                                             child.

HERAKLES What's happened to me? Have *I* done something—to
                                          make you weep?

AMPHITRYON Even a god—if he cared enough to know—would grieve.

HERAKLES That terrible? But you still haven't told me.

AMPHITRYON There. It's in front of you. If your mind's clear enough to
                                                              see.

HERAKLES Tell me! You act like things are changed—for the worst!

AMPHITRYON If your mind's not drunk—on death—then I'll tell you.

HERAKLES My mind? What's the riddle? What are you hiding?

AMPHITRYON I'm still not sure—if your mind's completely sound.

HERAKLES But I don't remember—any uproar in my mind.   1430

AMPHITRYON Old men, should I untie my son—or not?

HERAKLES Untie me. I won't let this pass. Whoever shamed me . . .

AMPHITRYON (untying him)   . . . What you've done is burden enough.
                                          The rest, let go.

HERAKLES So silence is all the answer that I'll get?

AMPHITRYON Zeus! Do you see what misery Hera's sent down on us
                                          from heaven?

HERAKLES Is it Hera's spite, then, that struck me down?

AMPHITRYON Let the goddess alone. Bear up under your own bitter life.

HERAKLES My life—is ruined then. You're about to tell me something terrible.

AMPHITRYON There. Look at them. The bodies—of children.

HERAKLES I can't bear to think of what I'm seeing!   1440

AMPHITRYON They weren't enemies—these children—when war broke
out against them.

HERAKLES War? Who did this? Who—destroyed them?

AMPHITRYON You. Your bow and arrows. And the god who lent a hand.

HERAKLES You're saying I killed them? You—my own father—messenger of this horror?

AMPHITRYON You were—driven mad. To answer you this way destroys
me.

HERAKLES And my wife—was I the one—responsible?

AMPHITRYON All of this . . . by one hand. Yours.

HERAKLES I can't bear up under all this. I'm swallowed up by clouds
of pain.

AMPHITRYON So now you know why I was weeping . . .

HERAKLES And I tore down my house in my madness?   1450

AMPHITRYON I only know this: Everything you had is changed to grief.

HERAKLES Where did I go mad? Where did my soul betray me?

AMPHITRYON There. By the altar. As you purified your hands with fire.

HERAKLES For murdering my sons—my dear little boys—I should
Take my own life. Be judge and jury

77

For my childrens' blood.

                       Hurl myself from
A sheer cliff. Stab a sword deep into my side.
Or set myself on fire and burn away
The shame that will make everyone turn
Their backs on me.

                        THESEUS *approaches in the wings.*

               There's—Theseus!   1460
My kinsman and my friend: He's in the way
Of my plans to kill myself.

                     He'll see my shame:
My childrens' blood will defile the eyes
Of my dearest friend.

                What can I do?
Wings can't fly high enough, there's no place
Deep enough for me to hide my shame.
I can't bear the sight of my own shadow!
I'll hide my head in darkness. Away from the sun.
I won't let my blood-guilt stain the innocent.

      HERAKLES *covers his head.* THESEUS *comes forward, with*
      FOLLOWERS.

THESEUS Sir, I've come from Athens. My troops are posted   1470
Down by the banks of the Asopos. I'm here
To offer your son a crack allied force:
A rumor reached us that Lykos had overthrown
The government and was pressing you—hard.
Old friend, whatever my hand or my spearmen
Can do, we're here to do it.

                    Herakles
Brought me back from the underworld—

                        alive.
For that, I owe him a helping hand.
What's this?

             Bodies—scattered about the ground.
It looks like we've come too late—your troubles   1480
Have outmarched us.

              These boys—who killed them?
That woman sprawled there—whose wife was she?

Children don't stand in the ranks of spearmen:
This looks out of bounds—some new atrocity.

AMPHITRYON Lord of the hilltop olive tree—

THESEUS   Are you all right?
Your voice—sounds broken—with grief.

AMPHITRYON We've been destroyed! Destroyed by the gods' hands . . .

THESEUS These boys you're crying over—who are they?

AMPHITRYON Their father is my son: He bred them.
He murdered them. Their blood is on his hands.   1490

THESEUS What you say—can't be!

AMPHITRYON   I only wish it weren't!

THESEUS It's unspeakable—what you just told me!

AMPHITRYON Our whole lives are swept away. Like trash.

THESEUS What happened? How did he do—what he did?

AMPHITRYON Madness like a wave shipwrecked his mind . . .
With arrows dipped in the venom of hydra's blood.

THESEUS Hera's hand is behind all this.
                                        But who is it
Lying there beside the bodies?

AMPHITRYON   My son—
My son who performed so many labors.
Who stood shoulder to shoulder with the gods   1500
And bloodied his spear against the giants
On the Plains of Phlegra . . .

THESEUS   Was any human being
Ever cursed with a fate worse than this?

AMPHITRYON There's nobody alive who's faced
Greater trials or suffered worse torments.

THESEUS Why is he hiding his head under his cloak?

AMPHITRYON Shame to meet your eye.
Shame before his kin and friends.
Shame at the blood of his butchered sons.

THESEUS I'll take my share in his pain. Someone uncover him.

AMPHITRYON Child! Uncover your face, hold up your head 1510
To the sun:
Against your grief,
friendship
Like a wrestler throws its weight.
Son, my old eyes
Can't keep from tears—I'm begging you
By your beard, your knees, your hand:
Don't let this rage
Run away with you—don't play the lion
Hungry for your own blood.
This race to death
Only swells the flood: There's been enough grief and
pain.

THESEUS You—huddled there—you think you're destroyed—
But look up:
We're your friends. Show us your face.
There's no cloud black enough that can hide this horror 1520
From the sun.
Why are you waving me away—
Warning me off from all this bloodshed?
Are you afraid your words will strike me down
With contagion?
But I can bear it if your suffering
Falls on me—you stood by me once:
You led me
From the underworld back into the sunlight.
I hate fair-weather friends—whose gratitude
Goes stale. Who'll take their share of a friend's good luck,
But won't sail with him when his luck turns sour.
Stand up and face us. Uncover your head. 1530
The gods shake the dice—
and we have to endure

80

Whatever Heaven sends. To face up to fate
Without flinching:
                    That's courage in a man.

                    THESEUS *uncovers* HERAKLES' *head.*

HERAKLES Theseus—have you seen what I did to my own children?

THESEUS They told me. . . . The suffering you point to—I see it
                                                    well enough.

HERAKLES So . . . why have you exposed my head to the sun?

THESEUS You're human . . . nothing human can stain what is
                                                    divine.

HERAKLES Steer clear of me. Run from my infection!

THESEUS No vengeful spirit of the dead can taint the love between
                                                    friends.

HERAKLES I have no friends. . . . But I'll never regret having been
                                            yours.   1540

THESEUS You helped me when I needed it—now I'm here to stand
                                            by you.

HERAKLES Stand by me? A man who butchered his own sons?

THESEUS Now that trouble drags you down—yes, my tears are for
                                            you.

HERAKLES Can any man alive have done anything this terrible?

THESEUS Misfortune like yours reaches from the earth . . . clear up
                                            to heaven.

HERAKLES So *now* you understand—I want to die.

THESEUS Do you think the gods care one bit about your threats?

HERAKLES The gods follow their own stubborn course . . . as I will
                                            toward the gods.

THESEUS Watch what you say—boasting will only get you in
                                                          deeper!

HERAKLES My hold's so filled with grief there's no place to stow   1550
                                                            more.

THESEUS What? If you're thinking of . . . Where is your rage driving
                                                            you?

HERAKLES To death. Back where I just came from—back to the
                                                    underworld.

THESEUS Now you're talking like any ordinary man.

HERAKLES And you—who aren't suffering—who are you to give
                                                          advice?

THESEUS Is this Herakles talking? Herakles, who's endured so
                                                          much?

HERAKLES But never this much! I've been pushed to the wall.

THESEUS You!—who made the world safe. Great friend to all hu-
                                                    man beings!

HERAKLES What good do they do me? Hera's the one who lords it
                                                        over us.

THESEUS Don't be a fool. Greece won't let you die such a pointless
                                                          death.

HERAKLES Hear me out. What I have to say will show up   1560
            Your advice. My life has been a botch,
            First to last:
                          I take after my father—
            Who killed my mother's father—and disregarding
            Such a blood-curse, married Alkmene who gave birth . . .
            To me.
                      When the foundation's laid so badly
            That the whole house tilts, the sons
            Inherit . . . grief.
                          Zeus (whoever Zeus is!)

Bred me as a target for Hera's hate.
Don't be angry with me, old man:

        You've acted
The way a true father would—more than this Zeus!   1570
When I was still nursing at my mother's breast,
The wife of Zeus sent gorgon-eyed snakes into
My cradle to poison me.

       When I grew up,
My arms and legs were sheathed in muscle
Tight-woven as a herdsman's cloak—

         but why go over
All those labors I endured?

       Lions;
Many-headed monsters with three bodies;
Giants; charging hordes of sharp-hooved centaurs—
I wiped them out. Slaughtered them all.

         Even that bitch
The hydra, two heads sprouting back for each one   1580
I lopped off—I killed her too . . .

        my labors
Stretched in front of me, horizonless
As the night sea—

      until I reached the dark world
Of the dead:

     At Eurystheus' orders,
I brought back from the gates of Hades
The three-headed watchdog snapping and snarling . . .
But my final labor—

      blood on blood—

         oh, I triumphed—
Was to butcher my own boys!—

       and set
The capstone on my house of slaughter.
My fate's come to this—the law says I have   1590
To leave: My own dear Thebes can't stand
The sight of me!

      If I stayed, what temple
Would let me enter? When they saw me coming,
Even my friends would cross the street.
A life as cursed and bloody as mine
—Just who will dare to speak to me?
Well, you say, there's Argos—isn't Argos

Home ground?
                    But Argos exiled me.
So how about some other city?
But there, they'd all look at me slyly   1600
Out of the corners of their eyes—
                                and they'd whisper,
"Isn't that him? the child-killer?"
                                        their tongues
Like doors slammed shut against me . . .
Gossiping the way people do behind locked doors:
"So that's Zeus' bastard! the one who murdered
His wife and sons! What's he hanging around here for?
Someone should tell him to clear off!"
                                        I counted myself
Happy once—and to find out that my happiness
Would come down to this:
                        Blood. Death.   1610
I can't bear to think of it.
                        That man's lucky
Who's known misery since his birth. His pain
Drags after him, familiar as the sun.
I've come to the end of everything—
My fate's unspeakable:
                        The earth cries out
Against me, forbidding me to touch the ground,
Rivers and waves shrink away from me,
Hissing, "Don't come near!"
                            I'm no better than Ixion,
Chained forever to a wheel of fire.
The best fate I can envision is that no Greek   1620
Who ever knew me when my luck was good
Should ever have to see my face again:
A life like that—what good is it.
                            I hate it:
Useless; bloody; cursed.
                        And all so that Zeus' wife—
The glorious Hera—can take pleasure in her hate:
Dancing on Olympos, her sandals ringing loud
While her feet pound the gleaming floor.
She's got what she schemed for—
                                she's smashed
To pieces, foundation and all, the pillar

That held up Greece:
                                        Who would stoop so low as   1630
To pray to such a goddess?
                                        Driven by
Petty jealousy — because this Zeus crept
Into a mortal woman's bed . . .
                                        And so
She's destroyed the one man all Greece looked on
As a friend —
                                        though that man was blameless
And did nothing to deserve such hate.

CHORUS It's Hera who's behind all this. No other god
        But the wife of Zeus. You're absolutely right in that.

THESEUS Listen to me:
                                        What's the point of killing yourself?
        Human beings have to suffer. So be patient.   1640
        Bear up. Show your true strength.
                                        Fate lets no one off,
        Not even the gods —
                                        if the poets haven't lied.
        Don't the gods trample on lawful love when
        They sneak off on the sly?
                                        And haven't they thrown
        Their own fathers into chains for the sake
        Of gaining power?
                                        But there they are,
        Still living on Olympos —
                                        managing just fine
        Despite their crimes.
                                        Do you think you're better
        Than the gods — you, who are only human?
        If they endure their fates without crying out,   1650
        Why shouldn't you?
                                        So leave Thebes.
        Live up to the law — and come with me
        To Athena's city.
                                        I'll purify your hands
        Of blood. And give you a home and a share

85

Of everything that's mine.
                                        All the gifts
My people gave me for killing the Minotaur
And saving the fourteen young people
That beast would have devoured,
                                        I'll give over to you.
Throughout my country, fields and pastures
Have been reserved for me—all these   1660
I'll cede to you and you'll hold them in your name
As long as you live.
                              And when you die
And descend to Hades, Athens will raise up
Stone monuments to your memory and make sacrifices
In your honor.
                         The honor that Athens wins
In serving you
                    will be our city's crown of fame
And make us renowned through all of Greece.
I owe this to you: You saved my life.
Now that you need a friend, I can pay back
What I owe.
                    But if a god makes up his mind   1670
To reach out to a mortal man, he needs
No human friends:
                         The god's help is enough.

HERAKLES   My troubles . . . what have they got to do with all your
                                                                talk?
I can't believe the gods shrug off unlawful love affairs.
Or wrap chains around each others' hands—
I've never believed that—and I can't be persuaded.
No god—
              if he is a god—
                                   lords it over another.
A god is self-contained. Perfect. Needing nothing.
He's his own atmosphere. And his own world.
All this talk:
                    It's only poets mouthing lies . . .   1680
I've thought it over—my head feels muffled
In dark clouds—
                         but to kill myself—
To blink or flinch away from what fate deals:

That's the kind of man who'll run from a spear
Thrusting in his face.
                        I won't turn coward.
I'll endure what I have to—and wait for death.
I'll go with you to Athens;
                        and I'll owe
A thousand thanks for all your gifts.
                                Theseus—
Look at the countless labors my fate ordained.
I didn't turn aside from one—even when   1690
My heart seemed to freeze inside me
And the air and light felt immovable as stone.
I never allowed myself a single tear.
And now here I am—
                        my cheeks—
                                are stained.
It's come down to this:
                        I'm chained to my fate.
No matter how hard I fight, I can't escape.

Old man. You see what's ahead of me:
                                Exile—
From Thebes.
                And you see that with these hands
I butchered my own boys.
                        Prepare them for the grave,
Wrap their bodies—
                        and bury them out of sight.   1700
The law won't allow murderers like me
To touch my own children.
                        Your tears are all the honors
That they'll get. Lay them in their mother's arms,
Their heads on her breast.
                        Mother and children
Together to the last.
                        I tore them from
Each other's arms . . . and killed them . . . not knowing
What I was doing:
                        Ignorant. Raging. The ache
In my mind blotting everything out.
Bury them, old man. And once the ground
Covers them, stay on here . . . painful though it will be.   1710

Force yourself to keep going. Don't lose heart.
I need your help to bear up under my own sorrows.

Boys:
            Your father—
                        who brought you into the world—
Destroyed you:
                        Herakles the Great. Heroic Herakles.
All the labors I went through to make your lives
Easier, and give you the best inheritance
I could:
            Glory. Fame. Honor—
You won't need them now . . . not ever.

And you, my unhappy wife—so patient
Through all those years of lonely waiting,   1720
So loyal to me and to our bed—
This is your reward . . .
                        my wife; my boys . . .
                                    and me,
The monster who did all this:
                        My head's splitting
With it . . .
            I've been unyoked from my children
And my wife.
            You can't know the bitter solace
Of kissing you like this—
                        or the bitterness
Of touching my bow and club,
                        my weapons
That I've loved and kept by me all these years:
Now I can barely look at them.
                        I can't bear
To keep them . . . or part with them either.   1730
Brushing against my ribs, they'll whisper over and over,
"With us, you killed your wife and sons:
                        If you keep us,
You keep your children's murderers."
How can I sling my bow and club over my shoulder?
What will I say to excuse it?
                        But if I throw away
My bow and club—these weapons that helped me

Do what no one else in Greece has done—
I'll be throwing away my life.
                              My enemies
Will come looking for me, and I'll die
In utter shame. I can't leave them behind too—   1740
No matter how much they hurt me.

                              Theseus—
One last thing—help me take to Argos
The savage watchdog of the dead.
                              The pain
Of my dead sons—I'm afraid of what might happen
If I go alone.

                Country of Kadmos!
And all you people of Thebes! Cut your hair
In mourning. Grieve with me. See my children
Into their graves. Raise your voices together,
Mourn for me and my dead—
                              for we're all
As good as dead . . . all of us struck down   1750
By a single blow from Hera's hand.

THESEUS   Come on now, get up. My poor, dear friend—you've
                                        wept enough.

HERAKLES   I can't get up. My legs are like stone.

THESEUS   Necessity is a hammer that breaks even the strong.

HERAKLES   I wish I were stone. Blank as stone. Past grief.

THESEUS   That's enough. Take your friend's hand.

HERAKLES   Be careful. I'll stain more than your clothes with blood.

THESEUS   Go on. Stain them. My love for you will protect me from
                                              infection.

HERAKLES   All my sons are dead. Now, you'll be my son.

THESEUS   Put your arm around my neck. I'll steady you. Come this
                                        way.   1760

HERAKLES The yoke of friendship. But one of us in despair.
Father—this man—choose a man like him for a friend.

AMPHITRYON The country that nursed him is blessed in its children.

HERAKLES Theseus! Help me turn around. I want to see my boys!

THESEUS But you're only wounding yourself more . . .

HERAKLES Oh god, I want to see them—and I want to hug my
father.

AMPHITRYON Child, I'm here. With open arms. What you long for, I
want too.

THESEUS Herakles! Have you forgotten who you are? All your
labors?

HERAKLES My labors—they were nothing—next to this.

THESEUS Herakles. This weakness will be scorned if someone sees
you.   1770

HERAKLES So my life makes you scornful . . . it didn't use to.

THESEUS Look, you're asking for scorn. Where's the old heroic
Herakles?

HERAKLES When you were down in the underworld, how high was
your courage?

THESEUS I was completely crushed. Less than the meanest soul.

HERAKLES Then how can you say that my suffering degrades me?

THESEUS Go ahead. Lead on.

HERAKLES   Father—goodbye.

AMPHITRYON   Goodbye, my child.

HERAKLES Bury my boys.

AMPHITRYON   But who's going to bury me?

HERAKLES I will.

AMPHITRYON   You're coming back? When?

HERAKLES   After you've buried them.

AMPHITRYON How?

HERAKLES   [I'll send word to Thebes and bring you back
To Athens.]
                    Now—

                              take in these boys. The earth itself   1780
Can hardly bear up under their weight.
Everything I thought was mine sank in storming seas
My shameful deeds stirred up.
                              Now, I'll follow
In Theseus' wake, a little boat in tow.
If in your heart you put wealth and power
Over loving friendship, I tell you—you are mad.

                    Exit THESEUS *and* HERAKLES.

CHORUS Flickering, uncertain, now we must go,
As if already we were ghosts
                              weeping and sighing,
Wandering
              the earth's depths.
                              Among all
Our other losses,
              we've lost our dearest friend.

                    Exit AMPHITRYON *and* CHORUS.

NOTES ON THE TEXT

1–126 The prologue consists of a typical expository monologue to orient the audience;
then there is an exchange between Amphitryon and Megara that es-
tablishes the psychological and ideological conflict of the play's first
part: between hope based on a view of life's fundamental mutability
and a noble determination to withstand one's enemies without compromise in a situation that, seen realistically, appears to be utterly without remedy. Mixed in with the first view is faith in Herakles' heroic
capacities, even in the face of death, while the second is felt to be
consonant with a Heraklean heroic ideal of dignified endurance—also
in the face of death. The main genealogical line referred to here is (as
relevant to the play):

$$
\begin{array}{c}
\text{Zeus} \\
| \\
\text{Perseus} \\
\end{array}
$$

Zeus
|
Perseus
Alkaios   Elektryon   Sthenelos
| | |
Amphitryon   Alkmene —— Zeus   Eurystheus
                 |
                 Herakles

3 *who shared his wife* Zeus came to Alkmene's bed while Amphitryon was off on a
military campaign.

8–13 *Thebes, where dragonteeth . . . from the ground up* The central foundation myth
of Thebes. Kadmos was the sower of the teeth. At the core of the story

there is fratricidal violence that recurs in Theban stories and is reflected in the civil war in the background of this play.

22–23 *a city so huge* The city of Argos, politically important in the fifth century, is in the legendary world of the play blended with Mycenae (and Tiryns) famous for massive stone structures (Cyclopean) but otherwise of no importance in the historical period.

38–44 *There's an old story* Mythographic tradition makes the older Lykos regent of Thebes after the death of Kadmos' grandson Pentheus. He is married to Dirke (an indigenous Theban figure with the name of one of the city's major rivers: see 736 and 1009–15) and in mortal conflict with another strain of Thebes' foundation stories, Amphion and Zethus, children of Zeus and Antiope; Amphion's lyre-playing was instrumental in building Thebes' famous walls. The play's Lykos may be Euripides' invention. He replicates his father's role of ambivalent outsider who threatens a more legitimate, local ruling line.

62 *to celebrate his great victory* Translates Herakles' primary, traditional and cult epithet, *kallinikos* (literally, of fair victory). It's used throughout the play (eight times in all), in the end with bitter irony.

73 *the city of the Taphians* Amphitryon's notable achievement as a young warrior. He was avenging the deaths of Alkmene's brothers (see 1382–83).

94 *Distracting them with chatter* Like *Tell them a story* at line 117. This is at once ordinary and realistic and draws attention to the lies implicit in all storytelling, including the stories told within the play: see lines 1642, 1680 and Introduction p. 22.

125 *That's what courage is* A striking and unconventional redefinition of courage (*aretê*), assimilating the warrior's traditional virtue to an ideal of behavior for the weak and helpless nonwarriors. Megara will reject this ideal in the name of unsubmissive heroic behavior that, she says, is alone fitting for the hero Herakles' family. The last part of the play will show a testing of the viability of a new sense of courage in the figure of the defeated hero himself.

127–160 *Parodos* or choral entrance song. There are fifteen chorus members accompanied by a player of the *aulos* — an oboelike reed instrument. They sing, here rather briefly, in two stanzas having the same rhythmic and melodic patterns, followed by a third (152–60) that shifts, as they respond to the desperate scene before them, to a more rapid tempo. They also dance in coordination with the rhythms of the song, we assume, because of their extreme old age, with deliberate, measured steps (perhaps indicating the effect old age has on their movements as they describe them at lines 142 ff). Their age links them with a more glorious and mythic world of the past while making it impossible for them to be of any practical help in the present.

152–54 *Look at those boys' eyes* Literally, "flashing a Gorgon's gaze like their father's." This evokes the family link to Perseus who killed the Gorgon Medusa and used her snaky head as a weapon. There is also a suggestion of the double-edged nature of such heroic achievement, engaging with and defeating monstrous forces then partly embodying them oneself. The Gorgon motif recurs at 1148, 1296 and 1572.

163–265 First *episode* (dramatic unit between choral songs).

176 *some slimy marsh snake* Lykos reduces the mythic monster Hydra's name to a common noun *hydra*, that is, water snake.

177–78 *He claimed he strangled* Again an untranslatable verbal maneuver on Lykos' part, playing *brochois* (with nets)—the normal and ordinary way of capturing a wild animal, off *brachionos* (the arm's or bare-handed)—the heroic way. Such verbal tricks were characteristic of contemporary speculative and sophistic rationalism.

198–99 *Zeus's thunderbolts ... Zeus' chariot* Herakles was often represented in Greek art as fighting alongside the Olympian gods against the rebellious earthborn Giants. He is usually in Zeus' chariot using his bow, complementary counterpart to Zeus' spear, the thunderbolt. See also lines 1103–4, 1500–2, 1578.

234–35 *while you keep / Your own head down* Renders the notion of being impervious to unforeseen circumstances. What follows in the play will make this claim deeply ironical.

284–309 The chorus probably in the single person of their leader, the *koryphaios*, speaks these lines, by far the longest such speech by a chorus in Greek tragedy. The length of the speech strongly underscores a frustrated anger of helplessness and the gap between an older heroic community of Thebes and the ruthless politics that, indifferent to the past, now dominate the city.

284 *Ares tore the teeth* Refers again to Thebes' founding myth (see lines 8–13), though here assigning the sowing of the dragonteeth not to Kadmos but to Ares. This may be in order to evoke the chorus's past as warriors.

393–582 First *stasimon*, a choral song with dance, usually consisting of paired stanzas (*strophe* and *antistrophe*), each pair with its own repeated meter, or rhythm, and melody. The formal structure of this *stasimon* is unusual, long overall (the longest in Euripides) and exceptionally stylized. There are three paired sets of stanzas and each individual stanza is followed by an additional shorter stanzaic unit. All of these shorter units are identical in rhythm and melody except the third pair, which is slightly varied and extended by one line. Overall, then, a musical refrain is intertwined with the usual succession of sets of *strophes* and *antistrophes*. Such continuing refrains, very rare in tragedy, are characteristic of religious cult songs, as are some of the rhythms of the rest of the *stasimon*. Thus a formal lament is suggested. At the same time the musical structure, certain stylistic elaborations and the recital of the hero's great achievements also recall the victory songs for athletes that we know from Pindar. Herakles was regarded as the founder of the Olympian games and the imagery of athletic competition often accompanies him. Athletic contests and the tests of the Twelve Labors are akin.

   The traditions of the labors and which particular ones make up a set, usually of twelve, are somewhat variable. Here the chorus celebrate the Nemean Lion, the Centaurs, the Golden Hind, the Horses of Diomedes, the outlaw Kyknos, the Apples of the Hesperides, the ridding of pirates from the seas (this is a unique item among collections of labors, also in its generalized character), holding up the earth for Atlas, defeating the Amazons, the Hydra, the monster Geryon (guardian of special—otherwordly—cattle that Herakles must steal), and the descent to Hades to get Cerberus. This choice of labors locates Herakles over a wide geographical range, which underplays his sometimes close association with the region of the Peloponnese and highlights his Panhellenic character.

419 *Zeus's wood* A sacred precinct at Nemea in the northern Peloponnese.

473 *Mycenae's king* Eurystheus.

498 *Singing Maidens* The Hesperides or daughters of the evening star.

594–804 Second *episode*.

608–21 Herakles' future plans for his three sons would have settled them at three sites in various parts of Greece important in his life stories. The play illustrates the roles of Argos and Thebes. Oechalia is a city associated with Herakles after the events of this play (he sacks it after a quarrel with its king over the king's daughter). The name of the city is a momentary, slightly disorienting reminder of what Euripides' choice of material for this play has otherwise excluded.

623–24 *And I was to choose / For each of you a wife* The extension of Herakles' presence in Greece through his sons was also to have been achieved through marriage connections. These, however, appear to have a more contemporary relevance: Athens and Sparta, at the time of the play's production in the next to last decade of the fifth century B.C.E., have been at war over ten years, and Thebes was aggressively allied with Sparta.

668 As Amphitryon concludes his farewell speech, Herakles (immediately identifiable by his lion-skin costume and the weapons he carries) appears coming down the long *eisodos* or passageway alongside the stage building (there is one at each side), probably at the audience's left, indicating the way to and from "abroad." (The *eisodos* at the right would then indicate the way into the city of Thebes.) By about line 680 he reaches center stage.

747 *Herakles the Conqueror* That is, *kallinikos*, as at line 62 (see note there).

778–79 *gift from the goddess? . . . The Mysteries* The goddess is the queen of Hades Persephone. This alludes to and rejects a version of the story of fetching Cerberus in which the hero simply gets divine help. The Mysteries are the Eleusinian Mysteries closely associated with Athens. They held out the promise of a blessed existence after death. Traditionally Herakles was said to have been initiated into them in preparation for the Hades journey. The more general support of initiation, which also makes a connection to Athens, takes the place of the particular assistance of a goddess.

785 *I stayed to rescue Theseus* Theseus with his close friend Peirithoos had undertaken the reckless project of abducting Persephone from Hades. They failed and were imprisoned there.

805–906 Second *stasimon*. Two pairs of stanzas, each stanza self-enclosed in content. The rhythms are Aeolic, similar in kind to those of the first pair of stanzas and all the refrains of the first *stasimon*. In form this is a song of praise for Herakles' newly demonstrated valor, combining stylistic features of a hymn and an athlete's victory song.

806–7 *Etna's / Stones* The weight of the volcanic mountain was said to imprison either the monstrous giant Typhon or Enkelados after their defeat by the Olympian gods with Herakles' help (see lines 1577–78 and 1193–4).

821 *old age* Herakles was represented on a number of Athenian vases dated to the first half of the fifth century B.C.E.—subduing the personification of old age, Geras. In his cults at Athens the hero is also most frequently associated with ephebes, young men on the threshold of maturity. In the version of his legend in which he is rewarded by the gods for his services to them and to mankind he is given Hebe, Youth personified, as his bride (see Euripides, *The Children of Herakles* 910–16).

864 *my muse is Memory* The goddess Memory or Mnemosyne is mother of the Muses.

878 *The girls of Delos* The Delian maidens or Deliades were an actual ritual choral group on Delos, the island in the Aegean sacred to Apollo, Artemis and their mother Leto who gave birth to them there. Athens took particular interest in the place for reasons of politico-religious legitimation and had "purified" it about ten years before the production of *Herakles*. The Deliades were also known in Greek poetry from the time of the Homeric "Hymn to Apollo" (ca. 7th century B.C.E.) as figures of legend. This combination of mythic past with contemporary religious practice is similar to the double role of the play's chorus who perform as Theban elders in a mythic story and as ritual actors in the Athenian festival of Dionysos (see Introduction, p. 22). The Deliades sing before Apollo's temple, the play's chorus sing before Herakles' house (887): the chorus seem to praise Herakles as a god, even as something more (compare lines 891–93 and 680), or at least as one who is a savior when the gods are not. Herakles is raised as high as possible before his downfall.

888 *A song the dying swan* See also line 132. The comparison is quite intricate: the chorus members' white hair is like the swan's plumage; the swan's song is thought to be strong and piercing, appropriate both to lament and victory-song; swans were believed to sing most beautifully just before they die—the chorus are very old and death pervades the play; and finally the swan is sacred to Apollo at Delos, which recalls the (para-

doxical) association of the young Delian maidens and the aged Theban men (see previous note).

907–66 Third *episode*. Between lines 942 and 966 the chorus sometimes speaks, perhaps only in the person of their leader, and sometimes sings. The sung lines are paired off to make rhythmic stanzas. The rhythm, called dochmiac (slantwise), has an irregular, staccato and excited feeling to it.

967–1058 Third *stasimon*. The opening call for dancing, already set off by line 965, is self-referential (the chorus are made to remind us that they are — lively — ceremonial dancers as well as actors in a play). The song is a celebration of Herakles' new victory over Lykos, marking a high point for both the hero and the civic and divine world of which he is meant to be a part. Such songs have a ritual dimension, and here there are repeated rhythms and words typical of ritual song form. In Sophocles there are often choral songs of joy or triumph just before final catastrophe. Here Euripides will make such a juxtaposition exceptionally abrupt and surprising.

1059–1326 The dramatic movement is now more fluid and continuous, less distinctly contained in the larger fixed structures. The fourth *episode* (1059–1129), the appearance of Iris and Lyssa, is prefaced by choral exclamations and followed by a nonstrophic choral song mostly in dochmiac rhythm (1130–62; see note on lines 907–66), which takes the place of a formal fourth *stasimon*. Further choral singing in a similar rhythm is now interspersed with cries of Amphitryon from inside the house (1163–97); this starts the fifth *episode* (1163–1326) and runs parallel to what is going on concurrently inside the house, the killing of Herakles' family (similar in structure and function to lines 942–66 that were sung, with interspersed cries from off-stage, while Lykos was being killed). An exchange follows between the chorus (singing) and a household slave (speaking) who has come out from inside the house to report what has happened there. His report, an extensive messenger's narrative, concludes the *episode*.

1064 *This is Lyssa* Again a mythic personification of a common noun meaning mad fury, used in Homer for that which possesses berserk warriors and by subsequent poets for god-sent madness. It can also mean rabies, dog madness, thought to be transmitted from wolves: *lyssa* appears to be derived from *lykos*, (wolf) as in the name of Herakles' antagonist.

1093 *my father Heaven* Lyssa's father is the primeval cosmic god Ouranos, father of
        Zeus' father Kronos. Literally Lyssa says here that she is born from
        Ouranos' blood, which may evoke the violent story of Ouranos' castra-
        tion by Kronos: Ouranos' blood falling on Gaia (Earth) produced,
        among others, the Giants and the Furies, avenging spirits with whom
        Lyssa is here associated (see 1159–62).

1104–29 The spoken rhythm, iambic trimeter otherwise throughout the play, shifts
        here to trochaic tetrameter, which has a quicker, more excited move-
        ment. It is, according to Aristotle (*Poetics* 4.1449a20–23), a rhythm orig-
        inal to the earliest tragedies. Euripides brings it back for occasional use
        in his later plays with an effect of stylistic archaism.

1187–88 *Look! A whirlwind shakes the house!* In a way characteristic of Greek drama's
        theatricality, verbal metaphor, actuality and an imaginary staging of that
        actuality are blended here in the representation of the destruction of
        Herakles' house. The metaphoric sense of the building's ruin is clear
        enough (later Herakles will apply the metaphor to his life: see lines
        1565–66, 1628–29). The actuality is variously reported. Lyssa had said
        she would "smash through his [Herakles'] roof" (1115), but also that she
        would be invisible (1129). The chorus from the stage imagine what is
        going on (1163, 1169) and evoke now what the audience should "see,"
        the house roof caving in. Then from offstage Athena is confusedly
        described in terms suggesting a natural disaster, an earthquake (1192–
        97). Next a household slave as messenger comes out of the house and
        describes the physical damage done by Herakles (1306–7) and by the
        earthquake or Lyssa (1315–17). Finally Herakles appears on stage tied to
        a piece of broken column (1319–20 and 1334–48). We do not know how
        the destruction was actually staged. (Similar questions are raised by the
        god Dionysos' destruction of a palace in Euripides' *Bakkhai*.) Probably
        the audience visualized most of it in their mind's eye, guided by the
        actors' words, though sound effects seem quite possible and could have
        been effective. The only actual, visible sign of the physical damage
        may have been the piece of column to which Herakles is tied.

1210 *The victims . . . to be sacrificed* This is a purification sacrifice to cleanse the
        house of bloodshed in the revenge killing of Lykos. It takes place in
        the house's inner courtyard.

1236 *I'm off to storm Mycenae* There is a strong irony or grim logic in having the
        hero who has traveled so widely confuse the space of his own home
        with those of his travels.

1266 *The blood of these upstarts* Amphitryon refers to a belief that shedding blood can derange one; the audience has been supplied with a quite different cause for the madness.

1310–12 *but something — a shimmering* Because the messenger's speech is in every other respect realistic or naturalistic, the supernatural appearance of the goddess Athena (for which we had been prepared at 1189–97) is described in a somewhat hedged way: her "shape" (1311) could refer to an apparition, as Iris and Lyssa had been called phantoms at their first appearance on stage (1060), but also to a statue, the visible form by which the goddess was known to everyone.

1327–41 Fifth ode or choral song. Like the previous ode (1130–62) this replaces a formal *stasimon* — it is brief, nonstrophic and primarily in the unsettled dochmiac rhythm.

1329–30 *the blood Danaos' daughters / Shed* The fifty daughters of Danaos faced a compulsory marriage with their cousins. All but one of them killed their bridegrooms on the wedding night.

1333 *How Prokne murdered* Daughter of Pandion, the king of Athens, Prokne with her sister Philomela killed her son Itys and fed him to her unknowing husband Tereus. This was revenge for Tereus' rape and mutilation of Philomela. Though he had cut out her tongue to silence her, Philomela represented Tereus' crimes by weaving a picture of them. Prokne, Philomela, and Tereus are then turned into nightingale, swallow and hoopoe respectively.

1342–1791 *Exodos.* Aristotle uses this term (meaning exit and outcome) to designate what follows the last choral ode of a play. In *Herakles* this is the extended aftermath of the catastrophe. It includes (a) an exchange between the chorus and Amphitryon, mostly sung; (b) Herakles' speeches as he awakens and then determines on suicide, framing one-line exchanges (*stichomythia*) with Amphitryon in which the hero realizes what he has done; (c) the unexpected entrance of Theseus leading to exchanges first between Amphitryon (singing) and himself (speaking) then himself and Herakles and then three longer speeches, two by Herakles, the first explaining his determination to kill himself, the second explaining his change of mind; these frame Theseus' speech to dissuade the suicide and offer help in Athens; a brief passage of exchanges among Herakles, Theseus and Amphitryon and then a few closing lines by the chorus will conclude the play.

1342–34 *The great doors / Are creaking open* This refers to the door of the stage building that represents Herakles' house. In all likelihood the sleeping Herakles, tied to a representation of a piece of broken pillar, and the corpses of the children and Megara were brought forward through this door on the *ekkyklema*, a wooden platform on wheels used to bring out into view figures from the indoors (not representable on the Athenian stage) — usually corpses (killing and even, in most cases, dying were not represented on stage) and sometimes those who were for some reason immobilized. The *ekkyklema* will then be the means of removing the bodies from the stage at the end of the play. Amphitryon here walks on through the door after the *ekkyklema* has been pushed out.

1383 *Vengeance on the Taphians* See lines 72–74 and the note on 73.

1434 *You. Your bow* For great achievements and great disasters Greek thinking and imagination tend to accumulate or overdetermine causes. Here personal agency, its instruments, the weapons (as though personified: see 1727–33), and a higher power, sometimes individualized (as Hera, for instance), sometimes abstract (as the god or fate or the like) are combined. Each of these has something like equal weight, though a character's perceptions and feelings about them may variously shift. Here Herakles responds as if he were simply the agent: "You're saying I killed them?" Later he will call himself blameless (1635). Theseus attributes what Herakles has done now to Hera (1497), now to Heaven and fate (1531–32, compare 31).

1461 *My kinsman and my friend* See Introduction, p. 17, on friendship, *philia*. It is usually tied closely to family relationship and especially to the network of kinship connections among the highborn. Theseus and Herakles are related through both their mothers, Aethra and Alkmene who shared a grandfather, and their divine fathers, the brothers Poseidon and Zeus. In the civic mythology of Athens, Theseus, the younger hero, is in many ways both modeled on and a more localized version, specific to Athens, of the older, Panhellenic figure of Herakles.

1469 *my blood-guilt stain* Any shedding of human blood, intended or not, created a pollution that was regarded as infectious to sight, touch and hearing. A homicide was forbidden all religious and social interaction, and to reduce the risk of infection his trial had to take place outdoors. This archaic belief was in force in civil settings, but there are indications of rationalistic views less impressed by it. Theseus in the name of friendship and in spite of Herakles' protests will disregard the risk of pollution to himself (1521–25, 1537–39, 1758).

1485 *the hilltop olive tree* This refers to the citadel of Athens, the Acropolis. The olive tree, located there, is iconic, sacred to Athena who had given the olive to the community; in return she became the city's patron.

1500 *Who stood shoulder to shoulder* See note on 198–99.

1514 *By your beard* This signals the traditional ritual gestures of supplication. Compare lines 1292–93.

1515 *don't play the lion* The lion comparison originates in Homer, standing for a heroic and often self-destroying ferocity. Herakles has both mastered the lion and put on its skin, that is, taken on the contradictory impulses of heroism. Amphitryon here urges a rejection of an older heroic temper.

1530 *Stand up* Herakles since waking up has been sitting, we may imagine, huddled up. At Theseus' arrival he covers himself with his (probably) lionskin cloak, out of shame and to prevent the pollution to one who might see him. He is now uncovered but does not find the strength to stand up—this seems implied by lines 1752–60 that indicate his being helped up and supported by Theseus. Up to that moment, then, only just before the play's end, Herakles remains as he had appeared at the beginning of the *exodos* (at line 1342), on the ground, surrounded by the corpses of his wife and children, and speaks from there.

1547 *Do you think the gods care . . . about your threats?* A pair of lines may be missing from the Greek text before this line. They must have made clearer the nature of Herakles' threats and his response in the following line. There is a general sense that Herakles wants to assert his autonomy in the face of his misfortunes. He would achieve this by taking his own life. Both the claim to autonomy and suicide are taken by Theseus as a challenge to the gods (the challenge may have been made explicitly by Herakles in a missing line)—a challenge, Theseus insists, that can only be useless if not actually dangerous.

1559 *Greece won't let you die* Compare Amphitryon's charge to the contrary at lines 253–59. In fact it will be Athens, through Theseus that will provide the conditions for Herakles' survival. Athens stands in for Greece as a whole: Thucydides reports Perikles making the claim that Athens is "a school for Greece."

1562 *I take after my father* This alludes to the archaic and tragic notion of guilt inherited through the family. Herakles sees himself cursed through both his fathers because of Amphitryon's blood guilt and Zeus' adultery.

1590 *the Law says* This is the contemporary religious and civic requirement that any one who has spilled human blood (except under conditions of war) must go into exile to be purified. This is what brought Amphitryon to Thebes (24–25).

1598 *But Argos exiled me* This is in a political sense. Herakles' rival cousin Eurystheus, under Hera's protection, holds the power there.

1626 *Dancing on Olympos* Hera is imagined dancing in triumph over Herakles' downfall, as the chorus had danced in triumph over that of Lykos.

1631–32 *Driven by / Petty jealousy* It should not be forgotten that legitimate marriage is the goddess Hera's particular domain. Her vindictiveness against Herakles is also part of the strong sanction she exercises on behalf of a social and institutional norm. The injustice or plain irrationality, of course, is that the sanction is exercised through Herakles because of the transgressions of his divine father.

1641 *Fate lets no one off* Fate translates *tukhê*, the uncontrollable turn of events, an abstract concept, not a mythic force. The same notion is expressed at line 1695 and, blended with the figure of Hera, at 1751.

1642 *if the poets haven't lied* Whether poets tell the truth or not is sometimes a theme of earlier Greek poetry. Its appearance in a dramatic setting is unusual, though characteristic of Euripides and his tendency to open up the texture of his drama and make his audience aware of an imaginative process at work. More often this is done by having a character or the chorus question some feature of a myth that is particularly contrary to normal human understanding, for example, Helen's birth from an egg (*Helen* 21) or the reversal of the sun's course (*Electra* 737–38).

1664 *Stone monuments* There were a number of shrines and monuments to Herakles throughout Athens and its environs. The temple called Hephaesteum or Theseion built around the middle of the fifth century B.C.E. in the agora, the city's central gathering place, had sculptures representing in parallel the deeds of Herakles (nine labors) and those of Theseus.

1685 *I'll endure what I have to — and wait for death* This translates a sense of the manuscript reading of the Greek. Finding such a sense too close to Herakles' rejected intent to commit suicide, many scholars have accepted an emendation that would translate as "find the strength to endure life." But this is unnecessary and perhaps a touch modernizing. Herakles says he will find the strength to endure the worst, including the most powerful adversary, death. For the relentless presence of death in the play see Introduction, p. 17.

1753–55 *My legs are like stone . . . I wish I were stone* Being like stone is proverbial for lack of feeling, sometimes due to an excess of feeling (as in the story of Niobe who in her extreme grief at the loss of all her children is turned to stone, though paradoxically still weeping: see *Iliad* 24.602 ff.). The image here may be additionally suggestive. It can recall a number of earlier references to the Gorgon who turns one to stone, first evoked in connection with the fear inspired by Herakles' heroic power, then for the forces that turn this power against him (see note on 152–54). Here the image refers as well to Herakles' physical weakness, so great that he can hardly move, and to the concomitant emotional weakness that keeps him clinging to his dead family. The figure on stage is caught in a death-like immobility — that could be seen to anticipate the stone monuments that had been promised to commemorate him at his death (1662–64). There is a powerful tension and connection, finally, between Herakles' desire to be oblivious of his grief, in effect, to die, as he had first intended after the catastrophe, and the public memorial that he is to become. The image of stone just as the play is about to end, may also draw our attention to Euripides' dramatic medium that is another form of commemoration wherein Herakles is less a fixed, monumental figure than a fluid and contradictory representation of what it might mean to be human.

1779–80 This passage is in brackets because the Greek text contradicts line 1710 where Amphitryon is asked by Herakles to stay in Thebes. Though there is a clear tradition of a tomb of Amphitryon at Thebes, there is no known connection between him and Athens.

1791 There are final exits in the three different directions available to human actors on the Athenian stage. Herakles supported by Theseus goes out (probably) at the left of the stage building, that is, in the direction away from Thebes (see note on line 668). The bodies of the dead family (on the *ekkyklema*: see on lines 1342–34) are brought back into the house through the door that marks the center of the stage; Amphitryon accompanies them. The chorus, perhaps as they sing their last lines, move out at the right-side entrance, that is, in the direction of the main space of the play's location, the city of Thebes. Each of these groups moves slowly, with difficulty.

GLOSSARY

ACHERON: underground lake or river that must be crossed to reach Hades.

ALKMENE: mother of Herakles, with Zeus as father, granddaughter of Perseus.

AMAZONS: legendary warrior women who live near the Black Sea; Herakles and other Greek heroes waged war against them.

AMPHITRYON: husband of Alkmene and foster father of Herakles.

ANAUROS: river near Mount Pelion in Thessaly.

APOLLO: son of Zeus and Leto, twin brother of Artemis; prophetic, musician, and healing god with major shrines at Delphi and on the island of Delos.

ARES: god of war, son of Zeus and Hera, father-in-law of Kadmos.

ARGOS: city in the north central Peloponnese, whose patron goddess is Hera.

ARTEMIS: daughter of Zeus and Leto, twin sister of Apollo; goddess of the wilderness and hunting.

ASOPOS: river at the frontier of Thebes.

ATHENA: daughter of Zeus, patron goddess of Athens.

ATLAS: god of the generation of Titans who carries the heavens on his shoulders.

BAKKHOS: another name for Dionysos, god of wine, ecstatic possession, madness and the theater.

CENTAURS: part horse, part human creatures associated with wild regions and at times with wild and violent behavior.

CERBERUS: monstrous dog who guards the entrance to Hades.

CHARON: boatman who ferries the dead to the shores of Hades.

CORINTH: city on the eastern end of the northern Peloponnese, site of the Isthmian games.

CYCLOPS: (Cyclopes in plural) gigantic, one-eyed (or circle-eyed) beings renowned as smiths and builders of monumental walls.

DANAOS: father of fifty daughters, the Danaids, betrothed to their cousins (see note on lines 1329–30).

DELOS: island in the Aegean, birthplace of Apollo.

DELPHI: town and shrine of Apollo on the southern slope of Mount Parnassos.

DEMETER: mother of Persephone, goddess of grain.

DIOMEDES: king in Thrace, in northeastern Greece, son of Ares.

DIRKE: river in Thebes; name of the wife of the older Lykos.

ELEKTRYON: father of Alkmene, brother of Amphitryon's father Alkaios; Amphitryon kills him, perhaps accidentally, in a quarrel.

ETNA: volcanic mountain in Sicily.

EUBOEA: island extending from the southeast mainland, across from Athens, up to central Greece.

EURYSTHEUS: son of Sthenelos, cousin of Herakles, king of Argos and Mycenae; Herakles' labors are undertaken on his account.

FURIES: deities of punishment for the bloodshed of kin.

GERYON: monstrous three-bodied guardian of cattle in the far southwest of Spain, the outer western limits of the world as the Greeks knew it; stealing the cattle is one of Herakles' labors.

GIANTS: children of Earth who challenge Zeus and the Olympian gods in battle.

GORGON: refers to Medusa, the mortal one of three sisters, killed by Perseus; the sight of, or the gaze from, her snake-haired head turned beholders into stone.

HADES: lord of the underworld and the dead; his name also designates his kingdom.

HEBROS: river in Thrace in northeastern Greece.

HELIKON: mountain, and mountain range, northwest of Thebes; home of the Muses who had a famous shrine there.

HERA: queen of the gods, wife of Zeus and his sister (a mark of her status); goddess of marriage.

HERAKLES: son of Zeus and Alkmene, foster son of Amphitryon; Greece's best-known and greatest hero, widely worshiped in cult. His physical capacities are enormous and his achievements are numerous, hard fought for and extraordinary. He is unusually close to the world of animals on the one hand (often in monstrous form) and to the gods on the other. In the literary tradition he is drawn more particularly into the human realm as a warrior with a family and as a figure subject to mental and moral as well as physical trials. He is rarely cast in tragic roles; his part in this play and in Sophocles' *Women of Trachis* are the only known examples.

HERMIONE: town near Argos where Demeter was worshiped as a chthonic or under-earth goddess.

HOMOLE: mountain in Thessaly.

HYDRA: poisonous, multiheaded water snake in the swamps of Lerna; Herakles destroys it, cutting off the heads and burning the necks before the regenerating heads could grow back.

IRIS: messenger of the gods whose name means rainbow.

ISMENOS: river in Thebes.

IXION: the first mortal to kill his own kin. Zeus purifies him of the killing but Ixion then attempts to rape Hera, for which, bound on a whirling wheel, he is forever punished in Hades.

KADMOS: founder of Thebes.

KREON: father of Megara, ruler of Thebes who is overthrown and killed by Lykos.

KYKNOS: son of Ares, savage warrior who preys on travelers; killed by Herakles.

LERNA: town south of Argos, famous for its springs.

LETO: mother of Apollo and Artemis; their father is Zeus.

LYKOS: former ruler of Thebes; his son of the same name is the usurper in this play who threatens to destroy Herakles' family.

LYSSA: daughter of Night and Ouranos (Heaven), embodiment of raging madness.

MEGARA: daughter of Kreon, wife of Herakles.

MINOTAUR: half man, half bull for whom Minos, king of Crete, exacted a tribute of Athenian youths and maidens; killed by Theseus.

MINYANS: inhabitants of Orchomenos, a city that is neighbor and rival of Thebes.

MYCENAE: a city notable at the time of the Trojan War, close to Argos with which it is identified in this play.

NEMEA: area north of Argos that includes a well-known sanctuary of Zeus.

NISUS: king of the city of Megara, west of Athens on the northern side of the Isthmus of Corinth.

OECHALIA: city on Euboea (see note on lines 608–21).

OLYMPOS: Greece's highest mountain, in the northeast of the central mainland; home of the gods.

PARNASSOS: mountain to the west of Thebes.

PELION: mountain in Thessaly.

PENEIOS: river in Thessaly.

PERSEPHONE: daughter of Demeter and Zeus, wife of Hades and queen of the underworld.

PERSEUS: son of Zeus and Danae, from Argos; grandfather of Alkmene; he cuts off and keeps the head of the Gorgon Medusa.

PHLEGRA: site of the battle of Giants and the Olympian gods, said to be in northeast Greece.

PHOLOE: a high plain in Arcadia, in the central Peloponnese, where the centaur Pholos entertained Herakles.

PLUTO: another name for Hades.

PROKNE: daughter of the Athenian king Pandion, wife of Tereus, mother of Itys (see note on line 1333).

SISYPHUS: one of the exemplary transgressors in Hades (Ixion is another), punished by having eternally to roll a boulder up a hill and have it always roll down again.

SPARTA: city in the southern Peloponnese.

TAINARON: cape at the southernmost point of the Peloponnese where a cave was taken to be the entranceway to Hades.

TAPHIANS: a people in northwest Greece against whom Amphitryon led a successful expedition to avenge their killing of Alkmene's brothers.

THEBES: city in south central mainland Greece.

THESEUS: Athenian hero, son of the god Poseidon (his human father is Aigeus). In this play he appears to be young and in the earlier phase of his heroic career.

THESSALY: large region of east central and northern mainland Greece, renowned for its horses.

ZEUS: ruler of the Olympian gods; father of a number of them and of human heroes, including Herakles.

THE 1600 KILLERS

THE 1600 KILLERS

A WAKE-UP CALL FOR CONGRESS

ANDY JACOBS, JR. U.S. REPRESENTATIVE, RET.

ALISTAIR PRESS
GREENWOOD, INDIANA

Text Design: Kevin Cook
Cover Design: Shelly Wells, Kevin Cook

Alistair Press

Alistair Press
A division of The Educational Video Group
291 Southwind Way
Greenwood, IN 46142

set in Trade Gothic

Printed in the United States of America

For Kim, Andy and Steve,
my greatest loves.

ACKNOWLEDGEMENTS

When I announced my retirement from Congress, I thanked all my constituents in general and several of them in particular. Those specified included my mother, Joyce Welborn Jacobs; my Father, Andrew Jacobs, Sr.; my "best gal, real pal" who is my wife, Kim Hood Jacobs; my little sister, Marjorie Jacobs Landwerlen; my big sister, Wanda Jacobs Strange and my brother-in-law, Robert Strange; and my super brother, Tom Landwerlen. Also of great help were Bob and Judy Aitken, Mary Kay and Mark Anderson, Mary Atwell, Sandy Augliere, Dr. Gary Ayres, Hoover Baker, Taylor Baker, Liz Bankowski, Steve and Sue Barnett, John Bartlett, Birch, Evan and Susan Bayh, Jim Beatty, philologist Phyllis Beatty, Judy Barrett, Walter Bell, Jerry Bepco, Mary Berry, Bill Blomquist, Ken Bourke, Dr. Otis Bowen, Roselle Boyd, Shell and Barbara Breskow, Jim Brower, Andrew and Roselie Brown, Billi Bueaux, Don and Ginny Burkert, Dr. Mary Bush, Catherine Butler, Max Brydenthal, Dan Carpenter, Shirley Chater, Pat Chavis, John and Eileen Christ, Cathy Clark, Tony and Phyllis Coelho, Ben Cole, Jim Corman, Bill Crawford, Grace Curry, John Day, Joe Deitz, Jack Dillon, Knute Dobkins, Winnie Donaldson, Keith Dooley, Paul Duke, Don and Edie Edwards, Frank Edwards, Dehaviland Elder, Bob Elliott, Pat and Eleanor Endsley, Nancy Endsley, Criss Fager, Carolyn Fay, Will Fay, brainy IBJ editor Ann Finch, Bessie Gasaway, Elton Geshwiler, Mart Gibson, Henri and Riley Gibson, Eugene Glick, John Godich, Charlotte Good, Dr. Mason Goodman, Charlie and Margaret Gray, Pat Grant, Stan Gregg, Theresa Guise, David and Elizabeth Haas, Jud Haggerty, Jay Haggerty, Dick Hann, M.C. Hansburough, Neal, Wanda and Priscilla and Jessica Holder, Buford Holt, Glen Howard, Dorothy Huffman, Mark Hulbert, Jed and Sidney Johnson, Mabel Johnson, Frank Jose, Bob Kaiser, Kay Kelly, Bob, Margaret, Colleen and Rob King, David and Maryann Kozak, John Krull, John Kyle, Nancy and Trixie Land, Dan Landwerlen, Greg Landwerlen, man-mountain Marty Landwerlen, Tom Landwerlen, Aurelia Little, Dr. Frank Lloyd, Tom and Maryann Logue, Miles Loyd, Cynthia Lyons, Florence Mahoney, Louie Mahern, Lou Maiden, Charlie and Gwen Mains, Joe Mansini, Louise Marr, Arlene Martin, Dave Mason, Bill and Marc Mathene, Elsie Mason, Jack McCann, Coleman McCarthy, Jenny McCarty, Pat and Rachel McGeever, Doug McDaniel,

Dan and Deb McGinn, Howard and Gussie Mills, Jeff and Jennifer Modisett, Owen Mullin, Marcia Munshower, Bud Myers, Helen Neihaus, Cathy Noe, Betty Nolan, Art Owen, Al Nolan, Jim and Helen Noland, Paul Page, Judy Pennington, Vic Pfau, Greg Porter, Max and Charlotte Potter, Francis and Ellen Quigley, Milana Riggs, Trisha Roberson, Joe and Theresa Romer, Liz Roslewicz, Dulcy Russell, Dick Salee, Bill Schreiber, Luther and Rosy Searfoss, Betty Selden, Dal Sells, Jim and Sylvia Shannon, Phil Sharp, Sue Shivley, Herb Shockney, Charlie Siegel, Greg Silver, Pete and Libby Singleton, Marie Smith, Jim Snyder, Andy Steffen, George Stuteville, Owen Sweeney, Joe Summers, Steve Taley, Gary Taylor, Grace Thompson, Bob Traugot, Pat Ulen, Sergeant Visher, John Preston Ward, Wilma Warren, Jim Warrum, Charlie Walton, Mary Ellen Weiland, Don and Liz Weiss, Patty Welch, Matt Welsh, David Wildes, Merle and Regina Wilgus, John V. Wilson, Ed Yates, and George and Silvia Zazas.

But in the beginning there was James Porter Seidensticker, Jr., whose sobriquets were *Sei* and *Sidewinder.* He was the first person, with the clear exception of myself, to broach the subject of my running for Congress. Having seen it all, Sei was the first to read it all in the manuscript. He made very much needed corrections. I am indebted to the practiced eye of my friend, Sei. Wonderfully talented fine-line editor Ann Finch provided the finishing and right touches for this work.

Though I typed each word of this book, I had indispensable help from others, including this Toshiba lap top. I had never touched such technology before September third, Nineteen Ninety-seven. That was eight months after my departure from The United States House of Representatives where I had served Indianapolis for thirty years. Before that September, I had used the *Smith Corona Sky Writer* manual typewriter given to me by my father and taught to me by my mother when I was in high school. I used it for forty years on such tasks as taking the Indiana Bar Exam, letters in my law practice and letters answering congressional mail.

The difference between this lap top and my old manual is like the difference between cutting our six-acre yard with the five foot swath *Dixie Chopper* my wife and I bought from the Carmel Welding Company, and cutting the large lawn with a nail clipper. After about two hundred sixty thousand words and wearing the letters off eight of these keys, I remain awed by this proof that "big things come in small packages." I made about twelve calls to the information section of the Indianapolis Central Library and each time, with efficiency and, more important to me, with warm friendliness, the scholars there found a dozen obscure facts for me. I think they could find a red needle in a haystack on Mars.

Shelly Wells applied her considerable talent to the task of making excellent graphic art of my idea for the dust cover. And Melissa Cooney at Kinko's Copies in Indianapolis was enormously helpful in the process.

Susie and Roger Cook own Alistair Press. With patience and with tolerance of the author's last-minute whims, they published this volume and, in the process, became my warm friends. Their son Kevin Cook used his magic fingers and tailored talent to provide the layout and to make beautifully enhancing modifications to the dust jacket.

My friend Andy Murphy, whose maiden name was Andersen and whose husband is Jim Murphy, was my literary agent. A well-received author in her own rite, Andy played a significant role in getting this book into your hands.

Kim Hood Jacobs, popular Indianapolis television journalist, cartoonist, master seamstress and Epicurean wizard, made invaluable suggestions as she was kind and patient enough to read the manuscript. She was also kind and patient enough to marry me and share the joy of rearing our two sons, Andy and Bronco (Steven) Jacobs. I asked for and received much good advice from my very literary sister, Marjorie Landwerlen, whose sons, my nephews, Tom, Marty, Dan and Greg were willing to read or listen to passages of this work and tell me what was wrong. My sister, Wanda Strange, an English teacher, was also helpful. *Indianapolis Star* feature writer Bill Shaw helped steer me away from some pitfalls of boredom. Another Shaw, Mark, legal scholar, author and radio talk show host, did much the same for me. And John Gallman, Director of Indiana University Press, helped bring me down to earth from some of my more tenuous flights of humor. Indianapolis Channel Thirteen's innovative television producer Kevin Finch enriched my understanding of historic events. James P. Maley made many useful suggestions, as did Loretta Raikes, The Honorable Julia M. Carson, Patty Welch, *Washington Post* columnist Coleman McCarthy, Author and financial whiz Mark Hulbert, Gary Taylor, Louis Mahern, Jr. and James Ward Beatty.

One of the principal and principled inspirations for this work was the Honorable Frank O'Bannon, forty-seventh governor of Indiana. He, his wife, Judy; and his Lieutenant Governor war-hero Joe Kernan, brought a refreshing wholesomeness and down-to-earth wisdom to the people of Indiana, of whom I am privileged to be one. The headline of the *Indianapolis Star/News* story that reported Frank's election was: **Nice Guy Finishes First.** Amen.

CONTENTS

PREFACE

"If a feller has any flare for writin', there's nothin' like being fired off a big government job ta' bring it out." Kin Hubbard's Abe Martin quote doesn't quite fit; I wasn't fired off the government job in which I served as a United States Representative for thirty years and from which I retired in 1997. Moreover, I have my doubts about any connection between a "flare" and my writing, but obviously I'm willing to give it a try. In fact, I tried once before, the result being *The Powell Affair: Freedom Minus One,* Bobbs-Merrill, 356 pages, Library of Congress 72-88272.

This is a stories book—a book of stories—all true to the best of my knowledge. However, the best of my knowledge is not good enough to guarantee absolute accuracy. "Tell it like it is." That was the slogan of the sixties—as well as an example of bad grammar—when people who are in *their* sixties at this writing were admonished not to "trust anyone over thirty."

Still, in the best reality we can perceive, no one can tell it the way it was, because it *wasn't* the way it was. It was the way each honest witness saw it. As one of those witnesses, one who had the privilege of seeing and hearing nearly forty years of significant American history up close, I have tried in this volume to tell it as I believe it was. What I saw and heard from my privileged position is what I tell you in the following chapters. Most of the stories are in chronological order and the ones that flash forward or backward are, I think, in logical order. Much of the material is controversial and you will inevitably find some of it at variance with your own view. Where that occurs, I ask that you credit me with an honest difference of opinion.

Some of my friends were a tad bit squeamish about the title I wrote for this volume. They wondered if it was too harsh. So I hesitated. Reconsidering, I concluded that the title is not nearly so harsh as the presidential misdeeds it describes. However, anticipating that *you* may not like the title, I have composed a few others for you. Feel free to pick one of them from the following list if you like:

THE WIMPS OF WAR
THE FALL OF THE CHIPS IN MAY

DOWNLOADING THE CUP
KNOWING WHAT I KNEW THEN
TO MOCK A KILLING BIRD
THE GREAT AMERICAN NOVELTY

I grew tired of repeatedly finishing this book "once and for all." So I clicked "Exit" on the laptop and breathed the sweet sigh that comes with closure. In a volume this size, it is probably inevitable that a story which could have been told was left out and that a person who should have been mentioned was not. However, since I have mentioned my mother, oversights in this book, though regrettable, can't be too serious.

My mother says that if you can't say something nice about someone, you shouldn't say anything at all. My country cousin Delmer Claise says he hates "to put a name on a bad story." So, except for cases of low-road campaigning and dastardly official deeds so prominent as to make the offender obvious, instead of naming names, I simply tell the tactics.

Government waste comes in many forms, but the one to which the title of this book refers, the presidential war, towers like a Sequoia over all the others. In my next book, *Slander and Sweet Judgement*, to be published at a later date, I attend to more domestic forms of waste.

THE 1600 KILLERS

"THE HONORABLE GENTLEMEN
REGRET THE LOSS OF LIFE."
—Rudyard Kipling

1

HOW TO GET A DATE WITH FATE

L et's start with this: Heroism consists not so much of inflicting pain as enduring it.

It is All Fools' Day, 1951; the ship glides silently into the port of Pusan, Korea. Hearts leap into throats. This was it. As if to confirm, bandoleers of thirty caliber ammunition are distributed. The green Marines would have to fight their way off the ship in the dark of night. Where was the enemy? Answer: about two hundred miles to the north. It would not be long before these Marines would learn that Pusan was a long, long way to the rear by the spring of '51. And safe. Why then the ammunition distribution? Simple, the Marine Corps maxim: There's the right way, the wrong way and the Marine Corps way. In other words, who knows?

The journey had begun almost two years before. Let's call our traveler, Jim. At 17, he had just finished high school. The scholastic ordeal was over and it was time to be something. Why not a Marine? It certainly was no longer a dangerous occupation. World War II had been over for four years. "With the help of God and a handful of Marines, MacArthur (had taken) the Philippines."

This was peace, but the uniform looked the same. And Jim could wear it every Thursday night for two years just by joining the Marine Corps Reserve. Might even slip it on for Saturday night dates. So in June he joined and became a home front hero. There was a bit of a problem, though. Just one year later the Korean War, which had been going on for some time in the form of border skirmishes, hit the headlines. It wasn't just that the forces north of the thirty-eighth parallel were getting the upper hand. More important was the fact that those forces happened to be Communist. So the President of the United States took the matter, not to the United States Congress as required by the Constitution, but to the United Nations Security Council where Communist Russian had the veto but was not there to exercise it.

The Soviets had outsmarted themselves by walking out in protest shortly before their friends in North Korea began the successful

7

offensive. Truman got his UN resolution to repel the aggression and quite unconstitutionally ordered U.S. armed forces into combat against the North Korean Communists.

At first, Jim failed to see any connection between his future and the news stories about that strange land whose name sounded like something people put into swimming pools. In fact, a whole month went by as he pursued his summer career of delivering concrete blocks to construction projects and unloading them by gloved hand.

Then, one afternoon in August while on his way with a load of blocks, he saw a headline on a newspaper stand: "16th Battalion Called Up." Hold it. That meant the local Marine Reserve Unit. Which meant *him,* definitely. College deferments came in handy sometimes and he had completed a year of college, but if a citizen were already in the service, college deferments didn't count. And of course he was already *in*. Deferments could keep you out, but they could not *get* you out. Those eight-inch concrete blocks got heavier.

The orders were to report to the Marine Reserve unit in his hometown on 10 August at 0800 hours, but our teenager didn't yet understand military time. He reported at 4:00 PM, thinking he was four hours early, but, in reality, he was eight hours late and the MP's had been looking for him. His superior officers accepted his explanation as an honest but stupid mistake. He preferred to call it an *uninformed* mistake, but was quickly learning that what he preferred would no longer be a factor.

The outfit left by train for California at 2000 hours, but not without first hearing some words of wisdom from the Governor. Boot camp was at the Marine Corps Recruit Depot in San Diego. It was eight weeks of aching muscles, calculated humiliation, isolation and assurance that his role as an infantry grunt was nothing more than that cannon fodder.

The boot camp ordeal did much for his physical condition and very little for his ego. Advanced combat training was somewhat less unpleasant, but still a long way from a lark. Showers at Camp Pendleton were ordeals; the hot water was cold and the cold water was frosty. The facility was either shunned by those who preferred a gamy smell to chattering teeth, or dashed into and out of in seconds, but Jim had an idea that worked; he gritted his teeth, stood for seventy-five seconds in the ice-cold water, then switched to "hot" which, by contrast, seemed warm. To the amazement of his buddies, he was luxuriating. Why wasn't the hot water heated? Your tax dollars at work—at something else to enrich a campaign contributing government contractor.

When the combat training was finished, his was "not to reason why...;" his was to board, not a U.S. Navy transport ship, but a privately owned and broken-down looking ocean vessel called the *Aiken Victory*. In fact it did break down in the middle of the Pacific. That wasn't good. If the military contractor who was paid to feed and deliver the Marines to Korea *had fed the Marines,* the Marines would have fed the fish as the ship teeter-tottered in the merciless ocean waves. However, the contractor made extra profit by not feeding them and about the best the "cannon fodder" could do was the "dry heaves". It is reasonable to conclude that the Marines did not soon forget the bad hand their own government had dealt them in dealing with the callous contractor.

Since plenty of tax-paid Navy ships with plenty of good chow were readily available, one was left to wonder whose cousin got the contract. It was not a luxury voyage. And the day before they sailed from San Diego, March 14, 1951, the title of what appeared to be a sympathetic and touching editorial in *The San Diego Union*, was TOMORROW, THE DAY OF SEPEARATION. The editorial was sympathetic but, under the circumstances, not very touching. It was not about the anxious fears of the Marines' families; it was about the income tax which was due the next day. At the time, March 15 was the deadline. Recalling the ironic editorial after a few months of soul and body battering terror in Korea, Jim penciled on a piece of a C ration box the following parody of a contemporary song, *That Lucky ol' Sun*:

> Up at midnight, out on watch; don't even dare to blink. 'But that lucky ol' c'vilian's got nothin' t' do but sit around all day and think.
>
> Fuss with my weapon, toil on my fox hole, shiver 'til dawn's first ray, but that lucky ol' c'vilian's got nothin' t' do but look for parkin' places all day.
>
> Good Lord above, don't you see me ever, down in this quagmire? Send down that dove with its peace forever; lift the enemy fire.
>
> Show me that ocean; take me across. Take all my weapons away. Like that Lucky ol' C'vilian, give me nothing t' do, but gripe about taxes all day.

At the port of Kobe, Japan, following two weeks of scant nutrition, the *"Aching" Victory*, as the Marines came to call it, docked long enough for sea bags with personal belongings to be warehoused. The "lucky ol'

Marines" who could survive a year in Korea would stop at Kobe for their things on the trip home. As fork-lifts carried pallets of sea bags into the dockside shelters, our Saturday night Marine thought about the odds against ever seeing his again.

With the exception of that hour on the dock at Kobe, the Marines had not put a foot on solid land for two weeks. And now in Pusan they would quickly learn they were indeed "in the rear with the gear." Therefore on that placid night in April, 1951, the newly arrived Marines slept safely and deeply on military cots. For most of them, such comfort would not happen again soon; for the others, never again.

At 0500 hours it was reveille and a change of dietary pace; the Marines were fed. Next came the six-by trucks and the short ride to the Pusan airport where an enormous number of DC-3 transport planes awaited. The green Marine replacements were heading for the front.

The view from the flight north was amazing. There were so many transport planes flying the round trip from Pusan that they appeared to form a gigantic sky-lift, the nose of each craft no more than a few hundred meters behind the tail of the next. Below, as far as could be seen, there were rugged mountain ranges, which for the Marines had already given birth to a new use for their initials, *Uncle Sam's Mountain Climbers.*

Jim and the other Marines landed on a field of blinding Korean dust, the color of which was unfamiliar to him. It seemed an eerie blend of red and orange. By the time the passengers disembarked, *this* Asian dust had settled and the fresh green dungarees were still green. Those who wore them proceeded to assemble on the south side of the runway. Though at least two hundred in number, they felt alone and vulnerable. There was silence and anxious curiosity. What were they supposed to do? Shouldn't there be somebody there to meet them? Could that somebody possibly be the enemy?

Presently around a curve on a makeshift mountain road, heading down into the valley of the airfield, came a convoy of U.S. six-by trucks. The personnel aboard those trucks didn't look like friend *or* foe. They didn't even look like Earth people, but they were. They were the heavily dust-encrusted Marines who, following a year of General Sherman's hell, were the lucky survivors. They were heading home.

The dusty and battle-weary veterans formed ranks across the runway from the frightened newcomers. The distance between the two groups was measured not only in meters, about eighty, but also in months of misery, twelve of them. If only our former concrete block delivery boy could change places with those "salts" over there. " So near and yet so far." Instead, he and his buddies climbed onto the trucks and headed farther north.

As it turned out, even the dirt airfield was pretty far to the rear. The enemy was still a long way off in terms of danger. In terms of time, too. The Marines were taken to the central Korean town of Hong Chong where Jim joined George Company, Third Battalion, First Regiment of the First U.S. Marine Division.

For about twenty-two days, war seemed surprisingly safe. There was a lot of mud and many cold nights of sleeping on the ground in shelter halves. There was snow and freezing rain with a lot of ups and downs over steep mountain ranges. Muscles ached and sometimes the Marines were soaking, but no one was shooting.

It seemed that war would wear you out, weigh you down, alternately soak and freeze you, but it wouldn't kill you. Were both sides getting ready to call it quits? General MacArthur had dramatically declared that, "In war there is no substitute for victory." Could it be that both sides had enough of the slaughter and destruction and now were seeking, not a substitute for victory, but a substitute for war itself?

That was not what the Third Chinese Field Army had in mind.

At about 1700 hours, 23 April 1951, George Company, which for three weeks had been climbing over and digging into the mud of what seemed like most of the mountains in central Korea, was suddenly ordered to "saddle up" and move out. This was strange. In all the maneuvering of those past weeks, the outfit had never moved so late in the day nor with such little notice, but on this day they marched north along rice paddies as the sun descended to their left.

After an hour of easy walking, not counting about thirty pounds on each back, they began to ascend onto a mountain which was destined to be recorded in Marine Corps annals as Hill Nine-O-Two. Darkness and real war were approaching. As George Company neared the summit, it was absolute hand-in-front-of-the-face darkness. The people of George Company were already cotton-in-the-mouth thirsty with nothing left in their canteens.

For a couple of hours, the Marines took turns sleeping. Then at about midnight, not with a bang, but with thousands of them and tracer fire to match, the replacements of George Company became combat veterans. Flares soared and parachuted above the chaos of battle. The Chinese could be seen with armbands fashioned from white rags obviously for the purpose of mutual identification among their ranks.

As if the massive gunfire did not shatter spirits enough, the Chinese chose to serenade the god of war with bugles. There were the horrible human shrieks from those cut down by the blizzard of tracer fire. The Bible speaks of "the quick and the dead." The battle speaks of the quickly dead. At daybreak, as a Marine aircraft swooped down in close ground support, Jim was struck violently in the head and began to bleed profusely. The pain was sharp as he fell back onto the rocks which were the roof of that mountain. "Oh my God." Those were the frightened words that faintly echoed his thoughts.

His mother's definition of courage flashed through his bleeding head, "Courage," she had written to him, "is fear that has said its prayers." He was saying his prayers as he noticed a shell casing. It obviously wasn't thirty-caliber from small arms fire. And it had blood on its rim, his blood. Deliverance! It was a much larger shell casing, one kicked out from a twenty-millimeter cannon aboard the Marine aircraft. He had been hit, not by a bullet, but by the cylindrical remains of a fired warhead projectile. The wound still bled and it still hurt like fury, but he certainly wasn't going to die from it. A miracle. For him, more would follow. Enough, in fact, to make him feel like Bill Mauldin's "fugitive from the law of averages."

Most people who waste their money on war movies have heard about limbs being torn from bodies and corpses riddled by shrapnel, oozing blood and viscera. And perhaps they have some sense of how a vibrant young person can become a hideous smear of dead flesh in the split second of a mortar explosion. Hollywood writers have little trouble making something heroic and glorious out of such stupid atrocities, but almost no one, who hasn't been there, has heard much about the other kind of battle casualty, deep psychosis.

There are of course dandy euphemisms for it, "shell shock", "post-traumatic syndrome", "battle fatigue". One might suppose a good night's sleep could take care of something that sounds like that, but it doesn't. "Battle fatigue" is the sudden scream of a combat infantryman followed by pitiful whimpers and decades of continuously painful nightmares and *daymares* in an unrelenting and torturous mental dungeon from which quite likely there will never be escape. No matter how brave the victim, in Hollywood terms, there's nothing very glorious about that.

The evil pandemonium of Hill Nine-O-Two had raged on through the night. In overwhelming numbers, the enemy eventually overran the entire Third Marine Battalion. In later reckoning, G Company would be credited with blunting the Chinese Spring Offensive of 1951. It was rather like being celebrated for blocking a kick with your face. War propaganda can be sardonically amusing. When the other side stands its ground, it's *fanatical suicide tactics;* when your side does the same, it's *heroic rear guard action.*

George Company took fifty percent casualties that night, but in the confusion of battle, its survivors managed to make their way south across mountains not occupied by the Chinese.

Marines don't retreat; they "attack in a different direction." This "attack" along the MBR, *Main Bug-Out Route,* had its own truculent events. And none of these events involved an armed enemy. The first was "friendly fire", but it was not a case of fellow Americans missing their aim. The Marine Corsair pilots hit their intended targets, but those targets were their fellow Marines whom they mistook for Chinese.

Fortunately the straggling unit on the ground had a good radio operator. His fast-thinking communication with the men in the cockpits averted a second pass. The initial attack shot off the heel of a South Korean who was attached to George Company. That made one more person to be carried out by the enervated Marines who were already carrying out the Marine tradition of carrying out both their wounded and their dead.

The trek back was no stroll. Moreover, along the way a controversy broke out between two Marines and it involved the unarmed enemy. Scott County, Tennessee seceded from Tennessee when Tennessee seceded from the Union. Something like that happened on Hill Nine-O-Two. In the chaos of the catastrophe of battle, where nobody quite knows "who's on first," George Company, even while being overrun by the Chinese, took three Chinese prisoners. They were young, they were smiling and they were emaciated. They literally looked as if they had not eaten in weeks. The Marines had C rations, but they had absolutely no appetite for them that day, suffering as they were from the kind of thirst most of them had never so much as imagined before.

Our own hometown Marine did what he was brought up to do; he offered his rations to the "starving Chinese", but another Marine vociferously objected. "Why should we give those bastards anything?" "Well," said Jim, "they took a lot of our guys prisoner last night and they're marching them north just as we are taking these guys south. What if God has a giant accounting system that balances out how they treat our guys with how we treat theirs?" The objector mellowed: "I guess that's right." Let's hear it for the Geneva Convention on how to be nice in war. Once the *two* Marines opened the cans for them, the Chinese had *American* that day. Jim, our young Marine philosopher, had no way of knowing at the time just how prophetic his words about the giant accounting system would prove to be nor just how soon.

As the survivors of G Company plodded on, up and down the ridge line, bearing the agonizing burden of their dead and wounded buddies, Jim found sublimation in the words of Kipling:

> "...force your heart and nerve and sinew to serve your turn long after they are gone and so hold on when there is nothing in you except the will that says to them, 'hold on.'"

And hold on they did—all of them. Somehow, some way, when the day ended, the agony ended too. They descended the last mountain into the Garden of Eden, a beautiful valley behind the new American lines. **Water!** Water in the fabled babbling brook, perhaps five feet deep and clear as Cascade-washed crystal. It was "Miller Time", except that at this moment of euphoria, water would do and do nicely. They praised the Lord and waded in, drinking while completely submerged, combat fatigues and all. For them, from then on, water would always be champagne.

For George Company it was reserve time and the living would be easy for a while. Replacements, fresh from the States, would arrive in a few days to bring the company back up to strength. The men would still be sleeping on the ground, still be eating cold C rations, but they would sleep a lot. In that happy valley, nobody would be trying to kill them. The training film was titled, *Kill or be Killed.* In the reality of the insane exchange of death, it was more like, Kill *and* be Killed, but for now, in this temporary peace, there was even time for politics, company politics, G Company politics. One evening as they sat around the fire, the Marines discussed who would replace their fallen squad leader. Jim, whose hometown was in the Midwest, said the new leader obviously would be Pete del la Santos.

All but one agreed. The exception was Hal Johnson from Texas. "You have to remember, Jim, that if Pete becomes squad leader, it will mean that three of our four squads will have Hispanics at the top." "So?" was the collective response. Everybody else was from some place other than the southwest. Jim was completely mystified. To him, Hispanic was the handsome matinee idol, Cesar Romero, the Latin lover to be envied. He quickly sensed that in at least one respect, Texas must be different. He knew about the mid-century prejudice against citizens who were Jews or of African descent and was sickened by that shallow arrogance, but this thing about Latin Americans, he had never before so much as heard a hint of it. He was growing up quickly. And in that valley, in that central section of Korea, he penciled this effort:

In life and death and youth and age
Some problems do arise
But often woes that seem the worst
Are blessings in disguise.

A nation's call to take up arms
Could breed a cynic's eyes
Or mold a boy into a man
A blessing in disguise.

The laborer who sweats and toils
Has no jewels that wealth buys
But his are gems of healthy limbs
A gift not so disguised.

The first of the month arrived along with the new Marines in those clean greens. This was the eighth draft and the lads of the seventh draft were not the fresh faces they had been on 1 April. They were not yet "old salts", but thirty days in general and thirty hours in particular had added seasoning.

Once again at full strength, George Company bade their safe haven a reluctant farewell and headed back to Hell.

It is said that the road to Hell is paved with good intentions. The road to the Marines' Hell that day was paved with nothing. It was mud, deep and sticky. Marching in deep mud is not only messy; it is strenuous. Each step is a study in prying a thermal boot from a natural suction chamber. Any attempt at cheerful thoughts that day was dampened, nay, drenched by driving rain. One of the uncheerful thoughts for Jim was, "Why me? What are my friends at home doing right now, sweating out exams in dry cloths in warm rooms with the prospect of warm dinners and maybe warm dates tonight?" Or perhaps a panty raid, which was the campus thing at the time.

When that night arrived in Korea, the driving rain had not subsided; it had turned into a downpour. And at about 2200 hours, the company was ordered into a rice paddy to make camp for the night. *"Make camp! In this mess?"* It was the only mess available at the time.

The rice paddy mud was much deeper than that on the road. Nonetheless the pup tents had to be pitched. How? Here's how: Each man had a shelter half in his backpack and a poncho covering his upper body. The upside-down poncho of one Marine would become the floor over the mud for both men. Two shelter halves buttoned together to make one two-man tent. That night in the middle of the inundation, in the middle of the rice paddy, our teen Marine, the one who was not back home in college, the one who had declined a last-minute reprieve from combat before leaving San Diego (we'll hear more about that later), doffed his poncho and, in the manner of Sir Walter Raleigh, spread it on the mud. Somehow the two Marines found some sticks, buttoned their shelter halves together and drove stakes with rifle butts.

Now they were roommates. "Be it ever so humble, there's no place like home." Still it wasn't exactly the Hilton, more your Motel 6-minus. Unlike even the humblest motel, though, there was no washer-dryer immediately available. So how do you dry the soaking combat fatigues on your back and legs? You leave them on, crawl into your goose down sleeping bag and sleep a couple of hours until you go on watch. Following that duty, you crawl back in. By morning, voila, nice, dry uniform. Feels good. You wonder where the water went. The evaporation is amazing. Of course, there is some residue of subtle dampness in the bag. When the rain stops and the sun comes out, if it ever does, you hang the bag somewhere for thorough dehydration.

The new day was promising. It was still raining, but the rain had become a blessing. There was a lot of mud to be washed off ponchos and shelter halves. Moreover, after only a few more miles of marching, the Marines would stop being pedestrians for a while. They would proceed east on six-by trucks. The Whachan Valley, where the U.S. Second Army Division had just been mauled by the Chinese offensive, awaited, along with clearing skies.

Located in the east-central section of Korea, the Whachon Reservoir was part of what the military called *The Iron Triangle.* When the Marines arrived, they found mind-boggling and soul searing devastation. Death dominated the countryside. Denudation had stripped nature of her mantle. The surface of the moon came to mind. Equipment was strewn everywhere; Thompson sub-machine guns and other small arms littered the ground. C ration cans made the place look like a city dump. On closer examination, one discovered that the cans had not been opened the American way with the thumb-sized can openers found in C rations. The bent tops had jagged edges from bayonet thrusts. Jim remembered that the Chinese prisoners from Hill Nine-O-Two had no idea how to open the American tin cans. Fortunately, they also had no bayonets.

As if he didn't have enough to carry on his back, Jim picked up a Russian carbine in mint condition. The odds of getting it or even himself home were pretty long, but if he did survive and did get the carbine home, well, what a trophy. There were a lot of Chinese canteens lying around too. And after Nine-O-Two, it seemed prudent to carry as much water as possible into the mountains. So Jim requisitioned one of those green aluminum beauties. Two canteens, one U.S. and one Chinese. They both came in handy during the days that followed.

Jim found something else on the field. It was a small, red, cloth-covered book with Chinese handwriting on several of the pages and nothing on the rest. He would learn much later that each entry was a congratulatory message and autograph from one of the dead soldier's classmates in a Chinese military academy. Jim used it as a diary. One of his entries, a line for a cartoon, had a Korean telling an American officer, "Me? I'm neutral; I was born on the thirty-eighth."

Up until now, neither the Chinese nor the North Koreans seemed to have artillery or mortars. And the Marines had long since discarded their entrenching tools, but when the Marines moved into position along the American line that night, they discovered that they weren't the only ones who requisitioned from the bleak landscape of The Iron Triangle. The Chinese had picked up some U.S. 60 mm. mortars and they proved to be better at mortars than at C ration cans.

Bill Mauldin had written that he never did a cartoon about mortars because, he said, they just weren't funny. Artillery screams a warning when it heads your way. So there's usually time to move leisurely into or behind something. Mortar shells do not scream across the sky. A nanosecond before they land and explode, you hear a whooshing sound. About all you can do is hope you are not precisely in the wrong spot.

When the first mortar round landed just before dusk, it missed its target, G Company, by about twenty meters, but the explosion with its black cloud of smoke spewed fear. And the men began frantically digging in. With what? Believe this: it was bayonets and fingers, bloody fingers. By the time the Chinese improved their aim, most of the Marines were in the ground little more than eighteen inches deep. And Jim was about to experience his second wartime deus ex machina.

As the mortar rounds exploded in G Company, an anguished cry pled for help. Another voice shouted, "Corpsman." That means "medic" in Marineese, but corpsmen are not Marines; they are sailors attached to Marine units. And their exposure to danger is no less than that of their Marine infantry charges. The same second voice added, "Let's get up here, Doc."

As the malicious mortar barrage continued, one landed on the edge of Jim's hole and he felt that sharp pain again, this time in his left arm. His left ear was deafened by the thunderous report and his head was buried by Korean earth. Once again he had been hit and once again he had not been hit very badly. The cuts were from shrapnel, but the angle was the miracle. The cuts were superficial. He didn't know this yet. Frozen with fear and covered with dirt, he lay there for another fifteen minutes when either fate or an exhausted supply of mortar shells ended the attack. By that time, the Marines were firing their own 60s which may or may not have reached the enemy.

As he struggled from the loose dirt, Jim still did not know the extent of his wounds, or rather the *lack* of extent. He did know that no sound was coming through his left ear. And the wooden stock of the M-1 carbine, which was lying next to him when the barrage began to hit home, was sliced nearly in half by shrapnel. Shrapnel that might have sliced through his chest?

Weeks later, when his outfit was fewer in number and back in reserve once more, he took his carbine to Ordnance, which was a repair shop on the back of a six-by truck. A new stock was issued. And that was fine until he received notice at the end of the month that the cost of the stock had been deducted from his generous pay, sixty-five dollars a day once a month. His protest that it was a Chinese guy and not he who damaged the stock was to no avail. "The right way, the wrong way and the Marine Corps way."

After the incoming mortars stopped coming in, the night was calm and some sleep was possible. The next morning, the Marines moved farther north with the understanding that the enemy had moved out and the Marines could advance on their feet rather than their bellies. They advanced in a horizontal line, ten meters from shoulder to shoulder, but not all of them were on the same ground level. Their ranks extended over terraced rice patties. The Marine to Jim's left, on the higher ground of a rice patty, was the unusually tall Bob Kirk from Brooklyn.

Suddenly, which is the way it usually happens, a machine gun on a wooded hill to their right front opened up. The Marines "hit the deck", which, in this case, was dirt. Jim, feeling the pain in his left arm, was lying on his stomach looking straight ahead. He could no longer see his New York buddy who was also in the prone position, but on the slightly higher ground. The Chinese gunner decided to go after Jim by "walking" the bullets along the side of the patty and toward the head of our hometown hero. Jim could see the puffs of dust as the rounds approached him and he judged they would enter his head at the right temple. Strangely, though, he didn't stiffen or grimace. He relaxed in resignation. With fleeting thoughts of his mother, father and sisters, he prayed, not for survival (not possible) but for a pleasant hereafter. Instead, it was miracle number three.

At that instant, Cpl. Kirk jumped up and headed for cover. In doing so, he distracted the machine gunner who jerked the unfriendly fire toward the tall Marine. Bullets found their mark in those long legs, and as the fortuitous diversion was occurring, "Sweed," another buddy from Minnesota, got his bazooka loaded and fired a recoilless round in the direction of the machine gun. It was not clear whether the machine gunner was hit or just decided it was time to move out, but the firing from the hill ceased and Jim was dizzy from one more improbable deliverance. He got up and pressed on toward a rendezvous with yet another miracle, one he would some day report to a very high ranking Chinese official.

The foothills of the next mountain G Company climbed were wooded. On the ground were hundreds of leaflets—Communist propaganda leaflets. The Communists could have used a better PR firm. The flyers were, unintentionally, just plain funny. Listen to this one. It has a picture of a man and a woman on a beach in Florida. The caption says, "Where are you this winter? Moneybags [sic—an outdated term in the American idiom] is having a wonderful time in Florida." There may have been some question about whether a Marine would live to return home, but he wouldn't have to be a *moneybags* to go to Florida and bask on the a public beach if he did make it out of Korea. Even if he had to hitchhike, he could get there. The Commies didn't have a clue.

Another masterpiece of ignorance described the construction of a new dam in Russia and asserted that "now life will be even more glorious in The Soviet Union." One Marine says to another, " What's so glorious about a dam?" The second Marine replies, "Damned if I know." Again, the Communists missed their mark. Unfortunately, they were better when it came to firearms.

When G Company dug in for the night, they tasted good fortune. C rations caught up with them and so did some mail, a lot of it. Jim even got a package from his mom. The popcorn in it was good, but it had been put there, not so much to eat as to keep those pineapple cookies fresh. Sharing them earned points with his pals. Not enough to acquire dry socks, but perhaps someone's C ration Fruit Cocktail. In fact, from farther up the hill a shout rang out, "Who likes Fruit Cocktail?" "I do!" replied at least ten other Marines. "Just checking," chuckled the first. No one gave up Fruit Cocktail.

Compared to the Communist propaganda, the mail Jim received was a symphony of poetry and penetrating logic. There were exceptions, including a letter from his girl friend and one from his sister's boyfriend. The girlfriend apologized for the long delay in answering his letter, explaining that she could "honestly say [she] hadn't had time." She went on to propose that they be honest with each other. If she went out with someone else, she'd let Jim know and he, in combat and a long way from civilians in general and young women in particular, should do the same for her.

The letter from his sister's boyfriend was even more bizarre. "Kill a million trillion of those dirty old Commies for me." It was nice to get those missives out of the way first.

He had several letters both from his father and his mother. And they brought wisdom, renewed faith and, therefore, joy. His mother knew, she said, that he would be delighted to learn that the local draft board had classified him 4-F because he'd had polio when he was twelve. The board obviously didn't know he had pretty much exercised his way out of the mild case, but it's always nice to know that though in the middle of hostile action against the enemy, one is not eligible to be. The right way, the wrong way and the draft board way. Anyway, he had enlisted for two years and his two years would be up in a few days. Now he was going home, right? Wrong. The Congress, by voice vote, had enacted a law that "abridged the right of contract" and extended his enlistment for another year. The official euphemism was "COG, *Convenience of Government.*" For a lot of Marines who thought they could count on their government to honor its contract, it was inconvenient.

Another Marine got a package. He was a Boston lad named Ford. The box of goodies came from the five-term mayor of Boston, James Michael Curley, politician extraordinaire. The mayor was definitely different. During one of his campaigns, it came to light that he had fraudulently taken a civil service exam for another person. Rough, but the mayor knew how to handle it. Overnight, billboards blossomed all over town saying simply, HE DID IT FOR A FRIEND. Swish. Put away.

G Company remained in position for several days. And that meant digging better, which is to say deeper, holes. It also meant some down time. Playing cards appeared. Improbable stories were told. No one ever met a Marine who wasn't a champion athlete in his hometown.

The stationary position meant something else. Marine officers back at battalion were curious about exactly where the enemy was and what the enemy was doing. That meant a patrol, which meant a few Marines venturing beyond their own lines into the proverbial *no man's land.* Night patrol? They wished. No, the Marines were to be visible on the next mountain to the north. Why? Well just to see if they could draw enemy fire—against themselves. When and if nightfall did arrive for them, they were supposed to sneak back to their own lines. Jim wrote a parody of *The Banks of the Wabash,* "Back Home Again In Any Bunker."

Selected to be part of the patrol, Jim recalled a World War II Bill Mauldin cartoon in which an army sergeant asks for volunteers: "I need a couple guys what don't owe me any money fer a little routine patrol."

At 0600 hours the patrol jumped off the edge of the earth. It was beyond the frayed outer fabric of the mighty American flag. They were on their own as they made their way down and through the underbrush of the valley ahead. They were welcomed there by some small-arms fire. No one was hit and they captured the upstart. Lo and behold, he was the first North Korean soldier the Seventh Draft American Marines had ever seen. His uniform was brown with red trim and it was immaculate. Most puzzling. Even more puzzling was his attitude. The Marines were tense with anticipation; the prisoner was relaxed and displayed an enigmatic smile. They took him along and he was an obedient prisoner, but they never did figure him out. Even when they encountered some "friendly" mortar fire, he seemed indifferent. They didn't.

When the patrol reached the assigned mountaintop and the samples of G Company proceeded to make themselves conspicuous, it was 1500 hours. And it was summer, too, with its long days. And the orders were for them to stay there until the end of daylight or for the end of their lives, whichever came sooner. There wasn't much to do there but move around, watch the prisoner and, well, pray. Ordinarily, darkness would fall at about 2100 hours, but dark clouds were forming on the western horizon, well above the next mountain range. A minor, but most welcome, miracle. Darkness fell an hour early that day. And the only fire the Marines had received during the mission was their own and a few thirty-one-caliber rounds misdirected by their paranormal prisoner. Maybe Intelligence would learn something from him. Otherwise, except for climbing the mountain "because it was there," the scary maneuver seemed fruitless. One of the Marines said it: "Life is so uncertain in this Marine Corps." But this time this patrol returned safely, tipping their helmets to the trigger men on the heavy machine guns at the outer parameter. The rest of the night was restful for the patrollers. The next day would be anything but.

At 0600 hours, the Marines of G Company left their temporary homes which really *were* holes in the ground. Northward again and this time their objective was to take space the enemy held by what lawyers would call *adverse position.* Speaking of lawyers, there was an item in the old *Saturday Evening Post* about a World War II veteran who remained in the reserves and was called up for Korea. Between the wars, he had become a lawyer and thought his highest and best use to the military was to serve as a Judge Advocate. When he shared the idea with the relevant officer at the Pentagon, he was told, "I think you misunderstand our mission in Korea. We're planning to fight the North Koreans, not sue them."

There was fighting and dying and wounding and mental breakdown that day, after which the objective, an east-to-west ridge line, was secured and the Chinese retreated. The Marines set up their "hasty defense". Good thing, because not *all* the Chinese had, in fact, retreated. Chinese mortar fire began to rain blood on the Marines. And then there was Lt. Lenseth.

Mr. (that's what Marine officers were called in the field) Lenseth was the idol of the younger Marines of G Company. "Swashbuckling" was a good way to describe him. He would remind you of no one so much as the actor, Steve McQueen. And he wore two pearl-handled revolvers. Life imitating art. To the young enlisted men, he was indestructible.

Lt. Lenseth was killed after the Marines thought the battle was over, but it wasn't. His chest was riddled by Chinese fire from a Russian submachine *Burp Gun*. Mr. Lenseth dead? Impossible. No one that alive could have come so far only to be so quickly dead. The rule in the Marine Corps is that there's no such thing as an unloaded weapon. And to the young enlisted Marines at that place on that day, there could be no such thing as the death of Lt. Lenseth. So four of them, including Jim placed the Lieutenant on a litter and headed southeast to an aid station, but just where was the aid station? The line had moved so rapidly that no one in G Company knew exactly which hill to climb or which rice paddy to cross. The ones carrying their probably already dead lieutenant made a bad choice. It was a rice paddy.

Marines in another company of the Third Battalion were in the woods next to the paddy and they were waving and shouting at the litter bearers. The men with the stretcher were confused for a moment and then quickly got the point. It was a Chinese Bazooka Team who were pointing their rocket launcher at the misplaced Marines in the paddy. The Chinese were no more than a football field from their logical target. Jim and the other Marines knew their luck had run out, but what you know isn't always so.

Do miracles run in fours? They did for Jim. As he said his final prayers once more and cringed, he looked back toward his executioners and stared in amazement.

The Chinese loader was signaling to the Marines to go on, obviously because they were carrying a wounded man. The Marines waved a bewildered wave of gratitude as they rushed from the paddy up a draw in the adjacent woods. They were immediately met with yet another threat. One of them caught his foot on the trip wire of a Bouncing Betty land mine. They had been kindly spared only to be doomed after all. One more miracle; the mine was a worn out and rusty dud. No explosion.

Having found the aid station and having found that their shining hero was indeed dead, the four volunteers trudged back to their company. This time the area really was secure, so secure that an interrogation official from far to the rear had arrived to question an elderly Korean man. He had been found among other civilians huddled in a cave safe from the fighting.

Heartsick, Jim arrived just in time to see the American interrogator raise his hand and slap the old man so violently as to knock him to the ground. Who knows what the Korean might have said to provoke the American? Everyone knew it was anger, not self-defense, which animated the clean-shaven screwball from the rear. This was too much for Jim. Had the cannon fodder, the grunts, the dog faces, gone through all those agony-filled days and nights of soul-shattering horror and carnage only to make way for the cruelty of this *Ugly American*?

As other Marines restrained and reproved the obnoxious offender, Jim went limp. In the calm that followed the storm of battle, windblown from the whirlwind of death denied, he sank to the ground. And there in the hand of God and the arms of Mother Earth, he began to sob. Coursing through his mind were ugly memories of the American military personnel who laughed boisterously as they exposed themselves to three lovely little girls who were selling hand-carved dolls from the equivalent of an American child's lemonade stand. He recalled the Marine on the back of a six-by truck who leaned over to knock the stovepipe hat off the head of an Abagee, the retired farmer, most dignified and venerable of Koreans. And his mind's eye saw that sadistic captain back at Camp Pendleton, California, who in a driving rain on a long march, cheered up the Marine trainees by assuring them that they had been born at the wrong time. Even those who weren't killed in Korea would never be civilians again. It would be Orwell's *1984*.

The unashamed tears flowed freely for nearly an hour. Friends saw him but did not disturb, sensing it best to let the grief run its course. As he began to calm, he wondered: Was he going into that thing euphemistically called battle fatigue? Not really. Maybe exhaustion. It had been a long day and, in only a few months, it had been a long war. And the phenomenon of his repeated deliverance continued to bewilder him. As for the Ugly Americans, they were of course exceptions. Most Americans in Korea did their country proud and showed respect for the Koreans they were supposed to be protecting.

The good life in the States was only a faint memory now. No longer did our friend Jim think of those fantastically fortunate friends back home. He had been swallowed by an entirely different reality. Now he wasn't asking, *why me?* Overwhelmed by his improbable survival, he was beginning to wonder, *why not me?* Adlai Stevenson told of a sign on a gandy wagon in Kenya which read, "The Lord is my shepherd...and I don't know why."

It was time to lick wounds, both mental and physical. The entire First Regiment, The First Marines, commanded by legendary Chesty Puller, was going into reserve, away from war. Jim would be living for a while in a tent city, sleeping on the kind of canvas cot that had proved so luxurious on that long ago night in Pusan. After a couple of days in reserve, he was assigned to a fateful KP duty.

C rations were the chow of the grunts on the line. Most would say the fare was not quite Spartan, but no one would mistake it for a banquet either. When a regiment went into reserve, however, it was "A" or "Able" rations, hot chow on a cafeteria-like line. Jim's assignment that day was perhaps the best kind KP could offer. He was one of those ladling out the food. As Marines passed through the line, he looked up to find himself face to face with the "rear echelon pogue" who had knocked the old man to the ground. This time he saw the face more clearly. It had the look of smug superiority.

Nothing snapped in our Marine this time. He was not fatigued and because of the ladle in his hand, he was somewhat in command. Would our guy deliberately hand over short rations to this monster? Was Pope John Paul a Pole? The homely American snarled, "Put some more on that gear." He meant mess gear, which proved he was stationed in the rear with the gear; combat infantry Marines had long since tossed such luxuries away in favor of lighter loads. Our Marine said nothing, but maintained a steady gaze into the eyes of this degenerate who had so disgraced America. The offender growled again. "I'll see ya' sometime." This time Jim quietly replied, "I've seen you."

The first treat to greet the First Marines was ice cream. As was the case with most modern facilities for the infantry in Korea, the ice cream machine was on the bed of a six-by truck. The lines were long and, with the taxpayers in mind, the commanders passed the word that each Marine could go through only once. Well, here's where the rank-and-file quietly overruled their leaders. How did one get two servings? The First Marines had been on line for more than forty days. Even nineteen-year olds like Jim had grown beards. That was the way to get extra ice cream. Go through the line bearded, then go through again clean shaven. With all due respect to Korea, let's hear it for Burma Shave. Delicious times two.

There was a big mail call which brought some advice from a friend at home, "Don't worry about the one bullet with your name on it; worry about the nine hundred ninety-nine marked 'to whom it may concern.'" Good point. There were newspaper cuttings in one of the letters from our Jim's dad. One of them reported a statement by a senator from Texas named Johnson: "The public will demand a showdown with Russia. We won't keep fighting her slaves while she stands by without firing a shot." Prophetic? Our Marine thought to himself, "Who is this guy and how many shots has he fired?" The senator's name was not exactly a household word then. In time, it would be.

Next to ice cream, what could be much better than a movie? Pretty young women in convertible cars. American city streets and super markets. The night was clear and warm when the Marines arranged themselves on the ground in neat rows parallel to the screen. At last, even if only by transparent celluloid, they would be back home. The screen brightened and came alive. Now they'd see the likes of Ava Gardner or Diana Lynn, maybe at Malibu, maybe in a Caddy convertible? Forget it, lads. The movie was *Kim,* Rudyard Kipling's story about India. Call it cinematic saltpeter.

The following day, Jim sat on the edge of his posh canvas cot and cleaned the thirty-eight caliber automatic his parents had given him when he left San Diego. The bore cleaner can was on the ground, resting against the toe of his right boot. Suddenly there was a deafening explosion, deafening and startling. After the surrealistic moment passed, what had happened was clear. Our Marine had finished his task, inserted a magazine in the pistol and had turned to reach for his field jacket. Violating that maxim of the Marine Corps against unloaded weapons, another Marine had picked up the .38, sighted it on the bore cleaner can and, assuming an empty weapon, squeezed the trigger. The good news: the other Marine was a good shot; he got the bore cleaner can, not our lad's toe. One more intricate extrication.

He had cleaned the pistol because he wanted to go for a walk in the woods and the regimental rule required that, in order to do so, a Marine had to carry a weapon. Accepting his stunned buddy's apology, he picked up his side arm and his composure and walked into nature's surrounding canopy. The weather was pleasant, the perfume of the forest pungent and encounter with enemy or even friendly fire was unlikely. It was a great day to be alive. By now Jim knew that any day was a *great* day to be alive.

He did not encounter the enemy. To the contrary, he very definitely encountered friends. In an unexpected clearing, he came upon an elementary school, but there was no schoolhouse. Instead, the children were assembled in groups on the bare floor of the forest. The ground was their copy books, sticks their pencils. The teachers, whose warm smiles greeted him, were small and their students, tiny. Our friend was invited to participate. Things did not go swimmingly for him in the literature class. He did his best to keep up with the first graders who were reciting a Korean poem. In rhythm, he called out the sounds they were saying. *Ba dgo gee noon. No ha go. Nuel shun da.* Since Korea uses Arabic numerals, he was a whiz at the fifth grade math. As he took his leave, bowing back to their gracious bows, he hoped he had helped them know that most American Marines were not ugly Americans. Well, at least in the sense of meanness.

The moons became many and the year that took a century to pass had somehow gone by. No longer green, our somewhat worn Marine got the news that brought immeasurable euphoria. He was going home— alive and pretty much in one piece. Maybe there were some bulging veins and some frostbite, the kind that prompted a Marine named Mott to declare that in Korea, "Many are cold, but few are frozen." Maybe there were a few scars from miraculously minor wounds for which he never took a Purple Heart, the Marine Corps maxim being that if you take one when you barely deserve it, the next time, you'll *really* deserve it. Here he was at last, sitting on that coveted and dust-covered side of the small airfield, heading out of, rather than into, the cauldron.

This time it would be high seas transport the taxpayers didn't have to pay for twice. It was the *William H. Gordon*; one of the Navy's finest ships. It didn't break down in the middle of the Pacific. It endured the early spring fury of the Sea of Japan. And its first stop was Kobe, Japan. This time the Seventh Draft was fewer in number. Many Marines did not come back to Kobe for their lonely sea bags. Jim did and this time he was even allowed to stay for a while in that pretty port city. His buddies and he made a beeline for the nearest bar. The others had beers; Jim had a glass of milk. All this time in the Corps and he still drank neither alcohol nor coffee—hadn't even learned to smoke. They forgave him.

Jim didn't care for wine, but he didn't have the slightest objection to women and song. While ashore, he wondered if it would be possible for him to get a date and go to a dance. The rickshaw operator could take care of that. The only thing was that "date" did not mean the same thing to him that it meant to Jim. The father of the young woman misunderstood, too. When Jim was taken to the sliding door and had removed his shoes, he entered to meet the lady and her father, who doubled as her (shall we say?) agent. To her father's proffer, Jim said that was not at all what he had in mind. He'd be happy to pay what the father required, but he just wanted to take the pretty daughter to a dance. At first there was confusion and incredulity. Then it dawned on the dad that all our milk-drinker wanted was to treat the daughter like a lady; they were to dance fully clothed. It happened. The money was paid and the young couple had an old fashioned date. It's not clear whether the other Marines forgave Jim for that.

A kiss at the door, a fond farewell to Kobe and the survivors of the Seventh Draft set sail, heading east away from The East.

The most memorable thing aboard the U.S. Navy vessel, aside from decent chow and plenty of it, was an announcement to, or, rather a denouncement of, the Marines aboard. It was the skipper of the ship. And here is how he said it:

> When you Marines came aboard our ship at Sokch-o,
> the vessel was in pretty good shape. Now it looks like a
> disgrace. You men will turn to and swab down fore and
> aft. The honeymoon is over.

The Marines "turned to." They cleaned the ship and they also cleaned the navy captain's clock with a cartoon, many copies of which permeated the decks. It depicted a wedding car, trailing tin cans and old shoes, speeding away from the kaleidoscopic carnage of Korea. The sign on the back of vehicle said, "The honeymoon is over." We don't know whether the captain saw any humor in it, but we can guess, can't we? Oh, maybe he did.

One morning there was a stir among the Marines. Something exciting seemed to be happening on the main deck. Along with the others, Jim stepped topside to see in the distant east a tiny bridge. As the sun rose higher, the bridge grew larger until it became the Golden Gate. The Marines came home through the west entrance of The United States of America.

They were deactivated and released from the same place they had endured boot camp, the MCRD at San Diego. Some things had changed. For one, the amount of change required to use a pay phone. Jim thought two public phones in a row were out of order before he discovered that a nickel, as in "It's your nickel; start talking.", would no longer do. In the year of his absence, the price had doubled.

Then there was the super pretty young woman he passed as they walked in opposite directions on the base. She was wearing a spiffy seersucker suit. After they passed, she turned and called to him. An old question in a new context came to mind, "Why me? How can I be this lucky?" He wasn't. She was a Marine lieutenant and she was calling him down for failing to salute. *Hope springs eternal.*

Before continuing the journey east, this time by train, Jim and his buddies spent some time in Los Angeles. They attended two radio shows where no admission was charged. The first was *The Charlie McCarthy and Edgar Bergen Show.* It was broadcast from an old movie theater and Charlie's guest was an actor named Wendel Corey who seemed strangely nervous compared to his super cool image on the silver screen.

Next, it was *Amos 'N Andy*, a show that to the naked ear was, sad to say, racist. The broadcast took place in a bare room of an office building. The polished hardwood floors were without rugs and the audience sat in wooden folding chairs on the same level as the performers. The front row was scarcely five feet from the chairs in which the actors awaited their turns at stand-up microphones. Jim sat in that first row facing a beautiful, young woman of African descent, the only performer not of European descent.

What looked like tokenism proved to be exactly that. She didn't have a line in the show until the very end; and that line was in a dialect obviously unnatural for her. After her split-second performance, she returned to her seat, looked at Jim, shrugged her shoulders and smiled a that's-the-way-things-are smile which he returned with an understanding look of disapproval. He was thrilled by the thought of dinner with her that evening. She was graceful and gorgeous and obviously a talented actress. They had had that moment of kindred communication, but there was one thing he had *not* had: the nerve to invite her. Anybody that wonderful could do a lot better than him, but on the trip home, he couldn't help wondering what she would have said to the idea of a dinner date. His mom had said he was in love with love and looking for someone to pin it on. Mother may not always be right, but it's a pretty good bet that she was this time.

A very nice lady on the train told the Marines her son was in the Navy, adding, "He's the one who took you boys to Korea." In a gentle and friendly manner, a wag replied, "He's also the one who forgot to pick us up for a year."

As the train proceeded east, cluster by cluster the Marines came home. When Jim's journey ended at the hometown, he saw a dream come true. His mother, father and sisters were there at the station. God had seen fit to let him live on; and this *was* living. For most of America, the return of Korean veterans amounted to two things, ho and hum, but that didn't matter to our friend. He was too busy counting his blessings. His deliverance was delicious. It was time to get back to the business of hitting the books and delivering concrete blocks to help pay for them.

His first visit to the barbershop brought an interesting encounter. Referring to the negotiations pointing toward a long-term truce roughly along the thirty-eighth parallel, a well-fed couch potato asked in a hortatory tone, "You left the job half done, didn't you?" "Well," replied Jim, "if you mean completely wiping out my company, you're right. We took fifty percent casualties in just one night." The smiles around the shop were reassuring. This spud was not for them either. The barbershop "Braveheart" reminded our newly coined civilian of that Texas senator (was his name Johnson?) who wanted Russia to fire a shot. And what about that government contractor who proved his patriotism by bilking the taxpayers and half starving the Seventh Draft Marines? The spud, the senator and the swindler. Brave fellows—at a distance.

Although it was time to continue his post-secondary studies, Jim had his doubts.

He knew the insight and wisdom of the Lincoln quotation, "I shall prepare myself and when the time comes, I shall be ready." But in our friend's case, would the time for using a college education ever come? This was 1952 and the Red Square Red Scare was in full swing. The chief exploiter of it, a senator from Wisconsin who was said to prefer whiskey to Wisconsin's milk and fraud to fact, was having the time of his life ruining other people's lives. Obviously, the senator was a phony, but that didn't mean Jim, himself, wasn't scared of Red Square.

The Soviets had developed the hydrogen bomb and Dr. Edward Teller was telling us that if we didn't surrender our wallets to the nuclear industry, the Russians would "leave us behind and way behind." Very scary.

In those days it was not altogether weird to wonder if any Earthling had a future. Jim confided to his father that he didn't know whether it would be worth the effort to finish college. Was it not likely that, in the musical words of the Kingston Trio, we would "all be blown away." Yes, replied his father, human capacity to make itself extinct might be exercised, the nature of humans being what it is, but what if, just maybe, the final nuclear folly didn't happen? Wouldn't his doubtful defeatist son feel a little silly facing a modern world without the educational tools it would demand? The son knuckled down and finished his formal education. Maybe there wouldn't be mutual suicide after all. Maybe the Russians liked to live, too.

2

COUNTDOWN TO CATASTROPHE

An amazingly large number of our fellow Americans have been con vinced that the Constitution places in the hands of the President the decision to go to war. It does not.

Article One, Section Eight, Clause Eleven provides that Congress shall have "the power to declare war..." Unlike bills requiring presidential concurrence to become law, not even so much as a presidential signature is involved in the declaration process.

In order to avoid ill-considered decisions to pull the lanyard of war, our founders wisely placed the war-making authority in the most representative of our three branches of federal government. It is, after all, the legislative branch that is most likely to be personally acquainted with the mothers and fathers of those Americans who have always done war's horrible bleeding and dying, our young.

Most presidents since the mid-Twentieth Century seem not to have understood this, but America's premier legal scholar, Abraham Lincoln understood it clearly. During Lincoln's first and only term as a United States Representative, he received a letter from his close friend and law partner, William Herndon, arguing that President Polk had the constitutional authority on his own to order the invasion of Mexico. This, in part, was Lincoln's reply:

Washington, Feb. 15, 1848

Dear William:

Your letter of the 29th. Jany. was received last night. Being exclusively a constitutional argument, I wish to submit some reflections upon it...Allow the President to invade a neighboring nation, whenever he shall deem it necessary to repel an invasion, and you allow him to do so, whenever he may choose to say he deems it necessary for such purpose—and you allow him to make

31

war at pleasure. Study to see if you can fix any limit to his power in this respect, after you have given him so much as you propose. If today he should choose to say he thinks it necessary to invade Canada, to prevent the British from invading us, how could you stop him? You may say to him, 'I see no probability of the British invading us' but he will say to you 'be silent; I see it, if you don't.'

The provision in the Constitution giving the war-making power to Congress, was dictated, as I understand it, by the following reasons. Kings had always been involving and impoverishing their people in wars, pretending generally , if not always, that the good of the people was the object. This, our Convention understood to be the most oppressive of Kingly oppressions; and they resolved to so frame the Constitution that no one man should hold the power of bringing this oppression upon us, but your view destroys the whole matter, and places our President where kings have always stood. Write soon.

Yours truly,
A. Lincoln

So why the modern misunderstanding about who decides about going to war? Because during the six decades since our country was most recently attacked militarily by a foreign power, most of our presidents have got away with the assertion that Article Two, Section Two, Clause One gives the President and not the Congress the authority to make the apocalyptic decision. That Clause reads, 'the President shall be the commander in chief...' As long as citizens are willing to believe the monumental myth that this clause in Article Two overrides the specific words of Article One, we are likely to see more un-Constitutional Presidential wars. When those Article One words no longer live in the minds and beliefs of the citizens, in effect, they have been repealed by extralegal arrogance, by presidential PR. This from the official who placed a hand on the Bible and repeated the prescribed oath, "I do solemnly swear that I will faithfully execute the Office of President of the United States, and will to the best of my Ability, preserve, protect and defend the Constitution of the United States."

To argue that the naked term, "commander in chief" supplants the specific and unambiguous language conferring the war-making authority on Congress, is as far-fetched as to argue that the term "chief of police" confers on that official the authority to enact criminal law. The duties of these executive officials are, respectively, to carry out the military and police policies other officials have established.

Beyond the Constitutional issue in foreign affairs, are the questions of what is moral and what is not and what is smart and what is not.

In the January 1984 issue of *The Atlantic,* Thomas Powers asked, "What Is It About? " He meant the military confrontation between The Soviet Union and The United States. In essence he points out that neither country really wanted to take anything away from the other. If the Russians wanted wheat, we wanted gold. That sounded more like a commodity exchange than a nuclear one. Instead, the confrontation was based on the fear each had for the other's military capability. "Carthage must be destroyed."

Perhaps the Russians had more reason for their fear than we had for ours. Remember, Russia had been invaded not only by the French and Germans, but once by the United States as well—or ill. For our part, the hankering of government contractors for more government contracts produced some pretty scary shrieks by self-seeking politicians. "The Commies are coming, the Commies are coming." This was the rough equivalent of the salesman's warning in the play, *The Music Man,* "There's trouble in River City. Buy band instruments from me." The distinguished U.S. Rep. Herbert Pell, father of U.S. Senator Claiborne Pell, wrote a pamphlet in 1951 entitled, *I Want Peace.* The writing was done when McCarthyism was riding high and destroying innocent people's livelihoods. Here, in part, is what Mr. Pell wrote:

> I know how easy it is for an ignorant politician to yell 'Communist' when he is at a loss for an answer or desirous of covering himself with a smoke screen. That is why I write this personal (preface). I should be among the first to be destroyed by Communism. I am nearly seventy and have never been in business. I have lived all my life on invested property as did my father and mother and my grandparents and most of my great-grandparents before me. Economically I represent everything to which Communism is hostile. I am one of the comparatively few Americans, everyone of whose ancestors became citizens of the United States on July 4, 1776.

I have always loved and enjoyed liberty. Since the day of my first effort in politics I have worked for personal freedom for all....

How much courage does it take for a Congressman or Senator to yell for blood?...How much courage does anyone think it would take for me, sixty-seven years old, living on an ample income quietly in the country , to clamor for gore, to demand the sacrifice of a million men forty years younger than I am and then end my heroic address with a bitter note of regret that my years or my grapevines prevent me from joining the brave boys whom I envy? Such words do not come from the mouths of heroes or of patriots, but from the lips of self-seeking politicians hoping to ride into office on a wave of excitement that will conceal their own shortcomings. I was in Congress for forty years. I was a member of Congress ten years before the oldest soldier was drafted, and I know.

Most of the political shouters think they are backing a winning horse—that's all. Loathsome insects gather round anything that is rotten. Twenty-five years ago thousands of American politicians attacked the Catholics to get the Klan vote. Today they follow McCarthy. Twenty-five years ago they said, as they swilled their bootleg liquor, 'There's one more election in Prohibition.' Today, safe behind desks, they think that war and hatred will keep their snouts in the public trough for two more years....

It is in the nature, as well as in the Constitution, of our country that our military accepts the orders of our civilian government. On two different occasions, decades apart, Douglas MacArthur was an exception to that requirement and tradition, but, in the main, the tradition has been honored to a fault. "Theirs is not to reason why...." Which makes even greater the responsibility of civilian officials to take care not to waste the beings of those loyal humans who serve in our armed forces.

To die for one's country is love, than which there can be no greater. To die for one's country's politicians as a campaign gimmick is to be victimized by a cold-blooded atrocity etched in eternity. May God have mercy on the politicians who have perpetrated this perpetual wrong.

In October, 1990, the Historic Landmarks Foundation of Indiana asked several Hoosiers including me to write messages for placement in a time capsule to be opened one hundred years later. These words of mine—and twenty-four of my father's—rest in that capsule.

Dear Century from now:

The Twentieth Century, which is rapidly drawing to a close, has witnessed the greatest share of physical scientific advancement since creation. The healing arts, the means of communication and transportation, shelter and food production have been advanced to stunning heights when compared with accomplishments of previous times.

The social sciences have not done so well. In terms of civilization, universal education and peaceful resolution of conflicts, the scant progress in this century has been a disappointment to those who long for the ancient vision of living 'in peace as good neighbors.'

The deadly conspirator of this social failure has been a rapidly expanding capacity to invent and produce machines of universal terror.

As politicians compete for vicarious military heroism, the world teeters between war and peace, 'peace with humankind's energy building an ever-greater civilization or war with the destruction of everything we have built up and everyone we love.'

If the latter happens, no one will read these words a hundred years from now. If the former happens, then you are probably living in a modern Garden of Eden. And we are happy for you. You are our children's grandchildren.

Will our great-grandchildren know the peace on Earth our great-grand-parents and we have not; will Earth know our great-grandchildren? That depends partly on us, doesn't it?

3

"THE UNITED STATES WILL 'SEND IN THE MARINES' TO ANY COUNTRY WHERE WE CAN GET TEN PEOPLE TO INVITE US." — WILL ROGERS

Colonialism is government, not by the people, but by someone from somewhere else. An indigenous dictator, bad as he might be, is usually better than a foreign one. Therefore, colonialism has usually been the most noxious of oppressions.

The French began their subjugation of Indochina at about the time British subjugation of America ended. As our fledgling nation took its first steps toward the free, independent and prosperous nation we were to become, Indochina, under the heel of France, was descending deeper into slavery and the deprivation of its own material resources. However, after a century and a half of cruel rule and economic exploitation, Vietnam found its own George Washington in the person of Ho Chi Minh.

Following the tragic stupidity of World War I, Ho went to Washington seeking aid in the quest for Vietnamese independence. He pointed out to the Wilson Administration that France was doing to his country what England had done to America, but to no avail. Our leaders yawned and the Vietnamese leader pressed on to Versailles where the French and other governments gave his appeal the same short shrift. One French group listened to him though, the French Communists. That's when he became one himself. His wife had died in a French colonial prison. Her offense? The dream of independence for her country.

The Vietnamese drive for freedom from France continued until the Japanese occupation of Vietnam during World War II. The French colonialists did not resist. Ho's army, the Vietminh, did. They were our allies in the war against Japan, earning the expressed admiration of General Douglas MacArthur. When the war ended and, by agreement at

Yalta, the Chinese occupied Vietnam north of the sixteenth parallel and the British occupied the south, our ally, Ho Chi Minh, was barred from forming the native and logical government. Instead, the British elected (so to speak) to delay disarming the Japanese for three months so that the defeated enemy could police our Vietnamese friends. General MacArthur was outraged at the treatment of "these little people who were our allies."

In the wake of World War II, Ho traveled once again to Paris, this time seemingly successfully. Under its first postwar provisional government, the France that had just been liberated from Hitler's Germany agreed to liberate Vietnam. Ho returned to his native land with the French document that proclaimed independence. And in the late summer of 1945 the Vietnamese celebrated their own *Fourth of July*. It seemed easy and it was—too easy, as events would soon show. By late fall, French actions spoke louder, thunderously louder, than the words of the French document.

In November, a French man-of-war lay off the port of Haiphong and in one afternoon of shelling, killed thousands of people in the Chinese section of the city. The first Vietnam War was under way. And it went badly for the aggressors, despite substantial U.S. aid for the nefarious enterprise. U.S. aid! How could that be? How could *The Arsenal of Democracy* with its freshly minted proclamation of *The Four Freedoms*, possibly have aided the French war to re-impose colonialism? Simple. When the Truman Administration proposed formation of the North Atlantic Treaty Organization as a defense against the paranoid bellicosity of postwar Russia, France quite understandably took a darker than dim view of re-arming Germany.

Charles de Gaulle, an egotist at best, threatened that France just might side with the Russians in the cold war if the U.S. denied his country the economic tart it had made of Vietnam. According to historian Barbara Tuchman, de Gaulle even indicated that, though he didn't really want it to, France might just be forced by the U.S. to "become Communist."

Interesting irony. France jilts Ho into becoming Communist in the World War I era, and de Gaulle warns the U.S. not to jilt France into becoming Communist in the World War II era. So the deal was cut. France would gargle the re-arming of Germany and the United States would help France in its unholy war to enslave Vietnam once more. By 1954, the United States would be financing eighty percent of the ignoble French cause.

The first Vietnam War went on for about nine years. It was essentially ended when the French were signally defeated at a place called Dien Bien Phu on May 7, 1954, but not before an adventuresome Vice President Richard Nixon and Joint Chiefs Chairman Arthur Radford urged President Eisenhower to send American B-29 air strikes to defend the ill-fated French who were clearly doomed with or without direct American military intervention. Radford even mused about using nuclear bombs. In any case, Ike quietly and firmly said no. My friend, the late Arthur Flemming, best remembered as the first Secretary of the Department of Health, Education and Welfare, was present when the vice president made the pitch for direct U.S. involvement. Dr. Flemming was then a member of Eisenhower's National Security Council. Reflecting on the meeting a decade later, Ike told Publisher Roy Howard:

> I tell you, the boys were putting the heat on me (about Dien Bien Phu). I was not willing to put the American prestige on one golderned [sic] thing in there.

Later when Nixon, Radford and others were again pushing Ike to send U.S. combat troops to Vietnam, Ike told a news conference:

> There's going to be no involvement of America in war unless it is the result of the constitutional process that is placed upon Congress to declare war.

Think of it: a president who could read the Constitution. I like, nay, love Ike.

Think of this too. Even when our country was directly attacked at Pearl Harbor, President Roosevelt did not violate the Constitution with regard to war. On the day following the attack, he went to Congress and *requested* a declaration of war against our attackers. In a speech following World War I, President Wilson said, "I was the one who *advised* the Congress to create the situation in which (mothers') sons died."

"Requested," "Advised." Those presidents, too, comprehended the Constitution. They knew that the founders, as Lincoln wrote, were so determined to make our presidents different from kings, that they left our presidents completely out of the official process of declaring war.

President Eisenhower and President Adams, the elder, had something in common—they both had the courage to stand up to domestic war hawks and say no to unnecessary war. Ike did it in three specific cases, Vietnam, the Mideast War in 1956—Adlai Stevenson took him to task for that one—and the Hungarian uprising. God only knows how many lives and tax dollars Ike saved for America. Instead of insinuating us into those fuses of others, he built an interstate highway system that is self financing. All this from a general whose critics insisted he'd get us into war if elected. I'll always love Ike.

As we have seen and shall continue to see, the whole dreary and deadly dalliance in Vietnam was quite bipartisan.

Dien Bien Phu was the final failure for the French in Vietnam. The French fortress was in a valley and the Vietminh were in the surrounding mountains. Thus the native forces held the high ground and the French the low ground, in more ways than one. The French soldiers fought valorously in a cause that did not deserve their sacrifice. In his newscast the night Dien Bien Phu fell, Edward R. Murrow quoted the poet Homer: "In a just world, there would be no need for valor."

Now that everything else had failed, the French had to leave, but how could they do so in physical safety? The French foreigners were not universally loved by the nationals. In fact, it would be most wise for the French to find some escape route as far from the Vietminh as possible.

So it was the diplomats' turn. They met in convention at Geneva. The participants were from several nations, including Communist China and Communist Russia, both of whom persuaded Ho to accept a little less than the unmistakable language he proposed for an agreement. Still, he got most of what his country had fought for. The convention produced a multi-lateral agreement called *The Nineteen Fifty-four Geneva Accords*. Among the provisions were safe conduct below the Seventeenth Parallel for the French retreat and general elections throughout Vietnam in 1956. The elections would determine the home grown government of Vietnam. Paragraph Six of the accord said, "The military demarcation is provisional and should not in any way be interpreted as constituting a political or territorial boundary."

While the United States was not a direct participant in the negotiations, we were a "unilateral declaratory," pledging in essence not to disturb the arrangements, but under the U.S. Secretary of State, we did. The Secretary, one John Foster Dulles was a strange man. In his masterful book, *The Ordeal of Power*, Emmit John Hughes wrote that Dulles had a particular knack for brutally boring his boss, the thirty-fourth President of The United States. In his memoir, James Reston told of an incident in New York involving a nasty fall taken by Dulles' wife down some stone steps. The look on John Foster's face, Reston wrote, "was not one of alarm nor concern; it was irritation." He had an unhealthy respect for, or really fear of, Senator Joseph McCarthy. Dulles was something of a flat-earth fellow himself.

When rioting occurred in a friendly foreign country during the visit of a U.S. official and the Eisenhower Administration was embarrassed by it, the Secretary implied that not much should be made of it. When he was a college student, he said, he "used to go out and riot *occasionally.*" No doubt about it; he was strange.

As the French withdrew from their safe zone in the south, a non-statesman named Bao Dai declared himself "Head of State," claiming that the "State" was territory below the Seventeenth Parallel. Before that, he had managed to land on his feet no matter who was running Vietnam. He worked for the French, the Japanese and, yes, even for Ho—but Dulles didn't think he could pull it off and forced Bao Dai to be the "exiled Head of State." Bao Dai moved to the rigors of the French Rivera and, at the behest of Dulles, declared one Ngo Dinh Diem, who was living in the U.S., the new Head of State in the south of Vietnam. Diem had worked for the French in Vietnam, but he was also a national-ist. He resigned when he became disillusioned with his French bosses. The Japanese offered him a job toward the end of their time in Vietnam, but he wouldn't put in with them, either. He wasn't a bad guy at the time. He became one later.

Diem was the man for Dulles, just right to lead (under the leadership of Dulles). The U.S.-invented state was dubbed "South Vietnam". Con-sidering paragraph six of the Accords and the U.S. pledge not to disturb their provisions, this U.S. fiat was hardly welcome to Ho.

Mr. Dulles did what he could (which was plenty) to disturb or, more accurately, *scuttle* the agreed-upon Vietnamese elections for 1956. Why? Because Dulles knew who was going to win at the ballot box.

In his memoir, Ike wrote about the required '56 election:

> I have never spoken with an informed observer of the
> Vietnam scene at the time who did not agree that had
> the election been held as scheduled, Ho Chi Minh, the
> Communist, would have received eighty percent of the
> vote.

Capitalism and Communism didn't mean much to the agrarian soci-ety of Vietnam, but Ho Chi Minh meant much to that society. Of course he did. Whether U.S. officials liked him or not, regardless of his politics, he was a national hero to the Vietnamese. In the manner of George Wash-ington, he had freed them from European enslavement.

The realities about Vietnam were completely lost on the American public, truth being "the first casualty of war." The two major political parties led the propaganda campaign. Dissent, like a "discouraging word," seldom was heard during those early days of American intervention. Commenting on freedom of speech in America, Alexis de Tocqueville wrote that there was plenty of it until a widely held consensus was reached. After that, he implied, "'tis folly" to disagree.

In order to thrive in politics, the demagogue does not need a stupid population. Ignorance will do. In the U.S., it was a revealed truth that the people of Vietnam desperately wanted protection from "that Commie bastard". The "Commie bastard" was Ho Chi Minh, who probably never would have thrown in with the Communists in the first place if only the Woodrow Wilson Administration had lived up to its lofty declaration that the world should be "safe for democracy."

When President Nixon lessened the tensions which he helped bring about with China, Senator Eugene McCarthy was asked how in the world the Chinese people could be so enthusiastic in their street welcome to the visiting U.S. President. After all, they had been taught for a quarter of a century that the Americans were the devil incarnate. Bear in mind, in the U.S. it had been "Red China" for that same quarter century. And now suddenly the President of the United States together with every cab driver was calling it The *People's Republic of China - People's Republic* for short. This was Gene McCarthy's answer about the phenomenon:

> Well, you have to remember that China is a closed society with an authoritarian government that controls public opinion and in the manner of Orwell's *Big Brother,* it can change public opinion overnight. By the way, when's the last time you heard anyone say, 'Red China' in this country?

In the case of those 1956 elections required by the Accords, fraud at the polls was more like destruction of the polls by Dulles' factotum, Diem. That destruction ushered in the second Vietnam War. The logo I composed for my Congressional stationery was, "The road to peace is paved with justice." The converse of course is, "The road to war is paved with injustice." In the case of the U.S. in Vietnam, the first road was the one not taken, much to our historic regret.

My father, Andrew Jacobs, Sr., a Representative in the Eighty-first Congress, had strongly opposed giving aid to the French war effort in Vietnam. He argued that starting down that road meant eventual direct involvement of American military personnel, adding that there were "too many people making history who never read history." First the guns, then the sons. In the early days of the war between Germany and The United Kingdom, Churchill had said to Roosevelt, "Send us the tools and we shall finish the job." Famous last words. American sons and daughters did go to a war in Europe, which a modicum of intelligence at Versailles could have obviated. By the close of 1941, it was too late. We had no choice. U.S. sons followed U.S. guns.

To Vietnam we had sent the guns and now fate was coming for the sons and their sisters. Before we left that sorrowful land, hundreds of thousands of our sons and daughters had been sent to what General MacArthur called "the quicksands of Asia." More than fifty-seven thousand never came home alive and tens of thousands of those who did were maimed for life. In those days, politicians competed with one another to show the voters who hated Communism most and which official was fearless—when it came to other people's lives. Many of those fearless leaders welcomed opportunities to become heroes "on somebody else's time."

Never mind whether the wars politicians drummed up had the remotest relationship to American security or even prosperity. The politicians had to show their willingness " to protect America," even if they had to fake the threats to America. And of course, being busy people, they just didn't have the time to go and do some of the fighting and dying themselves. They'd have liked to, but there were always more pressing matters, like arranging for others to do the unnecessary dying and arranging for this or that campaign contributor to clear a profit from it at the Pentagon. Politics is the place where it is *safe to be courageous.* Violence became the index to patriotism, but the violence was neither performed nor endured by the people in Washington. The leaders in Washington who so easefully did the "sending" to war, but in almost every case never had nor ever would do the "going," had no idea at all about the unspeakable horror to which they so recklessly condemned their victims, who happened also to be their constituents.

4

WE TOO, BUT WE CAN DO IT BETTER

Throughout the abbreviated Kennedy Administration, Vietnam continued to fester, far removed from publicly reported events. It was on
one of America's back burners, but politicians were easing the tempera-
ture upward.

Shortly after taking office, Kennedy had said, "If (Vietnam) were
ever converted into a white man's war, we should lose it as the French
had lost a decade earlier," but the fact that foreign relations were not
going well for JFK in the early days of his "thousand days" meant ominous temptations for foolish American moves in Indochina.

Kennedy had unfortunately given the go-ahead to U.S. clandestine
participation in a hopeless invasion of Communist Cuba by about twelve
or fifteen hundred Cuban exiles. The operation had been planned by the
Eisenhower Administration and Kennedy had unwittingly put his thumb
on it during the 1960 Presidential campaign. In fact, he talked about
liberating Cuba from Communism through a counter-revolution.

Little noted at the time was Castro's sarcastic comment on Kennedy's
platform: "If he weren't a rich man's son, he'd know there can't be a
people's revolution against a people's revolution." That was the theory of
the Bay of Pigs invasion. A relative handful of exiles would land with
weapons and the population would rise up and join them against Castro,
but the Left Wing Castro revolution against his Right Wing predecessor,
Fulgenico Batista y Zaldivar was fresh. And, by comparison, life for the
average Cuban had improved. The improvement was not a permanent
phenomenon, but the comparatively good times were still rolling in 1961
when the attempted invasion went down.

As the invasion became public, there was much rejoicing in the U.S.
That included the members of the Indianapolis Bar Association who gathered for lunch in its dining room. My father asked the group of celebrants
if they seriously believed the invasion would succeed and they brushed
aside his implication as loony. When news came the next day that the
surviving invaders were residing in Castro's prisons, my father's colleagues
asked him in wonderment, "How did you know?" His reply: "How could

45

Kennedy not have known?" The invasion planners' wish for success was father to the thought of it.

Because of the Bay of Pigs debacle and the perception that Nikita Khrushchev had bullied Kennedy during their early meeting in Vienna, the President wanted to show the world some U.S. military muscle. In his memoir, James Reston of the *New York Times* wrote that shortly after the meeting with Khrushchev, the President told Reston, "Now we have a problem making our power credible and Vietnam looks like the place."

Kennedy's awkward logic was echoed two decades later by White House aides when the Reagan Administration's blunder in Lebanon had left hundreds of hapless Marines blown to pieces. The overheard White House mantra was, "We [sic] have to win one *somewhere.*"

By autumn 1961, American military personnel were already on the ground in Vietnam. The Administration was calling them advisors in those days; they were about eight hundred in number. Their mission was to train and *persuade* our surrogate indigenous forces. Since most Vietnamese thought a lot of Ho Chi Minh, there was a lot of persuading to do. Of course, there were some Vietnamese who didn't like Ho. After all, Ike said Ho would have received "eighty percent of the vote," not one hundred percent, had the agreed upon elections not been sabotaged by his own Secretary of State.

Some American politicians claimed that about a million Vietnamese, mostly Catholic, "voted with their feet" by leaving the north for the American fiat government in the south. And those American politicians were quite right, but it is important to understand why the migrating Vietnamese were Catholic and why they didn't like Ho. They were to revolutionary Vietnam what the Tories were to revolutionary America, only more so. They had thrown in with the French masters who converted them to Catholicism and gave them colonial administrative jobs. That group of collaborators was doing pretty well, thank you, and had much to lose if independence came to their country. For them, colonial rule was anything but a bitter pill. I don't think they constituted the entire twenty percent who would not have voted for Ho, but, according to Ike, there were about twenty percent who for various reasons didn't favor Ho. That would leave just eighty percent for "our side," as Dean Rusk put it, to persuade.

Will Rogers said it: "The United States will send in the Marines to any country where we can get ten people to invite us." Decades later, President Bush, whom I personally liked very much, spent an enormous amount of American tax money persuading a few Mideast countries to invite us into the Gulf War. As was the case with Truman and Korea,

Bush went first to the United Nations, but, unlike the Truman "police" action, George Bush subsequently took the matter to Congress, arguing that the UN resolution which he obtained with some persuasive American-dollar diplomacy made it more or less mandatory for Congress to act favorably. Congress did, probably making the American war in the gulf constitutional, if not wise.

By the early sixties, the infection of Vietnam was spreading. Although it was still on the back burner of public consciousness, some scholars were beginning to ask about what seemed to be our growing involvement. Nervous about that themselves, members of the Kennedy Administration began to think about how to get out gracefully if we began to meet the same fate that finished the French. The President had an answer. "Easy," he said, "put a government in there that would ask us to leave." Will Rogers in reverse.

My first campaign for public office was an unlikely success because I ran in Marion County, Indiana, where Indianapolis is situated. Marion County usually went Republican, but there was a strange pattern of exceptions. You could just about set your clock by them.

The Democrats won the county in 1938 and not again until 1948 when Harry Truman was elected president. "My name's Harry S Truman; I work for the Government and I'm trying to keep my job." His plain talk infuriated the extremists who hated him, but it endeared him to the people. The Democrats lost Marion County handily in each succeeding election until 1958. That year they won once more and when they did, I was one of them. At age twenty-six, I was sworn in as an Indiana State Representative from Marion County. Birch Bayh was the speaker of the Indiana House in that '59 session. Four years later, he was United States Senator Birch Bayh.

In the 1960 election, I was a Democratic nominee for the Indiana State Senate. Bad year for Hoosier Democrats. JFK was on the ticket for president and Indiana had been the strongest Ku Klux Klan state outside the South.

The Klan had effectively controlled two Indiana state administrations during the 1920s. Their boss, a degenerate named D.C. Stevenson, boasted, "I am the law in Indiana." My father said it was about the only time Stevenson told the truth. This shameful background stacked the deck heavily against the Bay State Catholic Kennedy in Indiana. And with mandatory straight-party levers on the Indianapolis voting machines, other Democrats on the ticket, including me, shared the Hoosier fate of Kennedy. We were trounced.

Billy Graham was an avid supporter of Richard Nixon and on Billy's Sunday-night-before-the-election broadcast, he preached that the Bible warned against Kennedy's health program. That health plan came to be known as Medicare. One could wonder if Billy, himself, might eventually have become a beneficiary.

Graham was a saint in the 1960 presidential election compared to a holy sage named Norman Vincent Peale. Billy Graham never injected Kennedy's religion into the debate. Peale did. Norman's predecessors in spirit prompted a joke about the defeat of earlier Roman Catholic candidate for president. Following the 1928 defeat of Al Smith, the chuckle was that he cabled a one-word message to the Pope: "Unpack." By 1960 the Pope was John who had dismantled some of the sillier rules of his church. And when Kennedy was elected, I told my friends not to worry. Although it was true that we had our first Catholic President, it was equally true that we had our first Protestant Pope.

Throughout U.S. history, the religious pulpit has occasionally been used for political stump speeches—for both sides. Sometimes politics from the pulpit has nothing to do with ideology. As Edward R. Murrow said, people either loved or hated Franklin Roosevelt. And the ones who hated him tended to be those with upper incomes. At the time, *The New Yorker* ran a cartoon showing a sexton dumping a quantum of cash onto a table in the sacristy of an Anglican Church with the priest looking on. The sexton said to the cleric, "That crack you took at FDR sure paid off."

Jean Dixon, a tabloid seer and Kennedy critic, had predicted Kennedy would lose the 1960 election. When questioned about her error, she said there *was* no error, explaining that without Illinois Kennedy was a loser and that Mayor Daley had stolen Illinois in Chicago. Wrong again, Jean. I don't know what Mayor Daley was doing in Chicago, but I do know that had JFK lost Illinois in 1960, he still would have won the election. He went over the top in the wee hours of Wednesday morning when Michigan slipped into his column. Illinois had not yet reported. And when it did, it simply added to his margin in the electoral college. Thanks to the careful scholarship of James Maley, we know that the electoral vote was 303 to 219. Had a majority in Illinois voted for Nixon, Kennedy still would have won by thirty electoral votes.

The popular votes cast between Kennedy and Nixon numbered 68,000,335. Kennedy won by 119,000. His critics said it was just terrible that someone could become President by a mere 100,000-vote margin. Nine years later, as president, Richard Nixon proposed a Constitutional Amendment to change the electoral college in such a way that the one who *lost* by 100,000 in 1960 would have become President. DOA on Capitol Hill.

When I unsuccessfully challenged the Indianapolis incumbent Republican congressman in 1962, it was hard to get the voters' attention on the subject of Vietnam.

One foreign policy matter got their attention, though. It was the *Cuban Missile Crisis* and it was scary. The Soviets based some intermediate-range nuclear missiles in Cuba and they were discovered by our reconnaissance planes in the fall, indeed during the fall election campaign of 1962. President Kennedy stood tall and stood firm. Khrushchev stood down and stood the loss of his job as Communist Party Chairman because he backed down and took the missiles home. For a few days, though, the world bit its nails. This was real nuclear confrontation in which, unlike World War II, more than one side had *the bomb*.

As the Democratic candidate for Congress in Indianapolis, I was allowed five minutes on television to comment about the crisis. My remarks were very good because my father wrote them. He was the only one ever who did that for me and he did it only twice. Both were home runs. This is a brief sample of his powerful prose on the missile matter:

> We stand tonight on the precipice between war and peace, peace with humankind's energies building an ever greater civilization or war with the destruction of everything we have built up and everyone we love....

He wrote it; I memorized and recited it. "We killed a bear; Pa shot him."

By 1964, in the words of Chief Justice Warren, John Fitzgerald Kennedy had "been snatched from our midst by an assassin's bullet." Sen. Barry Goldwater, the Republican nominee for president, seemed to be saying that, if elected, he would be heating things up in Vietnam. Lyndon Johnson, no longer a senator from Texas, seemed to be saying he would not. On October 21 in Akron, the President said, "We are not about to send American boys nine or ten thousand miles away from home to do what Asian boys ought to be doing for themselves."

What Asian boys ought to have been doing for themselves was voting, but Dulles had precluded that. As keynote speaker at a radiant October banquet in Indianapolis, Sen. Hubert Humphrey, Johnson's running mate, emotionally declared that Goldwater and not Johnson wanted to play "war games" with the lives of young Americans in Vietnam. He added that it "does not take courage to make war; it takes courage to be a peacemaker." Listening to that vibrant and stentorian oratory, no one could doubt that this senator had that courage in quantums, but he didn't. He demonstrated that he didn't only months later with regard to the politics of Vietnam.

Johnson, despite being light years ahead in the polls, apparently thought it necessary to match Goldwater's tough talk. And he did it with more than words. Thus the two "incidents" in the Gulf of Tonkin. The Johnson Administration claimed that motor patrol boats under the command of the Ho Chi Minh authorities attacked the American destroyer, Maddox in international waters and later struck again. The first attack wasn't much of an attack; the Maddox wasn't hit. It happened in a dispute about how far Vietnam's coastal waters extended. Vietnam said twelve miles, Johnson said three. According to the Vietnamese we were in their waters and according to Johnson, we weren't, but we claimed that *our* coastal waters extended twelve miles.

The second incident simply didn't happen. Even Johnson acknowledged this in private conversation: "Well, those damned stupid sailors were just shooting at flying fish." The Administration seized the opportunity, however, and blew it up enormously out of proportion. It worked. Most of Congress and the public believed what the Administration reported at the time. Concerning a similarly successful government hoax, John Hay, personal secretary to President Abraham Lincoln and Secretary of State in President Theodore Roosevelt's Administration, wrote in his diary that he was surprised at the public acceptance of such a "concise impropriety."

The cock-and-bull story about the Gulf of Tonkin produced for Johnson a gift from Congress, the infamous *Gulf of Tonkin Resolution*. It granted the President authority in essence to do whatever he might choose militarily to protect our troops in Vietnam. Since fifty-seven thousand of them were eventually killed there, one might wonder just what was meant by "protect."

Walter Lippmann had written about "war whoop" politicians who didn't really want war, but just wanted to make a lot of noise about war so they would seem brave. It is my considered opinion that Johnson wanted some bloodless fireworks from our military just to show the American voters he was even tougher than Sen. Goldwater talked. So he upped the ante by ordering air strikes on some shacks along the east coast of Vietnam.

Johnson was out to make the voters happy, not to make the Vietnamese angry. So he radioed the so-called North Vietnamese in advance to warn of the strikes, giving "the other side" opportunity to evacuate people from the targets. His adversaries in the election pounced on the warning he gave the Vietnamese as proof that Johnson had no understanding of military tactics. They argued that as commander in chief, he didn't know what he was doing. He knew exactly what he was doing.

The purpose of this charade, of course, was to outdo Goldwater's campaign. Nevertheless, to add some seeming statesmanship to the mix, President Johnson phoned his opponent and former Senate colleague to tell of the pending air strikes. The foolishness that was being done for politics must be made to look as though it was above politics.

Lyndon Johnson very much did not want to escalate U.S. military involvement in Vietnam. He was, after all, one of those who had strongly advised President Eisenhower to spurn Richard Nixon's arguments for U.S. military intervention to help the French at Dien Bien Phu. He knew full well the disastrous dangers in the "quicksands of Asia," and he knew the risk he was taking with this campaign grandstanding.

One can imagine how Johnson hoped and prayed Ho would play the game. The air strike was designed to do no harm to humans. He knew Ho wouldn't "blink," to use the term that described the Russian capitulation in the Cuban Missile Crisis, but he hoped Ho might *wink.* It didn't happen. Instead, the Ho Chi Minh military retaliated for the air strikes. They attacked an American officer's billet. The seeds of disastrous escalation had been sewn in the rich soil of human folly.

Lyndon Johnson, even as he campaigned on a platform of peace, had gambled just once on a saber-rattling campaign gimmick. And as time has told, he lost. While Peter, Paul and Mary sang his praises with songs of peace, he consigned his nation to one of history's most punishing steel-jaw traps of war. And, by doing so, he set in motion the forces that would bring down his own presidency. "…When will they ever learn?"

Johnson already had all the votes he needed for a landslide, but he decided to crawl out to the far-right edge of that thin limb to get those few extra War Hawk votes. The limb broke and the President fell onto the hard rocks of history. He had played with fire and lit the fuse. He had trifled with the apocalyptic danger of unspeakably horrible deaths for thousands of his supporters' children and political death for himself, but you wouldn't have guessed it on election night, 1964.

To the folks in Texas, he was *Landslide* Lyndon, but he acquired that sobriquet long before the election of 1964. It referred to his first election to the U.S. Senate by an eighty-seven-vote margin. During the vote count, a Texas court house that contained uncounted official ballots somehow caught fire and burned to the ground. Here was an election that really *was* hotly contested.

On November 3,1964, Lyndon Baines Johnson had a real, no-kidding, even you might say, prodigious landslide. And a lot of Democrats, including me, slid in with him on his anti-Vietnam War platform. Popular thought had it that Barry Goldwater's perceived extremism explained his smashing defeat. I doubt it. True, he was saying some pretty weird things: e.g. "some children would be better off" without education; the use of nuclear weapons should be left to the discretion of field commanders (shades of *Dr. Strangelove*); and maybe Social Security wasn't such a good idea as designed. In 1964, few would call that platform a crowd pleaser.

My Dad's friend, Frank Edwards, known to Hoosiers as the showman newscaster—for good reason we may hear about later—thought the Democratic landslide of 1964 was a result of that shockingly sorrowful day in Dallas less than a year before. At Christmas time, 1963, Frank told us that if he were interested in serving in public office, he'd "try to get on the Democratic ticket next year." Why? Because the well of human emotion would make people want to let JFK's vice president continue, no matter what the candidates might be saying in the campaign. After the murder of John F. Kennedy, he was everybody's president; it was hard to find anyone who had not voted for him in 1960. Strange, considering that he won by only that one hundred nineteen thousand votes out of millions cast.

No matter what made it happen, November 3,1964 was undeniably Lyndon Johnson's day. It wasn't exactly castor oil for me, either, but Lyndon Johnson, clearly President of The United States, was the man of the hour and perhaps almost the year; very definitely of the first one hundred days of the Eighty-ninth Congress.

Publicly, he had been the candidate of peace while behind the scenes he had gambled on war. A year later the joke was, "They told me that if I voted for Goldwater, the war in Vietnam would escalate. I voted for Goldwater and, sure enough, the war in Vietnam escalated." The American comedian Roger Price said of politics, "You can't fool all the people all the time, but if you can do it once, you're good for four years." Which is true if you don't count President Nixon's second election.

By long-standing tradition, an inaugural gala is held a few days before the inauguration. In essence and to the naked eye, it is a variety show. As a member of Congress with all of two weeks seniority, I had a good seat very close to the stage and not very far from what looked a lot like a throne on which sat the thirty-sixth President of The United States. And did he ever look regal, replete with kingdom, power and glory.

He didn't look happy, though. Nor sad, either, just un-amused even by the master of ceremonies, the masterful humorist, Johnny Carson. One of Mr. Carson's jokes referred to the President's well-publicized insistence that White House lights be turned off when not in use. Carson said," Envy the guys who date the Johnson daughters, with the father going all over the house turning off lights." Good line; big laugh from everyone but the President. The expression on his face was somewhere between a frown and the rolled eyes of boredom. Was he being painfully regal, or was there something else on his mind? Even in that night of glory, could the fuse he lighted in Vietnam be nagging at him above the splendid frivolity and music of that magical evening? I had no reason to think such thoughts at the time—it might have crossed my mind that the President's shoes were hurting him—but in the ensuing years I thought about it often.

Some of the music was sung by the Caribbean star Harry Belafonte. Not counting the President, the audience, especially the woman seated next to me, loved it. My seatmate went berserk and confided at the top of her shrieking voice that she would be more than pleased to climb the entertainer's frame. Since she had just told me about her husband's recent accidental death at sea, I had to believe I was sitting next to the famous *Merry Widow,* but I don't believe waltzing was what she had in mind with Mr. Belafonte.

Now we come to the inauguration itself. The tradition at the time was to hold the ceremony on the east side of the Capitol. Many famous people were seated behind the podium with at least one who was not famous at all, me. General Omar Nelson Bradley, clearly superannuated, stared blankly from a wheelchair.

That night brought the Inaugural Ball, or rather several Inaugural Balls in various parts of Washington. I had phoned the inaugural committee to inquire about what one should wear for the occasion, hoping that President Johnson's announced policy of no black tie occasions any more at the White House might apply to the inaugural festivities. No such luck. The woman at the other end of the line, in a very British accent said the evening was to be black tie. She was a British subject who had accepted temporary employment at the committee. Grasping for reprieve, I asked, "Well, do I *have to* wear black tie?" The woman had no way of knowing that I was born and reared in Indianapolis, but, so help me, this was her reply: "Have to? Well I wouldn't say, 'have to.' There'll be some Indiana people there." Fortunately, I got to the rental store before they ran out of thirty-six inch sleeves.

The celebrations were over; it was time to go to work on Lyndon Johnson's proposals which he called *The Great Society.* His program was mostly noble in purpose and some of it was overdue. One part had unarguable logic, the 1965 Voting Rights Act. In his efforts to pass this law and a few others, Lydon Johnson was magnificent. Vietnam was his Achilles' heel.

By mid 1965 the Vietnam snare LBJ had set for himself began to tighten. He was faced with a bad choice. He could either push his country deeper into those Asian quicksands or suffer the ridicule of unworthy wimps whose roaring patriotism was confined to the vocal chords. Few, if any of them, would volunteer to face death in the warfare they demanded. And absolutely none of them would willingly endure taxes to pay for it, but LBJ had an unhealthy and fearful respect for the hawks. He could not get up the courage to face their forensic wrath. Lord Gilbert K. Chesterton said, "Sometimes it is easier to die for one's country than to tell her the truth." President Johnson chose neither. "With a heavy heart," he chose the insalubrious quicksands—for others.

According to the dean of political writers, David Halberstam, Vice President Humphrey did show the political courage to voice opposition to Johnson's escalation, for about seventy-two hours, but LBJ's icy stares were too much for "Hueby," as Johnson called him. In the words of Halberstam, Humphrey "signed on." In 1973 Humphrey claimed that he had no choice but to go along with Johnson's foolish policy, explaining that the relationship between a president and vice president is like a marriage.

Marriage? Lyndon Johnson, Hubert Humphrey's lord and master? Was it LBJ or as with RCA, "His Master's Voice"? Hubert was barking up the wrong simile. Consider the case of Mr. and Mrs. Bumble in *Oliver Twist.* Mr. Bumble is hauled before a court to answer for a crime his wife is alleged to have committed. Not surprisingly, Mr. Bumble asks, "Why me?" The court explains that the law presumes a husband controls the actions of his wife. To which Mr. Bumble replies, "Then, my lord, if the law supposes that, the law is a [sic] ass, a fool and a bachelor."

You couldn't help loving Hubert Humphrey nor being delighted with his rhetoric which sounded so much like strength, but as my mother was fond of saying, "The steam that blew the whistle never turned the wheel." Hubert's voice sounded fearless in the safety of the harbor, but he tended to be courageous only when it was safe to be so.

During the one term my dad served in Congress, Oleo margarine had burst upon the scene as a less expensive and more healthful alternative to butter. The dairy people were not happy. And they hit on a political way to smite their new and effective competitor. They would get their friends in Congress to pass a law against coloring margarine yellow. They argued that it was not fair for margarine to fake the *natural* color of butter. Having been a farm boy, my father pointed out during the House debate that yellow is not the natural color of butter, either. It was artificially colored, too, and there was no patent on yellow. Senator Humphrey was on the other, and successful, side. While the law was in effect, the consumer had to color his or her own margarine. The coloring came in a little plastic bubble attached to the clear plastic wrapping and one would squeeze the bubble to break it and then manipulate the color into the margarine. Margarine made it on the market, anyway, and the law was repealed by popular demand.

The margarine and civil rights issues animated my father to say to Humphrey one day, "Hubert, you're mighty courageous on Civil Rights with an African population of point zero, zero, zero one percent in Minnesota, but you have a lot of cows up there and you're sure as hell not going to let the margarine people use yellow."

After he was vice president and then the Democratic nominee for President, Humphrey was once again a senator from Minnesota. And he was dying of cancer. The U.S. House accorded him an honor rarely, if ever, before bestowed upon "a member of the other body." They asked him to address them in the House chamber. The ravages of cancer were sadly apparent. Before he spoke, various representatives were permitted to heap encomiums upon this historic figure.

The marvelous Morris K. Udall, whose presidency was most unfortunately denied the American people, said Humphrey was so liberal that he sometimes had solutions to problems that didn't even exist. It was said in fun and the gravely ill senator laughed. Mo Udall added that the prolix Senator had made hour-long speeches which Muriel, the senator's delightful wife, knew could have been made in fifteen minutes. Udall went on to declare, "In order for a speech to be immortal, it need not be eternal."

When Humphrey's close friend, Representative Paul Simon of Illinois, yielded the floor to the Senator, Simon said, "Now, Mr. Speaker, knowing full well the danger in what I am about to do, I yield such time as he may consume to the Senator from Minnesota." The phrase, "such time as he [or she] may consume" is boilerplate in the U.S. House. It usually implies a short period. Everyone howled.

Now Humphrey, the actual author of the Peace Corps, arguably the best debater of his time and the unfortunately weak figure of a failed foreign policy, too, began to speak as always, extemporaneously. I was sitting near the center of the well of the House which means that I was sitting close to the lectern from which the still vibrant orator began to speak.

The opening remarks were random. The speaker was adjusting his rhythm and balance, probing for the right rapport with his historic audience. Referring to his renowned reputation for speaking at length (he was never boring), he told the story about a few nights before when President Carter included him among invited advisors at the White House. The meeting was scheduled for an hour and Humphrey was the last to be called on. And there were only three minutes left. Referring to the President's hasty glance at the clock, Humphrey said to the House, "I shall be eternally grateful to your Speaker (Tip O'Neill) for what he said. The Speaker said, 'Mr. President, Hubert can't even say *hello* in three minutes.'"

The speech then turned serious. Humphrey said some inspiring things, and still forming his theme, his eyes met mine.

Hubert Humphrey was elected to the U.S. Senate for the first time when I was sixteen years old. And along with thousands of other young people, I was dazzled by his stentorian and eloquent oratory. Through the years my admiration for him only grew. When he competed with John F. Kennedy for the presidential nomination in 1960, he came to Indianapolis to address the Marion County Young Democrats. I was with him at his airport news conference when he was asked if he thought the health of the candidates was an issue. There he was, the picture of robust health and everyone knew Kennedy had some real health problems. Any politician could have made something of that. Not Humphrey. In reference to FDR, who was crippled by polio, and Ike, who was presiding over a recession and liked to play golf, the senator readily replied, "No. I think it's better to sit in a wheelchair and tell the country to go forward, than to walk all over a golf course and tell it to stand still." In later years, he would be less generous with another presidential primary opponent.

At the Indianapolis dinner, Humphrey's speech shook the rafters. "Don't tell me we have to sit by like Nero and watch our cities rot from within? Those who say we must, serve their country not well." He was dynamite and we loved him all the more.

Hubert Humphrey was a hero to me. During the 1964 fall election campaign, when he spoke in Indianapolis, he praised Pope John's *Peace on Earth* encyclical. That's when I heard him declare that it takes courage, by which he meant political courage, to be a peacemaker. When he failed in that regard and showed his feet of clay, it was a depressing disappointment. With the consequence of his tergiversation so vast, should he or, for that matter, could he ever be forgiven? He was well aware of the estrangement many of us felt.

Well, there we were in the U.S. House chamber, not eighteen feet apart with the eye contact of mutual recognition. Without breaking that contact, he said to the assemblage (especially me I presume to think) "…and forgiveness. That is one of the great human qualities." It was an emotional and defining moment for me. I relate profoundly to the Book of Matthew and try to be quiet and humble in my Christianity. Unlike most of the shouting preachers on television, I not only accept Jesus, but his teachings as well, especially The Sermon On The Mount. My response to my old and dying friend was a nod of the head that said yes…yes. "To err is human…." And could there ever be a being more human than Hubert?

There were several White House meetings with the freshman Democrats during those proverbial first one hundred days of that Eighty-ninth Congress. Our duty was disposition, one way or the other, of LBJ's legislative proposals, which were mostly successful in Congress.

When the "hundred days" began to fade away, the White House meetings began to change from domestic policy to foreign policy. There was LBJ's decision to send U.S. military forces to the Dominican Republic where an insurrection led by an alleged Communist seemed to be getting the upper hand. The alleged Communist likely was not that. He was later elected president in an election, which was accepted by our country as fair. And he was received with honors at the White House. The invasion, which cost American lives, was not only unnecessary and unconstitutional, but also wrong. And this is where I confess to my own lack of political courage.

After the action was over, Rep. Armested Seldon of Alabama offered a resolution of retrospective approval in the House. I cast my district's vote for it. The vote I cast did not authorize nor approve any future action, but it did approve of an unconstitutional act by the President, which had already resulted in human deaths including those of some Americans. It would be nice if I could say that the resolution was unclear or that I simply made a mistake; but I can't. I knew what the resolution meant and what it was likely to mean to me if I cast the correct vote, which was "nay". My opposition would harp on it.

I believe it is the only vote I ever cast in Congress that was intentionally wrong for the sake of political expedience. It happened during my first months in the House, but that is no excuse. And because of the smothering compunction I felt, I vowed it would never happen again. And I don't think it did. In retrospect, it occurs to me that I had also taken that vow before I cast the vote. I had sworn to uphold the Constitution of the United States, which clearly gives no president the authority to meddle militarily in the internal affairs of other peoples' countries.

By the opening months of 1966, the White House meetings were beginning to be about little else but Vietnam. In one of those 1966 meetings, there were about thirty of us from the House. Both the President and the Vice President were participants and the President made an off-the-cuff remark which seemed full-fledged Freudian. Whether he meant to or not, with the following phrase he bared his soul about his motive for reversing his campaign position on Vietnam: "I'm not going to let them (political simpletons) do to me over Indochina what they did to Harry Truman over China."

So there it was. This whole Vietnam adventure, in the President's own mind, was not for the security of our country. With a U.S. Naval base operating full tilt in Communist Cuba, ninety miles from Florida, a quarter idiot could see that technologically backward Vietnam was no threat to us. And anyone who knew anything about the history of Asia knew China didn't have a kerosene cat's chance in hell of taking over Indochina.

No, the sacrifice of tens of thousands of American lives and hundreds of billions of American dollars was not for American security. Those sacrifices were for a politician to avoid political slander from cheapshoters. The President could not, in the words of Kipling, "bear to hear the words [he should have spoken] twisted by knaves..." Listen to Lord Chesterton again: "Sometimes it takes less courage to die for one's country than to tell her the truth." It very definitely took less courage for LBJ to send *others* to die than for him to tell his country the truth.

The President seemed to have a primal fear of armchair war hawks. And Humphrey seemed to have some sort of weird fear of the President. By now, with so many of the "flowers" being senselessly and horribly cut down, Peter, Paul and Mary no longer sang for The President. Having lost the peace-loving vote (usually a majority) the President continued to court the hawks by deepening our military commitment to the quicksands.

The Administration called into active duty the Marine Reserves, including the Sixteenth Infantry Battalion at Indianapolis. As the U.S. representative from the area, I was asked to make a speech to the Marines on the occasion of their departure. My heart was both broken and not in it. Here's part of what I said:

> When a Marine lieutenant walked with his wife across
> the base, she noticed that each time he returned a sa-

lute, he mumbled, 'same to you.' When she asked why, the lieutenant explained that since he was once an enlisted man himself, he knew exactly what each Marine was saying under his breath. Fifteen years ago, as a young Marine member of the Sixteenth, I stood where you are standing now. And as I more or less listened to the speeches of political big shots, I was saying under my breath just about what you are saying now. So, let me begin by quoting that lieutenant, 'Same to you.'

I was the Marine who got "a date with fate" in chapter one. My high-school nickname was "Jim". Cousin Charles Browning, cousin Bill Westfall and I served as Marines in combat respectively during World War II, Vietnam and Korea.

1966 was a strange year with regard to Vietnam. The vocal public didn't like the war and didn't like the war critics, even the ones in Congress who were stating their opposition in civilized tones. I was ordered out of a cab in Indianapolis because the driver thought and said I was a "Commie Bastard." Actually I was not a Commie; I was a Democrat. And inasmuch as my mother and father were married three years before I was born, it's hard for me to see how I could have been the second thing. Oh well, at least he stopped the cab before he demanded my exit. And it was a nice day.

A news reporter in the Speaker's Lobby, an anteroom to the House Chamber, asked me one day if I were a *hawk* or a *dove*. I told him I refused to be *pigeonholed*. A few evenings later, I encountered the former chairman of The House un-American Activities Committee, which by then was also former. With what I can only describe as a smug smirk, he said, "Well here comes a dove." He thought for a moment and added in obvious reference to my military experience, "I guess you're a fighting dove." My reply: "Dick, I thought it over and decided it's better to be a fighting dove than a chicken hawk." He had done his Commie fighting in a climate-controlled Star Chamber with a pitcher of iced water and a few movie actors and college professors before him explaining why their political beliefs were not Communist.

David M. Shoup was one of what *Esquire Magazine* called *the brass lambs.* He had won the Congressional Medal of Honor in World War II at Tarawa. Eisenhower appointed him Commandant of the Marine Corps and Kennedy re-appointed him, saying Shoup was "my favorite Marine." Shoup was both a veteran of actual war and a student of history. He knew both well. So he was strongly opposed to the Johnson Administration

Vietnam policy. My much-loved and avuncular colleague from Indiana, Bill Bray was a supporter of the policy. We had a polite disagreement.

On Veterans Day 1966, in Indianapolis, I stood between Bill and a Pentagon Army general as we reviewed the traditional parade. While the tanks and ranks passed by, I asked the general if he knew Shoup. "Yes," he said, adding, "What do you suppose went wrong with him?" My answer: "You'll have to ask Congressman Bray; the same thing went wrong with me." No longer an enlisted man, I was not court-martialed.

In the summer of 1966, LBJ took a campaign swing through the Midwest. He campaigned vigorously for Democratic Congresspeople up for election, except when he got to Indianapolis. He did not mention my name once even as I sat on the platform with him. One might think my opposition to the war policy was the reason. It is fair to say that, because I had stayed with his campaign platform on Vietnam and he abandoned it, he was less than overjoyed with me. Yet, there was another, and, to him, more compelling reason.

LBJ had an inordinate proclivity to butter up newspaper publishers. He phoned them often. That included the publisher of *The Indianapolis Star* and *The Indianapolis News*, the late Eugene C. Pulliam, Dan Quayle's grandfather. Like Col. Robert Rutherford McCormick and Harry Luce, Gene Pulliam was a man of strong opinions and strong will, whose publication was his and not the public's. Even in the news columns, he let the public know his views on controversial subjects and officials, seldom bothering with the other side or sides. He didn't like my father even a little bit.

One of Mr. Pulliam's rules at *The Star* and at *The News* was that, as my dad put it, "[Dad's] name could never appear in those papers until [his] eagerly awaited obituary." Pulliam's son, who took over on his father's death, was different. Just as *The Chicago Tribune* evolved into an objective news source, the Pulliam papers in Indianapolis and Phoenix became exercises in fair journalism, under the leadership of Eugene S. Pulliam.

On that summer day in 1966, however, LBJ, President of The United States of America, was afraid so much as to mention my name in my hometown, knowing that to do so would anger the old-time publisher. It was funny. Later the same day, safely removed from Indianapolis, the President made a point of seeking me out to make amends. He said nothing about saying nothing about me to my constituents, but it was clear what he was getting at.

While the President spoke to a large outdoor crowd in downtown Indianapolis, some orderly demonstrators were arrested despite the fact that they were merely standing on church property, with permission, holding placards saying "Escalation Breeds Escalation." My dad took their case and easily won it. The Constitution worked OK in Indianapolis—at least after the arrests. On the trip back to Washington, I was re-reading William Shirer's *Berlin Diary* to see if there had been hindsight changes in the book I had just finished, Shirer's *Rise and Fall of the Third Reich.* A White House aide, who had few propensities toward warmth, noticed my book and remarked sarcastically, "You're really up to date." I glanced up at him and said, "Considering those arrests in Indianapolis today, you may be right."

I treasure a short letter I received upon entering Congress from columnist Drew Pearson. He was famous for his "predictions of things to come." In the letter he said that he was fond of my dad, even though he wasn't sure my dad was always fond of him. He went on to "predict" that I would do well in Congress. As irony would have it, he mentioned me in his last published column. The column item was about the LBJ visit in Indianapolis and the arrests. His reporter had asked me if there was any law under which citizens could be arrested simply for holding up the signs about escalation. My printed reply was, "Well if there is, I wasted my time crawling over half the mountains in Korea."

Mr. Pearson suffered a fatal heart attack about the time that last column was published. What LBJ suffered from the column was more like apoplexy. The next day a White House aide came to the Capitol to tell me that the President was wondering what I meant by my statement. I told him to brace himself, but I meant exactly what I said. To which he said, "Well, you know the Secret Service didn't have anything to do with those arrests. It was just some local cops." Looking at him evenly, I said, "What I know is that the 'local cops,' of whom I was once one, were asked by your Secret Service people to keep protestors out of the President's sight. I also know that the 'local cops'" [there was some heat in my voice at this point] "told your people such restriction would be unconstitutional. And the only reason the arrests were made was that the guys with hearing aids and dark glasses invoked that mumbo jumbo about presidential security. That's what I know. And while we're at it, just what makes you think a Secret Service Agent isn't a 'cop'?" This was not the White House aide who accosted me on the plane; this guy was pretty nice. He even smiled and quietly said that I had a point. I guess the Constitution does, too. My good and wise friend, Indianapolis lawyer Jim Beatty, sent his congressman a telegram which, referring to the Secret Service, said, "Their job is to protect his life, not his ego." Amen.

President Johnson tried to run the war on a credit card. There would be no tax increase to cover the increased spending. People might give the war more scrutiny if they knew they, and not some angel of manifest destiny, would have to pay for it. The government was pouring water into the economic soup by "printing" money to pay the military bills. And our country paid the dangerous and much higher inflation tax as well as interest on the increased government borrowing. My father said that if The Johnson Administration had been straightforward enough to raise the taxes for the war, it would have stopped two things: the inflation and *the war.*

In 1967 my dad and the Internal Revenue Service had a difference of opinion about how the tax code applied to a real estate deal of his. He had reported all the facts but did not see the law as the revenuers did. To avoid protracted litigation, he decided to throw in the towel and pay the additional tax. The amount he sent to the government was substantial, say around fifty thousand in 1998 dollars, adjusted for inflation. With the remittance he enclosed a note saying, "Regret unable to pay for more than a hangnail on a Vietcong soldier at this time."

By now our country had dropped one and one half million tons of bombs on Vietnam, seventy thousand more tons than we had dropped on Europe during all of World War II. And there was evidence that, in the manner of the British during the London blitz, the resolve of the Vietnamese was only strengthened. One diplomat said our war was making no progress because "their willingness to die for their native land exceeded our ability to kill."

As President Johnson sent more and more military personnel and equipment to Vietnam, the Vietnamese made it more and more clear that they could not be beaten in the absence of a U.S. military commitment even the most hawkish of Americans had not so much as dreamed of making. In a taped telephone conversation, the President told a friend that the carnage of "American kids" was weighing heavily upon him, but, in a masterpiece of misperception and superficial supposition, he added, "If you don't stand up to the Communists, the next thing you know they'll be in your kitchen." Yes, he was an intelligent man, but some times emotions take precedence over intellect.

President Johnson's standing with the public plummeted. The 1966 election had been a disaster for his party, and the year in which he was expected to run for re-election was fast approaching. By late 1967 the cat was out of the bag on the Gulf of Tonkin subterfuge.

"Respect," the late and irreplaceable Robert Bolt wrote, "...that's water on the desert." And the public was fast losing it with regard to LBJ. A lot of fibs had by now been told, fibs about the Gulf of Tonkin, fibs about the monetary cost of the war, and fibs about the progress of the ill-advised adventure. The jokes about the President were getting more demeaning. Gore Vidal declared that "[Lyndon Johnson] thinks of himself as an Abraham Lincoln, whereas in fact he's a sort of cornpone Genghis Khan."

In January, 1968, I was invited to the White House for dinner and, at last, a presidential pitch for a ten percent income surtax to pay for some of the war. By then the cat was meowing loudly about the money-printing scheme. The public was beginning to realize that, yes after all, this holy crusade was not a foreign policy freebee.

The meeting was in the West Room and about sixty House and Senate members were there. We were arrayed around twelve round tables. The President, being a chivalrous Texan, invited Representative Patsy Mink of Hawaii to sit at his table, despite the fact that she was strongly opposed to his Vietnam adventure. Seated on the other side of Representative Mink was General William Childs Westmoreland. He'd just blown into town on Pentagon business, said the President and nothing would do but that "Westy" give us a report on the war. We'd talk about taxes to pay for it some other time.

The setting was almost comical. There was a White House agent at each table, obviously for the purpose of monitoring congressional conversation. Then at the President's table, in addition to himself, Patsy Mink and the General was the Grigori Rasputin of the Johnson White House, Walt Rostow. Walt was one of Halberstam's *Best and the Brightest*. He was the White House wizard of war. He was—God forbid—an *expert*.

Here's what experts are like. A salesman invites himself into a home, dumps a sack of dirt on the living room carpet and announces, "Lady, if this vacuum cleaner doesn't pick up every bit of that dirt, I'll eat it." To which she responds, "Well, then you'd better get yourself a spoon, cause we got no 'lectricity." Walt had overlooked a few details himself, like how a people who had struggled for more than a century to keep foreign armies off their soil were not easy to subdue—no matter what the computers thought. Some say the Rostow computers figured the war would be won by the U.S. in 1967. "Nothing could go wrong, go wrong, go wrong..."

If he were wearing a private's uniform, you'd still know Westmoreland was a general. Tall, handsome, with well-cropped steel gray hair, he had the right look. Anybody who made a movie about a general and did not cast him in the title roll would be remiss. Westmoreland was not Rostow's intellectual superior. Not close, but Westy had full-throated confidence in the war and in himself. As Westmoreland began his report, Walt was relegated to turning the general's charts on an easel.

The general told us that when the U.S. first went to Vietnam, sixty percent of the personnel were in the rear as support troops, but by the next spring all that would change. It would be "thirty-nine percent" in the rear and the other "seventy-one percent," (No. I'm not kidding. It's exactly what he said.) "will be in combat." As audibly as my sense of humor dictated, I said to the White House man at our table, "I hope to God that guy never operates a mortar behind my position. The numbers on that little elevating wheel are pretty important."

Now the general got into the distress of the enemy. And here I believe it would help if you understand that Patsy Takemoto Mink is of Japanese descent. And she is bright times brilliant. The general declared, "The North is running out of soldiers. They're beginning to send old men, some as old as thirty-eight." As he looked around the room he noticed a lot of people who looked a lot older than thirty-eight. The general sensed his faux pas, but he did not correct it in the way one would expect. He did not say, "Oh. Right, but thirty-eight *is* old for a boxer or an infantryman." Westy had to show his arcane knowledge, his expertise about the Far East. He did so by saying, "Oh. Well, thirty-eight is old for an Asiatic." To Patsy the *correction* of the faux pas was the faux pas.

On our way down the steps to the exit level, Patsy was exclaiming, "Can you *imagine*?" To which some wag, possibly I, said, "Don't try to fool us. We saw *Lost Horizon* and what happened to that Asian lady when she came out of Shangri-la. When you hit thirty-eight, it's going to be wrinkle city, Patsy." Perhaps you have already guessed. When she did hit thirty-eight, she still looked like a schoolgirl. No wrinkles. No Oil of Olay. Ask John Mink.

General Westmoreland's upbeat report about our war effort and his downbeat report about the distress of "the other side" were followed in rapid order by the event which ultimately brought about the beginning of the end of the second Vietnamese War.

The Tet Offensive shattered the military illusions of the Johnson Administration. There was sudden consciousness in the U.S. that Ho's forces weren't just ragtag guerrillas whose ability extended no further that hit-and-run stings. There is controversy about how successful the offensive was in terms of what it cost "the other side." But the fact that there could even be an offensive was sobering.

In the barbershops and cabs of America, the mindless slogan was, "win or get out." This meant, of course that regardless of whether it was necessary, if it could be done, it should be done. And if it couldn't, so what? Rather like the joke about "Spantran", half Spanish Fly (an alleged aphrodisiac) and half tranquilizer. Take it and if the occasion arises, you can do it. If the occasion doesn't, you don't care. It seems obvious that if we could afford to "get out", we could afford to forgo "a victory". Indeed, getting out was enormously more affordable than a useless victory—by the '90s we as a nation were pals with the "Commie-bastard" government of Vietnam. The only way a Communist government in Vietnam ever could have affected American lives was as a pretext for a couple of U.S. presidents violently to snuff-out 57,000 of them.

Even at the time, "win or get out" was a strangely casual attitude considering the mounting casualties, but America was in no mood to discuss whether the policy was necessary and, least of all, whether it just might be morally wrong. Of course we were right, the thinking went. They were Commies, weren't they? What more did you need to know? You kill Commies. All cottage cheese is made in cottages.

The talk was also about saving face, the kind of logic Americans laughed about when it was annunciated by Japanese in World War II. Now some Americans were asking whether saving face was as important as saving another part of the anatomy.

On February 17, 1968, Paul Harvey's radio broadcast was magnificent. It was a symphony of truth *and* poetry in the rich rhythms of common sense. He made the compelling case *not* for "cutting and running," (The thing the chicken hawks said they wouldn't do and in fact couldn't do since they weren't there.) but for wisely acknowledging error, something a great nation could afford to do. He began with a simple statement of the inevitable:

> "Americans, we are going to get out of Vietnam…. To
> that we all agree…. The only questions we must con-
> sider today are how and when—and how many die
> first….. Some say to leave now would mean losing face,
> but how much face do we have left in Asia…? The places
> where we have meddled most we have the least
> 'face'…..Instead of waiting until we are bankrupt, let us
> revert to self-concern…on purpose, before we are drained
> of our blood and our sweat and our tears and our gold.
> Why not, instead, husband our resources—make of our-
> selves what we once were—strong and solvent—an oasis
> of arts and science and physical well-being…So honor-
> able, so admirable, so desirable….that the world will

then, again, have something better than a red star to
steer by."

Bravo.

Referring to the laughable logic of President Johnson's telephonic
reference to Communists in our "kitchen," Paul Harvey also said, "We
are told that if we don't fight them *there*, we'll have to fight them *here*.
Well they are here (Cuba) and we're not fighting them *here*."

People began to wonder if they should worry about what was best for
the American war effort or *what war effort was best for America*.

On March 31,1968, LBJ bowed out. He told the nation he would not
run for re-election. It was sad. He was the greatest civil rights President
since Lincoln and he might have been remembered that way. Instead,
through the ages he would remain the absurd architect of an Asiatic
Armageddon. That tall, proud man who had it all during those salad
summer days of '64, was no more. His kingdom, his power and his glory,
along with thirty-three thousand of his fellow Americans, had perished
somewhere in those quicksands of Asia. Five years later, he would join
those young Americans forever. A merciful God had allowed Lyndon Baines
Johnson to finish dying.

5

THE SECRET PLAN

Lyndon Baines Johnson's Vietnam blunder paved the way to the White House for Richard Milhouse Nixon who later declared Vietnam to be "our finest hour." No one else described the silliness of that assertion so well as David Halberstam who wrote, "Richard Nixon, who says Vietnam is our finest hour and is in public office today precisely because it is not..."

Somewhere along the way of his long career, Nixon had acquired from his adversaries the nickname *Tricky Dick.* His detractors were also fond of asking, "Would you buy a used car from this man?" The impressionist Rich Little even referred to Nixon as the proprietor of *Milhouse Motors.* It was therefore amusingly ironic that in his acceptance speech to the 1968 Republican Convention, using somewhat unpolished poetry, Mr. Nixon said he'd give America "the lift of a driving dream."

Nixon always envied John F. Kennedy's public prose, poise and poetry, even though quite a bit of the writing was Ted Sorenson's. Even if Ted had written for Nixon, though, it wouldn't have worked. Nixon's delivery was awkward; JFK's was nothing, if not graceful and charming.

Following a bruising, chaotic and tragic nomination campaign in the Democratic Party, Hubert Horatio Humphrey emerged as the Party's nominee to succeed LBJ as president, but he didn't.

The late and great Allard K. Lowenstein of New York led the so-called *Dump Johnson Movement* among Democrats in the 1968 presidential primaries. The issue, of course, was the war and the complaint that Johnson had done a "one-eighty" on his '64 campaign promise. Al had a hard time finding a Democrat to compete with LBJ. He tried Bobby Kennedy, but Kennedy thought it would be a futile mission and declined.

There was one senator who was game though, Eugene McCarthy of Minnesota. Tall, handsome, highly intelligent and witty, the former college professor was especially welcome to those who dreamed of another Adlai Stevenson. He was attractive to college students as well. The style for young men at the time was beards and long hair, but that appearance was not pleasing to older voters, probably including most of the Stevenson folks. So a lot of faces were shaved and a lot of hair was cut as young campaigners "came clean for Gene."

Running against the President's war policy, McCarthy did not win the initial match-up in New Hampshire, but he came too close for Lyndon Johnson's political comfort. At that point, Vice President Humphrey was sent in as Johnson's replacement and Senator Bobby Kennedy changed his mind in time to enter the Indiana primary. McCarthy had won the Wisconsin primary, but for some reason his success there brought a yawn. By contrast, his earlier close *loss* in New Hampshire had made him man of the hour. Who says close only counts in horseshoes?

In an hilarious presentation to the Fort Wayne Gridiron Club, McCarthy said:

> I lost in New Hampshire and they said I won; then I won in Wisconsin and they said I lost. Sometime in the evening Huntley and Brinkley just threw it out there. They said if I didn't get a certain percent, even if I won, I'd lose. I don't know where they got the numbers, perhaps multiples of seven from the Bible.

He had them rolling in the aisles and, since his remarks were sold on audio cassettes by a recording company, he, himself, may have been rolling in dough before the campaign was over. As a metaphor for escalation of the war, McCarthy said that barbecues at President Johnson's Texas ranch were different; "They don't start out to be barbecues; they're just branding parties that get out of hand."

McCarthy next took aim at Kennedy stalwart and one of the nicest guys who ever lived, Larry O'Brien. O'Brien had recently been Postmaster General for Lyndon Johnson, but now that Johnson was no longer running, Larry was campaigning for Johnson's nemesis, Bobby Kennedy. McCarthy told the titillated crowd, "A few months ago when Larry dedicated the new George Marshall twenty cent stamp, he said that if General Marshall (long dead) were here he'd be for the Johnson Vietnam policy. Now that Larry is backing a candidate who opposes that policy, we can only guess what General Marshall is saying to him tonight."

All in a day's work for Gene McCarthy. He got the laughs and the profound respect of thoughtful citizens who read history; Bobby Kennedy got the votes. Kennedy quite likely would have won the nomination and the presidential election of '68, but a latter-day Lee-Harvey-lunatic sneaked past security and murdered Bobby moments after his heartfelt expression of gratitude for having won the California Democratic Primary. Adolph Sabath wrote a volume called, *One With God Is A Majority.* By the second half of the Twentieth Century, it was beginning to look like, *One With Gun Is A Majority.*

Describing the pacifist demonstrations back in World War I, Gerald Johnson wrote, "The pacifists had no objection at all to fighting the police." The public demonstrations against the war at the Democratic convention in Chicago were, in some cases, rather warlike themselves. And some of the Chicago police weren't much better. Gloria Steinem criticized those officers for "breaking ranks." When asked, I told reporters, "Any public demonstration for peace which, itself, is not peaceful, is public hypocrisy." Some of the reporters themselves were physically assaulted by some Chicago policemen. This led my friend Jud Haggerty to propose name changes in the Sunday T.V. news programs. He suggested *Beat The Press* and *Mace The Nation.*

Once inside the convention walls, McCarthy and late-entrant Sen. George McGovern didn't have a chance. The pols in the back rooms had wired it for Humphrey, whose job now was to shake the Johnson-Humphrey foreign policy off the soles of his shoes. Shaking it off his other soul was foreclosed. Even at that, Humphrey came close.

I'm not sure whether the independent candidacy of George Wallace (R-Ala.)—No, the "R" stood for racist—helped Nixon or Humphrey. I've heard and read it both ways. Since Goldwater's 1964 campaign and Richard Nixon's "Southern Strategy" were effectively beckoning the racist elements of the southern Democratic Party to the Republican Party, one might assume Wallace took votes from Nixon. Whatever the case in that regard, as election day drew near, Nixon was losing ground.

In his book, *The Selling Of The White House,* Joe McGinnis claimed that the public was beginning to see through the staged "spontaneous" question and answer sessions Nixon conducted on TV. There certainly was a contrast between the rehearsed and, even so, wooden Nixon presentations and those of Humphrey who sat on the edge of a desk and fielded unrehearsed questions phoned in to a TV studio. However weak the flesh, Humphrey's spirit was engaging and endearing, but Nixon cleared the hurdle for his long-dreamed dream.

Richard Milhouse Nixon was the President-elect and here a little-noticed irony occurred. When Nixon lost to Kennedy in 1960, as Vice President it was his duty to read aloud in the U.S. House chamber the vote count of the Electoral College. When Nixon did so, he made what was probably the best speech of his career. He beautifully stated the case for good sportsmanship and the profound duty in our country of the losing candidate to accept the result as an adult.

Now it was eight years later and another vice president had lost the election for president and would be the one to announce the results in the House. It was legal for Humphrey to send a *pro tem* to do it. I couldn't imagine he would, but he did. I had sent a letter to him, urging that he personally announce the results and make an inspiring speech of the sort Nixon had given. I implored him not to let history compare his example badly with Nixon's. When I took a seat in the chamber, Humphrey was nowhere to be seen. The distinguished Senator from Georgia, Richard Russell, did the job. Life is filled with lost opportunities, but some are more difficult to understand than others.

Nixon's inaugural address was undistinguished. In fact, of the seven presidents with whom I served, only one said something in his inaugural that touched me. That was George Bush, generally not thought to be a good "talker" as Calvin Trillen put it. Bush said something to the effect that the sum of our possessions did not measure the sum of our worth.

When I was asked by reporters to give my opinion of Jimmy Carter's inaugural speech, I said, "I liked the invocation better because it hit the issues more squarely and made fewer references to scriptures." The inaugural speeches of Jefferson, Lincoln, Franklin Roosevelt and Kennedy are ones that could be set to music.

In his campaign, Richard Nixon essentially said that when he dealt with Vietnam, he would follow the example of Eisenhower in Korea. He would get us out quickly. He said to reporters:

> If this war goes on six months after I become president,
> it will be my war. I don't intend to end up like Johnson,
> holed up in the White House, unable to show my face
> on the street. I'm going to end this war fast.

"I'm going to end this war fast." Concerning the Korean War, Eisenhower used a phrase designed to be more dramatic, one that would ring through the ages. On paper it was stirring: "I will go to Korea." It did not sound quite so good one of the times Ike said it. This is how it came out that time: "I will go, a, to Korea." That was unfortunate. After all, Douglas MacArthur was Ike's rival, at least for the 1952 Republican nomination. And think how beautifully Dugout Doug intoned, "I shall return," when he left a certain set of islands in the Pacific—just ahead of the Japanese. And he did return. "With the help of God and a handful of Marines, MacArthur took the Philippines." Neil Armstrong had a dandy when he stepped onto the Moon: "That's one small step for man; one giant leap for mankind." Seems to me it would have been more poetic had he dropped the "That's".

But, so what? Ike got us out, perfect meter or not. Nixon neither got us out of the *quicksand* nor used much eloquence when he said he would.

In his campaign, Dick Nixon said he had a "secret plan" for extricating the U.S. from Vietnam, but it wouldn't do to spell it out before he carried it out. Sounded like vintage "Tricky Dick", but it wasn't. He really did have what he thought was a put-away idea. It was an idea that scarcely reflected the thinking of a foreign policy expert, but it was sincere. He believed that if he arranged some juicy U.S. trade concessions for the Soviet Union, the Soviets, in turn, would make the Vietnamese give America favorable terms for an armistice, a compromise of Ho's position.

What Nixon did not understand was that, though the thought of such a deal would probably make the Russians salivate like Pavlov's pups, the Russians could not pull off their end of it. The Vietnamese had help from the Russians, but the Russians weren't going to get that kind of help from the Vietnamese. That would be about as absurd as our getting Israel to require its citizens to attend daily mass.

In the late Fifties and during the Sixties, the John Birch Society was fond of asserting that the rest of America did not "understand the nature of Communism." Here was a place where the Birchers and Nixon – there was a big difference between the two in Nixon's favor—did not understand the "true nature of International Communism."

International Communism was mainly international along the Soviet borders, the *Satellite States*. Beyond that, things got a little thin for them. A popular play and its title song, *Love is a Many Splendored Thing,* was parodied by a *Scripps-Howard* columnist at the time: "Asian Communism Is A Many *Splintered* Thing.*"* There was no monolith, no giant computer in the Kremlin with keys that could be pressed to move distant pawns to please. Not Tito, not Mao and certainly not Ho, when it came to compromising a lifetime struggle for independence—especially after the compromises Russia and China had talked him into at the '54 Geneva Convention. President Nixon's secret plan was nestled high on a *pie-in-the-sky*.

Our objective in the Cold War should have been twofold; keep ahead of Soviet military capability and practice democracy here so that very few would have the slightest interest in the stupidity of Communism for our country.

Stupidity, that's what Communism was. In a sense it was foolishly idealistic, each would produce according to his or her ability and each would consume according to her or his need. Lots of luck. Like Walt Rostow, the Commies overlooked human nature. Prohibitionists suffered from the same oversight. So did the Boy Scout who wanted to help the old lady across the street only to learn she didn't want to go.

The boisterous American Cold Warriors, or "patrioteers," as Jud Haggerty called them, overlooked something also, their own argument. Communism, they argued, was unworkable. They were right, but it was only unconsidered rhetoric to them. They seemed like the congregation who assembled to pray for rain. The pastor asked, "Do you have faith in the Lord?!" "Yes!" from the good people. "Do you believe in his mighty omnipotence?!" "Yes, yes!," was the thunderous reply. "And do you *believe* that in his infinite love and mercy, he will give us rain?!" "We do, we do!!" they cried. "Then where," demanded the minister, "are your umbrellas?!" Had our super patriots really believed that Communism would, in the manner of other failed societies in history, collapse from within, they would not have clamored for U.S. military action to make it happen.

When Communism finally did fall of its own weight in Europe, the *patriotic-er than thou* anti-Communists were either surprised or claimed that Star Wars, a figment of government contractors' profit-making imaginations, had scared the Communism out of existence. Of course, if that were true, Communism would have fallen in China as well. It was unworkable in both Russia and China, but the Russians had a third-of-a-century head start on the Chinese in the process of proving it. With the blossoming of free enterprise in China and Vietnam, though, Communism's ideological posterity seemed headed for the Potter's Field of history in those countries as well.

When the Communists first mounted the saddles of authority in Iron Curtain countries, they kept hungry populations in line with machine guns and preposterous, yet fervent, propaganda. Except, when you stop to think about it, in a sense, so did the U.S. Prohibitionists.

Leaders do not control large populations by machine guns alone. Even slick slogans will succeed only until ignorance recedes. After that, the populations can only be *persuaded* by leaders with logic. Otherwise those populations will go their own ways. If the leaders wish to remain leaders, the leaders had better change directions themselves. "There go my people," said Napoleon, "I must lead them." Of course people like Stalin and Joseph McCarthy are less likely to be questioned by the public and more likely to continue their mischief if, in the manner of Orwell's

Big Brother, they are able to convince their respective populations that their authoritarian rule is necessary for protection against dire, lethal and *mythical* threats that lurk beyond or even within their borders.

When he found his secret plan not viable, President Nixon was confronted by the same choice that had plagued LBJ. He could suffer the politically harmless vocal chord violence of domestic chicken hawks by making a "decent interval" deal with the Vietminh (which Nixon actually did 24,000 young American deaths later) or he could put his trust in the same dice that had, in turn, rolled *snake eyes* for both the French and LBJ. The third time was no charm.

Because of his emotional make-up, Richard Nixon probably didn't have much of a choice at that. Like the Russians, Richard Nixon had a fixation on "firsts." He insisted that he would not be the first U.S. President to lose a war. And he was right. We certainly didn't win the War of 1812. We did win a battle in New Orleans *after* the war was over.

In 1960, Richard Nixon declared himself the *first* presidential candidate to take his campaign to all fifty states, a distinction of dubious merit since it made him look worn and sudoriferous during his first and pivotal television debate with the rested and cool JFK. He gloried in being the first to do this and the first to do that. He was, in 1952, the first national candidate to reveal the sources of every penny of his income. That was the *Checkers* speech in which he skipped over how he got a lot of the money he "came out of the Navy with." The profitable poker he played in the Navy might not have played very well in 1952 Peoria.

There were some things President Nixon did not want to be the first to do—resign from the presidency, for example. Certainly not lose a war. No! He would not "be the first American President to lose a war."

He knew that the path he followed was the one followed by the French and LBJ, but he rationalized that this time it would be different. The war would be over "with honor" before the end of the six months he said it would take to make it "Nixon's war". Unlike his lesser predecessors, *he* knew what he was doing. War was like football he told an astonished group of severely disabled Vietnam veterans at the White House one day. The people who managed the war before him didn't seem to understand that. (Neither did his combat veteran audience.) However, with his excellent coaching, he implied, this country was going to win the game and use B-52's to kick the hell out of the Vietminh for the extra points. Let's call this one the *football fallacy.* As is usually the case where the wish is father to the thought, this wishful thought turned out to be illegitimate.

For his secretary of state, President Nixon picked another "expert". Chutzpah was the word for Henry Alfred Kissinger, whose German accent tended to make him sound sage and mask his record of pedestrian thought and salient error in foreign policy. It was "Henry the K" who, on the eve of the Soviet collapse, charged gargantuan fees to tell well-heeled clients that it "vouldn't happen." And despite all the pages of history that dripped with evidence to the contrary, Nixon's Secretary of State stated, "I refuse ("refuse" was the operative word) to believe that a little fourth-rate power like North Vietnam [sic] doesn't have a breaking point." Half a decade before, the Swedish sage Gunnar Myrdal had said:

> The conviction that this (American Vietnam) policy will
> end in failure is commonly held in all countries outside
> the United States.

It is said that when Kissinger was teaching something or another at Harvard, the title role of the play *Dr. Strangelove* was modeled after him. Nixon's Secretary of State, then a bachelor, fancied himself a "make-out man," declaring that "power is the ultimate aphrodisiac." One assumes he meant his own "power" as a high U.S. Government official. If that is what he did mean, then by saying it he betrayed additional ignorance about political science. I would defer to Kissinger on the subject of aphrodisiacs, but I do know that "Power" with reference to a United States Government official is an obscenity in this land of the free where public servants are supposed to be servants of the public. "Here, Sir, the people rule," said Alexander Hamilton. And when Thomas Jefferson left the presidency, he said, "I go forth to accept a promotion from servant to master." Here, Sir or Ma'am, the term, *"powerful* public servant" is an obnoxious oxymoron.

I will say this much for Kissinger: he did say a funny thing at a political roast/dinner I attended shortly after President Nixon announced reversal of his isolation policy toward China. Kissinger was scheduled to fly to Peking a few days after the roast. He and Senator Frank Church of Idaho were the headliners and Church spoke first.

Referring to Kissinger's cultivated reputation as a Casanova, Church said, "Secretary Kissinger is about to embark upon an historic journey and every thoughtful American wishes him success, but it is comforting to know that just in case the venture turns out to be a bust, Dr. Kissinger will know how to handle it." Kissinger began his response by saying, "I think I have been called on to determine whether one can commit suicide after first being assassinated." I thought that was pretty good even though Church's joke was better.

Let's see now, President Johnson averred, "I'm not going to let them do to me over Vietnam what they did to Harry Truman over China," President Nixon insisted, "I'm not going to be the first American President to lose a war." And the official "make-out man" *refused* "to believe that a little fourth-rate power like North Vietnam [sic] (didn't) have a breaking point." Interesting how three different people can say exactly the same stupid thing, each in a different way.

In a national television interview at the time, soft-spoken and powerfully eloquent Congressman John Conyers of Michigan was among the first to point out that Nixon had abandoned his campaign pledge to extricate America from the Johnson Administration's blunder in Vietnam. Playing upon Nixon's favorite preface, John said:

> If President Nixon has made anything 'perfectly clear,'
> it's that he has no intention of getting us out of Vietnam
> any time soon.

So with Nixon and Vietnam, it wasn't going to be the same as with Ike and Korea after all. Nixon could have emulated Eisenhower without political harm just as he came away politically unscathed from reestablishing contact with China. He knew that despite Ike's having made two concessions to Pyongyang, concessions that Truman had refused to make, the criticism of President Eisenhower's peace policy was pretty much relegated to the marginal and somewhat disturbed John Birch Society. They called Ike a "Conscious and dedicated agent of the international Communist conspiracy." *Ike*!

Richard Nixon ignored his Republican benefactor's successful statecraft in foreign policy and, instead, emulated his Democratic predecessor's *un*successful statecraft in foreign policy. Johnson got into trouble because of his inordinate fear of loudmouth chicken hawks, but it was strange that Nixon worried about them. In 1962 when he ran for Governor of California, he, himself, joked about a flat earth group. The Birch Society was against Nixon and to allay his supporters concerns, Nixon told this metaphor to underscore the Birch Society's relatively few members: "A farmer contracted with a restaurant to supply 100,000 frogs each week. The first week, he brought in five, the second week it was one, and none thereafter. The restaurant sued him for specific performance of the contract. In court he testified, "They sounded like a hundred thousand a week.""

Still, like the moth and the irresistable flame, with his country in tow, Nixon headed for more years in the furnace of Vietnam. He was, of course, aided and abetted by his faithful indian (of Germany) companion, Doctor Kissinger. Well, maybe not so faithful. Kissinger's permanent principal was the Rockefeller family. The Secretary was even caught on tape making fun of his President to Nelson Rockefeller, who replied, "I love it."

Why couldn't Nixon and LBJ sense the basic common sense of the American people and give them reality rather than myth about foreign policy? It was, I think, because in both cases there seemed to be emotional insecurity, a fear that they would be viewed as cowards if they didn't talk tough and send others to act tough against ideological infidels in other countries. Were the kings of old moved by the same motives? They "defended the faith" by sending crusades to kill religious infidels in other countries. Such abuse of authority does not prove heroism, though. Far from that, it is the ultimate cowardice. These American presidents seemed to think that violence is the index to patriotism.

The play parodied above, *Love Is A Many Splendored Thing,* made a more sensible point. The heroine says to the hero, "You are stronger than I," the hero replying, "I've always thought of you as being stronger than I." "Then you are wrong," concludes the woman, "because you are gentle. And there is no greater strength than gentleness." It does take great strength to prevail over the bad side of one's human nature, the side George Orwell called "the little fat man within, the voice of the belly protesting against the soul." Another British subject, Rudyard Kipling, described the moments of truth badly faced by these presidents:

> Then it is, the brave one chooses, while the coward stands
> aside, doubting in his abject spirit, while his Christ is
> crucified—and the multitudes make virtue of the faith
> they had denied.

Kipling's multitudes, the American public in this case, have long since seen the virtue of not borrowing money to borrow trouble in other people's countries. Here's a good rule: We should go to war when we have to, not when we have a chance to.

The foregoing probably would lead a reader to believe that I have a personal animus for the presidents who led, nay, sent our country into Indochina. I do not. I detest what they did, but I do not detest them. They were responsible for horrific wrong, but they each accomplished great good, also. My mother seemed never to tire of quoting Edward Wallis Hoch:

> There's so much good in the worst of us and so much bad in the best of us, that it hardly becomes any of us to say very much about the rest of us.

Richard Nixon's domestic policy accomplishments have been over-shadowed by his troubles, but they are there. Under his administration, our country began to take seriously threats to the air we all breathe and the water we all drink. The EPA was begun. He advocated sensible, not ideological, welfare measures. LBJ's domestic policy achievements are towering. With all the attacks against Medicare, where would we be with-out it? The '64 Civil Rights Act was literally centuries overdue. It insured that if you are a law-abiding citizen, your money is as good as anybody else's at a public accommodation. The Act removed from the soul of our body politic a dastardly hypocrisy that should shame any decent citizen. LBJ's 1965 Voting Rights Act ended the clearly "un-American" practice of denying the Constitutional right to vote, to participate in the process of national decisions that determine how much you are required by law to "do for your country," including the possibility of laying down your life.

There is no perfect hero and, if you don't count a few people like Hitler and Al Capone, no perfect villain.

I have a special empathy for President Nixon. First, I am sorry for the agony of his childhood. Second, he was my father's friend. As fate would and did have it, my father served in the U.S. House on the same commit-tee with both Richard M. Nixon and John F. Kennedy. Nixon and my dad even traveled together for debates between them and, despite the de-bates, became fond of one another.

When my father got into a public fuss with a not respected but widely feared columnist named Westbrook Pegler, most of my father's congres-sional colleagues continued to like him, but were afraid to be seen with him in public. Not so Nixon. He went by my dad's office for an hour on each of several evenings just to cheer Dad up. I believe Nixon did the same kind of thing for Ted Kennedy after the Chappaquiddick tragedy. Nixon seemed to be like the fellow who is the picture of civility as a pedestrian and becomes a road rager when he gets behind the wheel of a car. One on one, Nixon was caring and eager to help, but when he got behind the wheel of a microphone, when it was that amorphous mass of enemies, the paranoia he suffered from childhood wrenched his being.

Shortly after Nixon became President, he went to the U.S. House to hold a reception for the Members. Representative Richard Bolling of Missouri, who had served with the new President in the House, acted as spotter, calling out the names of the representatives as they stepped up to shake hands. When I was introduced, the President asked, "Are you Andy's boy?" which I proudly acknowledged. I'm afraid we held up the line a bit. The President said, "Your father was one of the great speakers of the House." Of course, it would have been more "perfectly clear" if he had said "orators". My colleagues had a hard time figuring how my father could have been one of the Speakers of the House since he had served only one term. The conversation was pleasant and I'm not sure that some of my Republican colleagues weren't a tad envious at the time.

I was among Nixon's guests for breakfast at the White House one morning and had the good fortune to be seated by the towering historic figure Senator William Fulbright of Arkansas. In the early days of the Nixon Administration, Fulbright had kept his fingers crossed and also kept his silence in the hope that Nixon would be wise enough to follow Ike's footsteps and extricate our country from an already clearly foolish military involvement in Asia. By the time this White House breakfast meeting took place, however, Fulbright's hope was fading.

The President was table-hopping that morning and when he got to us, he did what he always did face to face with people of contrary views. He spoke of something else when he greeted his former Senate colleague. "How's your golf game, Bill?" In his rich baritone and delightful Arkansas drawl, the Senator said, "It's coming along, Mr. President." The President continued, "You play a slow game." That tripped the Fulbright wit. The Senator made a metaphoric reference to his recent and uncharacteristic silence on Vietnam. And everyone present, the President included, understood it. Fulbright looked up at Nixon and twinkled—tweaked too—"I could speed up, Mr. President." I was embarrassed for the President. He couldn't handle it. Reddening, he walked awkwardly to the next table.

During 1969, U.S. opposition to U.S. involvement in Vietnam was growing rapidly among the public. Therefore, it was doing the same among members of Congress, including some members of the President's party. As criticism mounted, the President invoked the "bipartisan tradition in American foreign policy." The cliché went, "Politics ends at the water's edge." I was curious and did some research. And sure enough, I found a juicy quotation from a member of Congress during the Truman Administration: "It is a (foreign) policy that did not deserve respect (in the beginning) and it does not deserve respect now." Need I tell you that it was then-Congressman Richard M. Nixon who said that?

I placed the inconsistent quotation in the Congressional Record and it was widely reported in the news media two days later. If it slowed the President's insistence about the "tradition", I did not notice. The President just kept on trumpeting the tradition and the newspaper reporters, having forgotten *yesterday's newspaper*, went right on printing the President's repeated assertions. The Congressional Record is no match for the "Bully pulpit".

Public demonstrations against the war continued, some noble and inspiring, some the opposite. The latter were most welcome to the Administration; they turned the public's attention away from the outrageous waste of sons and money in Vietnam. The uncivilized behavior of those mindless demonstrations was outrageous, too, and played right into the Administration's hands.

One of the *decent* demonstrations occurred in October, 1969. A variety of citizens, prominently including many mainstream religious leaders, filed quietly past the White House one evening, each with a lighted candle in hand. The demonstration was called, "The Vietnam Moratorium".

Some of my colleagues and I organized an all-night House debate on the war policy for the night before the candle procession. In a speech on the House Floor the day before the debate, Rep. Wayne Hays of Ohio, who had entered Congress as a freshman with my dad, labeled us "self-appointed emissaries of Hanoi." One of our number, Rep. Abner Mikva of Illinois, told Hays on the Record, "I happen to be one of the people who expect to take part in the special orders tomorrow. Is the gentleman suggesting that I am an emissary of Hanoi?" "No," said Hays, "just an unwitting tool..." Mikva was generally recognized as having one of the best intellects ever in The Congress. Hays was generally recognized as...well, read on.

I ran into Mr. Hays later in the day and mentioned his slander. His reply was, "Jacobs, your old man was always getting into stupid controversies...." I'm afraid I interrupted long enough to say, "You'd better damn well leave my father out of this, Hays." I believe he did from then on. I must have made myself "perfectly clear."

In his speech, Hays had said that he had been planning to go to Europe that evening to attend a meeting of the North Atlantic Treaty Organization, but that he might just cancel the trip in order to be in the House Chamber and break up this disloyal session. My friend and co-worker, Louie Mahern, predicted that Hays would "opt for the junket." Lo and behold, Hays decided on Brussels, at taxpayers' expense.

Hays called the all-night debate disloyalty. *The Washington Post* called it something else:

> Rep. Andrew Jacobs, Jr. (D-Ind.), an organizer of the debate, set the tone as leadoff speaker, saying the purpose was 'not to stir up hatred for the President; we have too much hatred in this country,' but to discus Vietnam....

> Despite the Republican reluctance to let it happen, they soon became involved in a lively back-and-forth discussion that was polite and intelligent and provided the most illuminating debate the House has had on the war...

Because of the national notoriety which accrued to me in consequence of the all-night debate, mail gushed into our office during the following few days. Most of it was supportive, some not. One in the latter category came from the state of Virginia:

> Honorable Andrew Jacobs, Jr., Washington, D.C.
> Sir:

> I use the term 'Honorable' in addressing you merely as as a courtesy to your office because I think you are a disgrace to our country particularly in view of the fact that you are an ex-Marine and I am certain the Marine Corps is happy you are no longer a part of their fine organization.

> Any representative who participated in the disgraceful Vietnam moratorium which I believe you are credited with proposing (not so) should be turned out in the next election.

> Sincerely,

The letter was signed "Oscar F. Baxter..." not "Junior," not "II," nor "III," but *"IV."*

My reply:

> Sir:
>
> I use the term, "IV" in addressing you merely to point out that you may be in violation of one of your own Virginia state statutes. Perhaps you recall the case of Buck v. Bell (274 U.S. 200) in which the Supreme Court, in passing on the constitutionality of a Virginia sterilization statute, held in the opinion of Mr. Justice Homes that 'three generations of imbeciles are enough.'

I sent a copy of the exchange to Senator Steve Young of Ohio. Sen. Young was the master of Congressional replies to abusive mail. His classic was:

> Dear Sir:
>
> I thought you would want to know that some nut has been sending letters to this office and signing your name.
>
> Sincerely,

I asked Senator Young to "grade" my letter and he did. He rated it a "humdinger." I'm sure that was not a failing grade.

The news media reported my correspondence with Oscar *The Fourth,* whereupon a lady sent a message informing me that the public paid me to do "something besides looking up obscure law cases." To allay her concern I wrote back:

> Dear Mrs._____:
>
> Rest assured I did not spend so much as a split second looking up that case; it was a matter of common knowledge among the students at my law school. In fact, when one of the professors facetiously undertook to announce the birth of his first child in legal terms on the bulletin board, someone came along and scribbled at the bottom of the announcement, 'See Buck v. Bell.' Now that

I think of it, it may have been the only useful thing I
ever learned in law school.

Sincerely,

Up to the time of the all-night debate, the level of House discussion
about the war—on the few occasions when discussion was not blocked
by the Democratic and Republican leadership—boiled up to something
on the order of, "Yer' a Commie" and "LBJ, how many did ya' kill today?"

John B. Anderson, an Illinois Republican and one of my most admired friends, was my polite counterpart in the debate, although many
other representatives, including Gerald R. Ford of Michigan, joined in.

On the night of the debate, a Gallup poll reported fifty-eight percent
of the public opposed to our involvement in Vietnam and thirty-six percent in favor.

Another representative from Illinois, Roman Pucinski, asked me to
yield the floor, which I did. I controlled the time for an hour and was not
required by House rules to yield any of it to anyone, but I carried out my
plan to yield to anyone who asked, even if I were in the middle of a
sentence. Rep. Pucinski said, "....What assurances do we have that this
(debate) will not cause hoodlums in this country to churn up young people
and cause more violence?" I responded: "I might say to my colleague
from Illinois that I know of no member in this (debate) who would utter
the kind of hateful words that inspire violence...."

John Anderson asked me to yield and I was more than happy to do
so. He reminded the House of President Nixon's Vietnamization plan
which I must say on the surface sounded promising, but, in essence, was
pretty much where Lyndon Johnson started, "We are not going to send
American boys to do what Asian boys ought to be doing for themselves."
Nevertheless, John Anderson was sincere in his belief that with additional American equipment, our clients in the south of Vietnam could
prevail, a "triumph of hope over experience."

Of course, events discredited the Administration's plan. The final
negotiated agreement for U.S. withdrawal was announced by the Nixon
Administration in January, 1973, with the assurance that our confeder-
ates in Vietnam would prevail militarily by themselves, but the
announcement was made with tongue-in-cheek. The Administration knew
perfectly well—even though it did not make it "perfectly clear"—that
our indigenous clients in Vietnam were not about to do what we had been
unable to do ourselves. The term used in the deeper recesses of the
White House was, "a decent interval" between American withdrawal from

Vietnam and the collapse of the "government" we had set up there. Our clients would lose a war, not Nixon.

In order to secure release of American prisoners in the north, the Nixon Administration quietly dropped its demand that the forces from the north be withdrawn from the south and the Hanoi authorities dropped their demand for dismantling our puppet government in the south. Hanoi knew "our side" would collapse in short order anyway and had no real problem with allowing the Nixon Administration the fig leaf of a "decent interval". After the squandering of 57,000 American lives, hundreds of thousands of American arms, legs and livers and tens of billions of American dollars, the Government of Vietnam ended up being just what President Eisenhower said it would have been if the elections scheduled for 1956 had not been sabotaged by the great John Foster Dulles.

As the all-night debate continued, my friend, Sam Steiger of Arizona, one of the more interesting members of Congress, asked me, "A cease fire. Is that what the gentleman is after? An immediate cease fire?" To which I responded, "A cease fire so far as attacking with 'search and destroy missions' is concerned; yes." Sam inquired further, "With no quid pro quo?" And I answered, "I do not know what the gentleman means by 'quid pro quo', but if I were the father of an eighteen-year-old kid who would not have to march up *Hamburger Hill* and be shot dead, that would be quid pro quo enough for me...."

Clark MacGregor, the tall, handsome member from Minnesota, presently made a point of order that a quorum was not present and the roll was called. Those were the days before electronic voting in the House. The roll call took about forty minutes, during which the Speaker of the House, legendary John McCormack approached me outside the chamber. He was laudatory about the progress of the debate and suggested that I finish up by reminding people that, despite differences among us, we are one nation and no other nation should be unclear about that. The Speaker was saying that when the House had a debate of this sort, the world would watch. I thanked him and followed his advice.

When the roll call ended and a quorum of two hundred thirty-seven members was declared present, Speaker McCormack announced that "the gentleman from Indiana is recognized for the nine remaining minutes of his time." Three more members asked me to yield and I did. After that I finished the hour with this:

> Let me close. I probably have about two minutes remaining and I just want to say this: First of all, to the foreign governments that no doubt will be reading of

this debate, we are a nation (where) politics does end at the water's edge in abiding our lawful decisions, but in discussing the making of those decisions, we do a lot of fussing and that is why we can claim to be a free people. When the decision is made we abide by (it), but we have every right to continue to (try to) change it. For the future, dear friends, let us remember what has happened too often in the past. A politician makes a brave speech, and a lad lies dead. How easy it is to be heroic on the House floor, but that means 'being a hero on somebody else's time.' When the call for war is made by a member of Congress in the future, let that member decide if he would be willing to give his own life in such a war. And the next time we have a chance to go to war, let us decide if the giving of American lives would not be better reserved for the defense of our country than for the defense of some dictatorship far removed from the security of this land we love.

Let us bear in mind that there are two concepts of 'saving face.' In a hospital in Houston there are scores of American soldiers. One of them is from my district and I spoke to his wife this very afternoon. *His* face was burned (in Vietnam). Sixty-five percent of his body was burned. I want to leave you with this thought. Which kind of face, really after all, if we really, really believe in priorities—which kind of face really most needs saving? The face of a mistaken policy or the face of that American boy who either will or will not come under rocket attack a year hence. Consider the difference between diplomats…and soldiers. At noon, (diplomats) go to lunch; (soldiers) go to eternity.

A year later, in what had long since become, by his own definition, *Nixon's* war, American sons were still under rocket attacks in Vietnam and continued to be for two years beyond that.

On the candlelit night that followed the all-night debate, President Nixon went to the Lincoln Memorial to seek conversation with college students who were there to join the peace demonstration. They were surprised, of course, to see a real, live President standing there beneath Abe's steady gaze. The President's attempt at conversation with the young citizens was difficult, even awkward. When he asked which school they attended and was told, he began discussing its football team. That wasn't exactly what they went to Washington to talk about.

President Nixon loved football, and I shocked a few people by referring to that love at a dinner I addressed one night near Baltimore. Perhaps it was a little rough on this President who had been so kind to my dad. I said, "We have a President who thinks war is like football; and he loves football." It was hyperbole, but it made a point.

On October 19, 1969, *Parade Magazine* said this:

> ...The electorate believed Nixon and voted the Democrats out of the White House, because they felt the lives of their sons were at stake. If Nixon fails to end the war as he promised, he and his team will also suffer politically, for what's at risk here is human life, which to most Americans is still more important than money—or the survival of the Thieu-Key (the two generals running our client government at the time) government in South Vietnam [sic].

In essence, Richard Nixon and Henry Kissinger had prolonged for their entire first term the martial agony their predecessors had set in motion. It had been "four more years"—the Nixon re-election campaign slogan—of senseless human slaughter and wanton property destruction.

After the peaceful procession for peace in October, 1969, something called the *New Mobilization* demonstration descended on Washington and destroyed most of the public goodwill built up by the Moratorium. Though billed as a peace demonstration, the *New Mobe* was anything but. Its march was in the street, some of its participants carried Viet Cong flags and much of its behavior was truculent. Middle America was turned off and its attention was turned away from the stupidity of the war itself.

Some radicals crashed a meeting Sen. George McGovern had planned with the civilized element or peaceful part of the peace movement. One of the firebrands leaped up and shouted that the U.S. had gone to Vietnam to steal oil. McGovern politely replied, "I think you overlook the stupidity factor." The wild man denounced the senator as a weakling. McGovern was a World War II combat veteran. His accuser was a frail wimp of the left.

New Mobe provided cover for the Nixon Administration to intensify the fighting.

Despite the fact that the United States had dropped 70,000 more tons of bombs on Vietnam than it had dropped on Europe during all of World War II, the chicken hawks claimed the U.S. had not made a sufficient war effort in Vietnam. Of course they, themselves, had made none at all.

Kissinger, the principal architect of the notorious and indiscriminate Christmas bombing of both civilian and military targets at Hanoi and Haiphong, showed a kinder and gentler disposition toward the Watergate felons. He said, "Ve should be compassionate." After all, none of the Watergate offenders had committed the heinous crime of wanting foreign armies off their native soil.

Not only did the November demonstration embolden the Nixon Administration to broaden the war, it led to a new concept of White House propaganda, *The Great Silent Majority.* Sure, the White House said, "there are a lot of noisy people demonstrating against the war, but the good people, the folks who get up each morning, go to work and obey the laws, these citizens are with us and they are the majority." For a while the savage demonstrators did savage the poll numbers which favored a halt to our Vietnam involvement. Fortunately the setback for good sense was short-lived. In fairly rapid order, the public consensus against the policy formed again.

As the effects of the non-peaceful peace demonstrations began to fade, White House aides dreamed up a ploy to undergird their mythical Great Silent Group. The White House announced receipt of countless letters and telegrams in support of the war policy, but some news people did count and something happened that the Administration had *not* counted on.

The reporters discovered that most of the messages were fakes, letters and telegrams the *White House* had sent to itself. There is an old song that goes, "I'm going to sit right down and write myself a letter, and make believe it came from you." A parody come to mind: "I'm going to sit right down and write myself a letter, and make believe it came from the Great Silent Majority."

The Mylai massacre was not make-believe. One Lt. William Calley led his men into the village and, with U.S. weapons intended for use against an opposing army, they methodically committed the ghastly murder of every civilian man, woman, child and baby who had the terrifying fate to be there.

For reasons too bizarre for ordinary psychologists to figure out, Calley became something of a hero to the chicken hawks. How dare the army prosecute this poor boy. Shooting a six-month-old baby through the head with a military rifle doesn't make anybody bad. Lt. Calley was just doing what he was trained to do. President Nixon accidentally called him "Captain Calley." This made me wonder if, instead of prosecuting the monster, the Administration, forgetting Nixon's 1962 "hundred thousand frogs" story about the John Birch Society, had decided to promote him out of fear of the Far Right.

Governor James Earl Carter even declared a special day in Georgia to appease Calley's chicken hawk supporters there.

One newspaper ran a front-page editorial cartoon showing Calley being crucified, cross and all, leading my father to write to the cartoonist, "I knew Jesus said, 'Suffer little children to come unto me;' I just hadn't heard that when they got there he shot them." An Army Judge Advocate officer put the matter nicely in perspective by saying, "The difference between what those men were trained to do and what they did is the difference between a disciplined military unit and an armed mob."

During a Lieutenant Calley canonization session in the U.S. House, the very honorable John Sieberling of Ohio, tall to begin with, stood even taller when he took the floor to declare they could count him out in their effort to commend a man who had shot a little baby through the head.

I met Jesse Jackson for the first time while the Calley flap was raging. In discussing the matter, Jackson charitably and somewhat rhetorically said, "You don't know what you might do in the same situation." To which I responded, "I beg your pardon, Rev. Jackson. I do know. I was in the same situation more than once."

In the late spring of 1969, fifteen or twenty quiet Quakers assembled on the East steps of the U.S. Capitol and by turns read the names of the young Americans killed in Vietnam during just one week. The number was about four hundred. The purpose of the Quakers was to remind members of Congress that the dead were not just statistical numbers, but American kids who meant much to our country and *everything* to some of our fellow countrymen and women. The response from our fearless congressional leaders was an order for the Capitol police to arrest the Quakers and cart them off to the D.C. jail.

The Quakers posted bonds and were right back on the Capitol steps the next day, this time accompanied by three members of Congress— Abner Mikva, Ben Rosenthal of New York and me. Also standing with us was Methodist bishop James Armstrong. The four of us joined in the reading of the list. We were there to bear witness that the Quakers were violating no law and neither were we. Arrest them; arrest us.

During their World War II occupation of Norway, the Nazis ordered all Norwegian Jews to wear Stars of David on their sleeves. The very next day, Norwegian King Haakon, a Christian, appeared in public with a Star of David on his sleeve. In the case of the Quakers at the U.S. Capitol in 1969, two Jews and two Christians appeared in public to show support, not only for the Quakers, but for the Constitution as well. The police refused to arrest us, but they carted the Quakers away once more for doing the same thing we had done. The Quakers were charged with "unlawful assembly." Judge Harold Green threw the cases out, declaring, "The people's Capitol cannot be declared off limits to the people." Just so.

On June 25,1969, I was pleased to read this editorial in the San Francisco Chronicle:

> Every Wednesday for the past five weeks groups of Quakers have peaceably gathered on the steps of the Capitol in Washington to read aloud the names of servicemen killed in the Vietnam war in protest of its continuance.
>
> Each day they have appeared, the participants in the read-ins have been arrested by Capitol police, photographed, thumbprinted, charged with unlawful assembly (Speaker McCormack had denied them permits to assemble) and prosecuted in court. A few have been sentenced to jail.
>
> Last Wednesday, as the Quakers stood on the steps outside, and were again reading the death toll, Representative Andrew Jacobs, Jr. of Indianapolis stood on the floor of the House to deliver the following remarks:
>
> Mr. Speaker, 'Sticks and stones can break my bones, but words can never hurt me.'
>
> Churchill said: 'You see these dictators on their pedestals surrounded by the bayonets of their soldiers and the truncheons of their police. Yet in their hearts there is unspoken, unspeakable fear.
>
> 'They're afraid of words and thoughts; words spoken abroad, thoughts stirring at home, all the more powerful because forbidden. These terrify them. A little mouse, a

little, tiny mouse of thought appears in a room and even the mightiest potentates are thrown into panic.'

Does that sound like America?

Then why, in the land of the free must one be brave simply to stand on the steps of his Capitol and quietly remind us to remember that once there were thirty-five thousand living, breathing, laughing kids who are no more because of a war to protect freedom in Vietnam where there is no freedom to protect?

What kind of logic tells us a transparent gallery shield against the sneak attack of some maniac inside this Chamber is unnecessary separation between people and government, while a rule against the words of an unobstructing few outside this building is indispensable to security.

Mr. Speaker, it is the function of congressional security to protect lives, not consciences. Yet, from the steps of their Capitol, without blocking anyone's way, Quakers go to jail for making public the identities of our war dead, after the John Birch Society receives a prize from the American Legion for doing the same thing in Indianapolis.

Mr. Speaker, the document reads, "No law…abridging the freedom of speech…peaceably to assemble, and to petition the government…" It does not read, "Unless the speaker and Vice President think otherwise."

Mr. Speaker, a quarter of a century ago Pastor Niemoller said of Nazi Germany:

'…They came for the Jews. And I was not a Jew, so I did not object.

'Then they came for the Catholics. And I was not a Catholic, so I did not object.

'Then they came for the trade unionist. And I was not a trade unionist, so I did not object.

'Then they came for me. And there was no one left to object.'

Now it is the United States of America, 1969, and against the wishes of our founding fathers and nearly every other American, first they come for the Quakers. And I am not a Quaker, but I do object.

On the day following Congressman Jacobs' speech, a General Sessions judge in the District of Columbia ruled that reading aloud the names of war dead on the steps of the Capitol in a peaceable and nondisruptive assembly is nothing the government can forbid...

There was one amusing aspect to the incident involving the Quakers on the Capitol steps. The day I stood with them, a crowd gathered in front of us. Among them was my co-worker Louie Mahern, who joined me to walk back to the Longworth House Office building where we worked. It was about noon when Louie told me that the woman walking just ahead of us was in the crowd at the steps and had just said that if she had a bee bee gun, she would shoot me. I caught up with her and asked, "Why would you want to shoot me?" In a reverse echo from some future Tiananmen Square and scarcely a year before the fatal gunfire at Kent State, she angrily declared, "Something has to stop these demonstrations." "Well," said I, "that might do it, but if you think about it; the Quakers were expressing their wish that people not be shot and you were expressing your wish that a person be shot. And they're on their way to jail while you're on your way to lunch. Doesn't that strike you as somewhat paradoxical?"

A few weeks later the same woman and her little girl walked by our congressional office and saw me and my Great Dane, C-Five, who tended to be a dog and pony show in and of himself. The girl ran in to attend that show, the mother somewhat sheepishly following. I made a pronounced ducking gesture and, I'm happy to say, we both laughed. She and her husband became friends of mine. Emotions about the war ran high in those days. She probably had violated the letter of the federal assault law, but not the spirit of it. It was not she, but her anger, that had spoken. And I remembered my dad's sage advice: " Do not hold against anyone what she or he says in anger during a twenty-four hour period. If it's repeated after that, it is another matter."

A year after the Quaker incident, a group of U.S. combat-disabled amputees from the Vietnam War went to the Capitol to petition for U.S. withdrawal. When they tried to speak to some of the most hawkish members of Congress, the ones who made brave speeches about supporting "our boys" in Vietnam, the congressmen brushed by them and gave looks of scorn. I saw it.

The veterans had not eaten for quite a while and I offered to go to the Ray's lunch counter in the House cloakroom and buy sandwiches for them. Somehow news of my mission preceded me to Ray's emporium. Ray was all for selling me the sandwiches, but a few members were hostile in their insistence that, even though I was there first, they, as members of Congress, should be served before the riffraff outside. Members who had not made the vicariously brave speeches about supporting "our boys," were more than sympathetic and even offered to help pay the tab. I declined their offer, but the offer itself was a tonic of fellowship.

The scene of the chicken hawk members' showing scornful condescension to the young Americans they had condemned to being maimed and whom they celebrated in the abstract, brought to mind a Bill Mauldin cartoon. It showed three expensively attired women startled at the appearance of an unkempt, scraggly, raggedy and unshaved Revolutionary War soldier with out-stretched arms. One of the women had fainted into the woman standing behind her. The caption read:

> The battle-scarred ghost of Ezra Mulligan (Thompson's
> Pennsylvania Rifle Battalion) pays a visit to his great-
> great-great-great granddaughter's D.A.R. meeting.

My father's good friend, Indianapolis Attorney Tom Scanlon, sent me a copy of a letter he had written to another U.S. Representative. The sentence that stands out in my mind was, "Don't ask me to support our boys to graves in Vietnam."

The same William Fulbright who had handed President Nixon the golf satire during the White House breakfast launched another laugh in the President's direction. When the first manned mission to the moon went down—up?—President Nixon became effusive, too effusive. He said it was "the greatest event since the dawn of creation." The poetry was getting better, but it was misplaced. It offended Nixon's old friend and supporter, Billy Graham, who held that the birth of Christ was the greatest event since the dawn of creation, and said so—publicly.

Not long after the *dawn of creation* flap, President Nixon was in Vietnam and declared our dictator of the moment, General Key, I believe, to be "the greatest statesman in the world." Modern communication being what it is, only an hour or so later in a hallway of the U.S. Senate, reporters asked Sen. William Fulbright's opinion of the encomium. It went like this, "Senator, President Nixon has declared General Key to be the greatest statesman in the world..." Sen. Fulbright quietly interrupted, "Since the dawn of creation?"

Gotta be careful. For example, then Vice President Nixon played a decisive role in settling a steel strike just before he launched his 1960 presidential campaign. Some of his campaign managers were enthusiastic about labeling him, *Man of Steel*. Think of it. Superman! Stalin, too. Oops. Then there was President Bush's slight faux pas. After the collapse of the Soviet Union, the President said he was planning a *New World Order.* One more "oops". Someone should have checked the Bible. The Religious Wrong was not pleased. Jimmy Carter managed to *piss* off the Mexicans by joking about Montezuma's revenge during a state visit south of the border. I pulled an unfortunate boner, too.

Whatever else it is or isn't or ought to be or ought not to be, Congress is long hours. For two days in a row I had slept not much and on the third night I was worn out to the point of languidness. That night I was able to go to bed by ten. By one minute after ten I was deliciously in the land of Morpheus. By six A.M. the world would be looking much better. Thank the Lord.

Except that at about three A.M. the phone rang. It was a stateside non-combat Army sergeant, drunk and quite definitely disorderly. What did he want? Your guess is as good as mine.

The next day, having not been able to get back to sleep until five A.M., I was taken on a tour of the Indianapolis Western Electric plant. The company made telephones and I joked with one of the production workers by asking if she could make a phone that would block three A.M. calls from drunken soldiers. Ha, ha. Well, not so funny. Her husband, being a sober Army combat infantryman in Vietnam, had been killed three days before. I apologized and explained the thing I could no longer call a joke. She was understanding and nice about it, but I know I inflicted a hurt which I sorely regret to this day.

On May 27, 1971, it was my privilege to testify before the Senate Foreign Relations Committee in opposition to the Administration's Vietnam policy. J. William Fulbright was in the chair with the gavel. By chance, my near-brother friend from California, Representative Paul (Pete) N.

McCloskey, winner of the *Navy Cross* in Korean combat, was scheduled to follow me.

I accept the *Washington Post's* judgement about how best to summarize my prepared statement. In the paper's regular editorial page column, *For the Record,* the following appeared under the title, *An Ex-Marine Suggests A Peace to End All Wars*:

> From a statement before the Senate Foreign Relations Committee yesterday by Rep. Andrew Jacobs, Jr. (D-Ind.), who served as a PFC in the First Marine Division in Korea.

> One hears it said that a continuation of intervention will mean a generation of peace—it will teach the Communists a lesson. Yet in the very midst of our mammoth effort in Southeast Asia, did the Russians even so much as hesitate to invade Czechoslovakia?

> Who would ever believe that the underdeveloped tip of the Asian tail could wag the World?

> A generation of peace? A war to end all wars?

> I was 13 when World War II ended all wars. And I knew that sort of thing was only for my father's generation. I would be spared. And so at 18 I was sent into hell with a M-1 rifle to bring back a generation of peace.

> My little sister's boyfriends would be spared—long enough to serve in another crusade, this time with M-16 rifles and another promise of peace.

> And next month my little sister's little boy will be 16. A generation of peace? A war to end all wars? How about a peace to end all wars?

> Mr. Chairman, if our country ever goes to war again it should be because we have to, not just because we have a chance to.

And we don't need to borrow money to borrow the trouble of a war to protect freedom where there is no freedom to protect.

The only way to avoid future Vietnams is to recognize our error in becoming involved in this one.

And that recognition—that realization will not result from declarations that Vietnam has been "our finest hour."

Generally, the U.S. House was more supportive of the Vietnam misadventure than the Senate, but because of the Senate's much earlier willingness to have its proceedings televised, the "People's House" tended to drop from the people's consciousness—also from the consciousness of sonorous-voiced T.V. news paragons.

In the early '70s the U.S. Senate passed a resolution which in essence said that our country should end its deadly foolishness in Vietnam. Shortly afterward, President Nixon was the guest of an annual television program called *Conversation with The President,* an event subsequently and sadly abandoned by the networks. The anchors of the major networks joined together for a sit-down question and answer session with the President. One of the anchormen asked Nixon what he would do "now that *Congress* has passed a resolution calling for an end to U.S. involvement in Vietnam." (emphasis added) Obviously the sage anchorman had forgotten his high school civics, which is to say the Senate did not comprise the whole of Congress. Nixon nailed him. "Well, Mr. (let's be kind) ..., the founders, in their wisdom, provided two Houses of Congress. And I'm sure that when the resolution reaches the House there will be a responsible disposition." Meaning the House would help the President persist. It did.

Because of the unfortunate events collectively called Watergate, President Nixon would not be remembered for his prolongation of the Vietnam War and the consequent additional deaths of 24,000 young Americans. Instead, he would be remembered for an attempt, a failed attempt, to subvert the foundations of our freedom for a capsized cover-up a bungled burglary—that didn't kill anyone.

6
MORE WAR IN STORE

The "Decent Interval" between U.S. military withdrawal and the Vietminh victory throughout Vietnam was about twenty-four months. The popular slogan in the U.S. at the time was in the nature of "Remember Pearl Harbor." "No More Vietnams," however, meant different things to different people. To some it meant that the policy cost more than it was worth, which implied that it was worth *something*. To a few students of history it meant what it should have meant: "don't meddle in other countries' internal affairs, especially when the rest of the world, friends and foes alike, knows you are on the morally wrong side of history." To still others it meant, "Go ahead and meddle, but meddle enough to *win* and win without paying for it with taxes."

Whatever the respective sizes of the various groups, one phenomenon was demonstrative. Sales of toy firearms were off substantially for about half a decade. Such sales would not pick up again until the Reagan years when his nostalgia for World War II—during which he made government training films in California—would lead the nation once again to glorify war, but it didn't take five years for unconstitutional presidential foreign warfare to resume.

As we shall see, forty-two marines were sacrificed to the god of war on the altar of politics by the Ford Administration. The Carter Administration, or a part of it which included Mr. Carter himself, callously condemned innocent Americans to death in an asinine effort to steal a march on the presidential election of 1980. The public seemed to learn little from these two improprieties which were perpetrated to promote the two presidents respectively involved.

The two assaults on common sense and human life went by almost as quickly for the American public as for the brave and hapless military victims of the presidential politics that sent them to their graves.

The lessons of Vietnam faded. Fifteen years after U.S. withdrawal from that enormously costly misadventure, a high federal official was asked if he thought sending expeditionary forces there had been in our best interests. Well, yes, he said because "the Domino Theory proved out to be true."

I do not believe that official even knew what the Domino Theory was. The theory was that if U.S. policy in Vietnam didn't have its way, China, "Red China", that is, would take over all of Southeast Asia. Of course U.S. policy did not have its way; and China did not take over Southeast Asia. In fact, following the defeat of the U.S. clients in Saigon, Communist China fought two border wars with Communist Vietnam—and lost both of them. My father was right, "There are too many people making history who never read history." One aspect of history isn't history at all. That aspect is human nature. It remains essentially the same, modified for the better usually only by the limited supply of good child-rearing that can thicken what my dad called the "thin veneer of civilization."

History, then, is the warning label for life. If an activity was poison in the past, it very likely will be poison in the present. If we don't read the warning label of history, we are more likely to swallow the poison of some politician's superficial sales pitch for unnecessary war. To use the Oklahoma expression favored by Sen. Mike Monroney, "When you want to find out what a cowboy will do if he gets drunk, you find out what he did the last time he got drunk."

When I introduced a bill requiring presidents to submit cost/benefit statements before getting us into wars, a critic called the proposal "silly". Really?

It was possible for Representative Gerald R. Ford to become President Gerald R. Ford because of the Twenty-fifth Amendment to the Constitution of the United States, and because of the dishonesty of Spiro T. Agnew. President Nixon used the amendment after Agnew resigned in disgrace and Nixon was under fire for Watergate, to place Ford in line to become president. He did so because of his well-founded belief that Ford would remain loyal to Nixon no matter what.

Ford was our first president never to have been elected president *or* vice president by the people. Section 2 of the Twenty-fifth Amendment provides:

> Whenever there is a vacancy in the office of the Vice President, the President shall nominate a Vice President who shall take office upon confirmation by a majority vote of both Houses of Congress.

A vacancy did occur when Agnew's corruption in public office was uncovered and he resigned. His crookedness, among other things, was ironic. During the 1972 presidential election campaign, former Attorney General Ramsey Clark and a movie actor named Charlton Heston jointly appeared on television respectively to represent the candidacies of George McGovern and Richard Nixon. I believe that an objective observer, which I was not, would say that the actor's demeanor was smug and condescending.

McGovern had picked Sen. Thomas Eagleton to be his running mate only to discover later that Eagleton had failed to mention a clinical treatment for emotional problems in his past. This of course was an embarrassment to McGovern who, after first indicating he would keep Eagleton, decided the Senator must be replaced. Arnold Swartzenegger's future father-in-law, R. Sargent Shriver, was tapped.

During the TV discussion, actor Heston languidly rolled his open hand outward and sanctimoniously declared that at least President Nixon was competent enough to choose a good vice president (i.e. Spiro Agnew). In retrospect, you might wonder if the actor was competent enough to judge competence. A quarter of a century later, the same actor, Heston, opined that the solution to gun violence was more guns. By then, as head of the National Rifle Association, an organization that spent a lot of time promoting handguns, he represented the people who made money selling them.

President Nixon had good reason to believe that his second choice for vice president might well become his successor as president. Obviously, it would be handy to have a very good friend in that spot in case serious legal problems arose for Nixon.

Ford fit the bill nicely; he was a Nixon loyalist bar none. Moreover, he was warmly liked by most members of the Congress where the question of his confirmation would be decided. When Nixon nominated him, Ford was confirmed handily. As everybody knows, Ford did replace Nixon. Before the vote in Congress, Ford was asked at a Senate hearing if, under some circumstance, he would be in a position to issue a criminal pardon for the one who had nominated him. Ford's reply was that "the public would never stand for it." Ford was likely right; his pardon of Nixon was probably the main reason the people wouldn't stand for his election to the White House in 1976.

Even though Ford was by then the incumbent president, as a candidate for the 1976 GOP presidential nomination, he faced a serious obstacle. That obstacle was the candidacy of the sturdy former Governor and former actor, Ronald Wilson Reagan. Here was where American presidential history happened again.

Reagan was the darling of the heavy-duty Republican Right. Ford, well he had done some suspiciously un-doctrinaire stuff like supporting the Panama Canal Treaty. Perhaps the most troubling thing about the treaty from view of the Right eye, was that it was bipartisan. To paraphrase Hoosier comedian Red Skelton, that just didn't look right to the Right. Then there was the unacceptable notion of our giving back a canal which, in the words of California Republican Senator S.I. Hayakawa, we "stole fair and square."

Seventy-two years before the contest between Ford and Reagan, another Republican vice president had succeeded to the presidency under the *Tyler Precedent*. He, too, faced strong skepticism from his own party's Right as he sought the presidential nomination to be elected in his own right. Both in 1904 and in 1976, foreign events presented juicy political and inappropriate opportunities for the respective incumbents.

For Teddy Roosevelt, it was the Perdicaris incident. A Barbary pirate named Raisuli kidnapped Ion Pedicaris from his vacation home in Tangier. Raisuli demanded substantial ransom from the United States of which Perdicaris was erroneously thought, even by the President, to be a citizen.

Roosevelt's Secretary of State, John Hay, declared to the world, "This Government wants Perdicaris alive or Raisuli dead." According to my dad, when the statement was read to the Republican Convention in Chicago, the delegates went wild: "There wasn't a dry pair of pants in the house."

The words that excited the folks in Chicago, however, were only some of the actual words delivered to our chargé d'affaires in Morocco. In essence the second part of the message instructed the chargé d'affaires to ignore the first part. The ransom was paid for the Greek national who had immigrated to the U.S. and back to Greece when it looked as though the American Civil War, from which he had made a fortune, might require him to serve in the Union Army. As mentioned in Chapter Four, Hay wrote of his amazement at the public acceptance of that "concise impropriety".

The history of Teddy Roosevelt's "concise impropriety" was repeated, as we have seen, when in his effort to appease chicken hawks, Lyndon Baines Johnson used the Gulf of Tonkin essentially-non-incident to wham up U.S. involvement in Vietnam.

In 1976, Gerald Ford's Administration followed suit and perpetrated another deadly public hoax.

Reagan ran for president in '76 on a tough-guy platform. He'd brook no nonsense from foreign bad guys, which meant he wouldn't do the sort of thing Ford had done on the Panama question. Now the question was, how Ford could respond to a challenge like that?

At first, the Ford campaign ran this clever ad:

> Governor Reagan could not start a war; President Reagan could.

Eventually, there *was* a President Reagan and he did start war—four times.

The 1976 Reagan camp cried foul, the ad was pulled, and it was back to square one for Ford.

Then it happened. What turned out to be some renegades in Cambodia captured the American merchant ship *Mayaguez*, claiming it had violated Cambodian waters. The Ford White House smacked its lips. Secretary of State Kissinger knew what to do with that one. The Ford candidacy, in the manner of the Johnson candidacy before, thought it needed to show the world it wasn't a wimp as the opposition implied. It could be just as reckless and foolhardy as the Reagan camp. The Administration wasted little time on effete and non-macho negotiations with Cambodia. Ford's campaign needed fireworks. There would be a rescue mission ASAP.

U.S. intelligence indicated the ship's crew was being held on Tang Island which was not thought to be heavily fortified. Not confirmed, and not true on either count. Things were just right politically, though. Now the Ford Administration would show Reagan a thing or two. Fate had locked it up for Ford.

So the raid was ordered. It would be carried out by the Marines from helicopters. Although the matter is in dispute, there is good reason to believe that before it actually began the Cambodian authorities radioed our government that the ship and crew had been released. So much for trumping the Reaganites, unless.... Well after all, if the raid went forward, no one, or at least not too many of our people would be hurt. Shades of Lyndon Johnson's post-Tonkin air strikes.

The attack went forward. Forewarned is forearmed which the Marines were *not*. Forty-two of them were killed and the others barely escaped from the island, which was armed to the teeth and held no hostages.

A revealing photograph appeared in newspapers across America the next day. It showed the President and his men celebrating in the Oval Office with huge smiles of triumph—political, not military—on their cleanly shaven faces. To paraphrase Frost's words, they, not being the ones dead, turned to their celebration. Of course, the Marines did not lose their lives to free the hostages. The hostages weren't there, they had already been released. However, the raid certainly let the hot air out of Reagan's campaign.

President Ford, standing next to Archibald Leach, a rather better actor than Reagan, won the Republican Nomination in Kansas City. Leach was also known as Cary Grant. Ford's gain was only temporary. The loss for the forty-two Marines was forever. To the best of my knowledge, the Marines' lives were not listed on the campaign spending report, but they were spent for the campaign all the same.

Gerald Ford, of whom I was personally fond, served out President Nixon's second term fighting inflation with lapel buttons that said "WIN", which was suppose to mean "whip inflation now." He made one half-hearted attempt to obtain from Congress another quarter of a billion dollars to prolong the agony of the fiat government in Saigon, and didn't seem too upset when the request was denied.

James Earl Carter was the improbable Democratic nominee for president in 1976, but he picked the right year. Despite his disastrous interview with the risqué magazine *Playboy*, he was elected. As the president he did one very good thing and one hideously bad thing for which forgiveness cannot come easily.

It was Jimmy Carter's perseverance which helped bring about an international settlement not only of historic, but also of Biblical proportions. With delicious fresh air, the world breathed a sigh of relief when Egypt and Israel called it quits on killing each other. It was a feather in Carter's cap, but when Carter threw his hat in the ring for re-election in 1980, he committed one of the most horrific abuses of presidential authority ever.

I was not around as a member of Congress for the Ford foreign policy fiasco. I had displeased some local politicians by refusing to help them chew off an expensive piece of federal pork and their efforts to gerrymander me out of Congress in 1972 were successful. In the words of Jefferson, I was given "a promotion from servant to master," from public servant to private citizen. *C'est la vie*, but following a delightful two-year sabbatical, I went back to Congress two years before Carter arrived in Washington.

Carter took the next logical step from President Nixon's restoration of contact between the U.S. and China. He re-established diplomatic relations and ambassadors were exchanged. Shortly after arriving at his embassy in Washington, the Chinese ambassador went to the Capitol to meet members of Congress.

This was my opportunity to deliver a message about an incident which had occurred a quarter of a century before. The reception line formed in the hall outside the Speaker's Dining Room on the first floor of the Capitol. It moved along fairly quickly until I shook hands with the envoy. "NEXT," ordered a voice from behind the still camera. I said, "No, not next. I have something to say to the Ambassador." Whereupon I proceeded, with the help of the interpreter, to relate the story about the two Chinese soldiers who had spared my life and those of the three other Marines in that Korean rice paddy all those lifetimes ago. *Lifetimes* because every instant since was another grant of life for me. I concluded, "It just occurs to me, Sir, that this is my first opportunity to express my gratitude and I do thank you." The Ambassador said, "Even in the savagery of war, there can, at times, be humanity." We smiled and I moved on to savor some more of my borrowed time.

The sorry saga of Carter's foreign policy promiscuity began when the Shah of Iran lost his peacock throne. We have the excellent scholarship and skillful research of Mark Hulbert, author of the book *Interlock,* to thank for some of the more obscure details of the outrage.

Chase Manhattan Bank is one of the Rockefeller properties, as is Henry Kissinger in a sense. At the time of the Iranian Revolution which removed the Shah, Chase owned a loan to Iran, payable in regular installments. Iran had huge deposits in the London branch of Chase—*demand* deposits. This meant that Iran, no matter who ran it, could withdraw its deposits quickly while paying its loan slowly.

The relationship between Chase and Iran seemed safe enough. The Shah was in firm control with an entire military division constituting his personal bodyguard. As if that weren't enough, the name of the division was *The Immortals.* With the "expert" advice of its permanent retainer, Kissinger, Chase believed the Shah was there to stay, but he wasn't. Overthrown, he went to Mexico.

When the advice of Kissinger proved, as it frequently did, to be wrong, Chase saw that it might have a financial problem. This new Iranian theocracy would surely do all its "rendering" to Allah and not to Caesar or Chase. That might be all right though. All Chase had to do was apply Iran's deposits to the loan as soon as the holy men defaulted on this temporal matter, but the mullahs turned out to be worldlier than the bankers had supposed—smarter, too.

Iran played a dirty trick on Chase; it continued making its payments on time. Chase could only stand by nervously and watch the deposits rapidly disappear while the loan balance declined at a snail's pace. Once the deposits were gone, would the revolutionaries continue the payments to the Shah's favorite bank? Not likely. At this point, Chase's financial problem was substantial. It looked very much like checkmate. There just wasn't anything Chase could do, *unless*....

Kissinger, the Rockefeller retainer, had an idea which was not good in the moral sense, but very good in the effective sense. Suppose there were a full-scale international crisis between Iran and the U.S. Wouldn't the first duty of the president be to freeze Iranian assets in U.S. institutions? Would that not immediately change Iran's demand deposits into *forget-it* deposits at least until the crisis ended? It is reasonable to assume that Kissinger probably proudly presented this plan to his patrons.

One can almost hear the royal David Rockefeller imploring in Shakespearean shouts across the fog-laden moor, "A crisis, my kingdom —or a little bit of it—for a crisis!"

Revolutionary Iran was less than hospitable to Americans. It was our CIA that had saddled the mullahs with the Shah decades before, and now the mullahs themselves were in that saddle. The U.S. embassy had already been raided by revolutionary mobs three times when Chase began to realize its financial predicament. Both U.S. Ambassador William Sullivan and later Chargé d'Affaires Bruce Laingen had sent warnings to U.S. Secretary of State Cyrus Vance. The Shah was so viscerally hated by the new Iranian government that his admission to the U.S. would be the last straw. It would trigger an assault on our embassy that would make the three previous raids seem like Sunday strolls.

For Chase, opportunity knocked. Because of their connections, both Rockefeller and Kissinger quickly learned about the cables from our diplomats in Iran. The rest would be simple. Start a propaganda campaign to convince Americans that the Shah was a wonderful friend of ours. This was especially ironic considering the rumors that the Shah had previously led the OPEC oil price gouge against us with smiles from Kissinger. Since the Shah was in Mexico suffering from cancer and some other as-yet-undetected ailment that gave him a jaundiced appearance, he must be *admitted to the U.S. immediately* for health care he could get nowhere else. Pass the grain of salt.

Except for the soon-to-be diagnosed gallstones, the Shah's health was being looked after by his doctors in Mexico as well as could be anywhere on earth, not to mention that the best doctor to remove the stones resided not in the United States, but in Canada.

Once the "good buddy" campaign was launched, Rockefeller and Kissinger descended on the White House and the State Department to insist that the Shah was in danger of imminent death and must be taken to New York for unique treatment. Carter did not turn them down, but at first did say the time "was not right." Later he would claim that when he did cave in to his New York betters and admit the Shah, it was because he was convinced by the imminent-death yarn, but was he? Even if he was, was the Shah's "medicare" more important than the ghastly harm that would almost certainly befall American personnel in Iran if the Shah should be admitted here?

Carter's Administration had plenty of evidence that the Shah's long-standing cancer was not coming to a head just then, and the claim that sufficient medical care was available only in the U.S. was inherently incredible anyway. Also inherently incredible is the notion that Carter, among the most intelligent of U.S. presidents, did not fully cognize the foregoing. Even if he had been a ninny, he would still have understood that bringing in the Shah would mean some sort of sudden doom for our embassy people in Teheran.

Carter probably got a pleasant pat on the back and hearty hand-shakes from those paragons of the Empire State. They could very well have quoted from the Jonathan Winters Hefty Bag commercial, "You've done (us) a favor, Strange Person."

So the Shah came up from Mexico, the doctor came down *from Canada* and the Chase money was secure. If you don't count forty-four miserable months of American hostage captivity, humiliation for our great nation and a misperception about our military strength that led Americans to elect the Reagan Administration and lay their wallets and their children's wallets on the curb to squander on patently unnecessary—but profitable—military contracts, all was right with the world—at least Chase's world.

Of course, this disingenuous Carter catastrophe didn't end with the hostage taking.

In 1979 Senator Edward Kennedy was gearing up to take on President Carter in the 1980 Democratic presidential primaries. The Senator was walloping Carter in the Gallup Poll, but now, in the late fall of seventy-nine, no matter how contrived the cause, America had a genuine international crisis. As has always been the case, *at first* the country rallied to the President—bad political news for Kennedy. The two men exchanged positions in the polls and did so long enough for Carter to take a decisive lead in the actual primary vote.

Carter would get the nod at the summer convention, but we as a nation are an impatient lot. We'll put our presidents on pedestal horses in international crises for only so long. By spring, with no end to the crisis in sight, Carter began to slip in the polls. So, utterly ignoring the lessons of long-standing and recent history, as well as specific, contemporary intelligence reports, Carter sipped that old presidential political bromide, the campaign fireworks of military action.

Once again, the wish would father the thought. Apparently, Carter took the famous Israeli hostage-freeing raid on Entebbe as his model for the raid he ordered on Teheran. Of course, he didn't want his thinking confused with facts. Fact number one: The Entebbe airport was so remote that the Israelis had been there, collected the hostages and were gone before Idi Amin Dada could even get his army to the scene. Fact number two: Our Embassy consisted of several buildings in downtown Teheran where practically every other teenager was roaming the streets with firepower. Our military had no way of knowing where the American hostages were at any given moment.

Damning fact number three: Both the CIA and Army Intelligence told Carter that even if the raid were *successful,* from one third to one half of the hostages would be slaughtered. Oh well, how could that be very important compared to Mr. Carter's political career? In John Wayne movies, lots of people got killed, but if the battle was a success, folks always seemed to walk away from the theater pleased. The hero was still standing. Of course, Carter was to be the vicarious hero in this deadly scenario.

Mr. Carter also brushed off something else he was told—by his own Secretary of State. Cyrus Vance told the President he would be honor-bound to resign if the President deliberately condemned to death otherwise safe Americans in Iran. By the time Carter decided on the raid, he knew and knew well that the hostages were no longer in the hands of street mobs. He knew they were in the hands of the new government, which assured our State Department regularly that the hostages were safe and would be released once the banking issues were settled. In the manner of Kissinger and the *Mayaguez,* Carter did not call off the reckless raid. As was the case with his recent predecessors, he wanted to show his opponent how tough he, the President, was—one more political "hero on somebody else's time."

Thank God the raid aborted at *Desert One,* the name given to our base of operation for the raid inside Iran. It was scrubbed there when eight Americans lost their lives and five more were wounded. Military equipment, ill-suited, which is to say ill-chosen, for the mission, performed badly. One of our aircraft crashed into another.

The idiotic plan was to fly American commandos to that remote spot in the desert and from there by helicopters to mountain caves north of Teheran. From the caves they would then be driven to the embassy in trucks operated by Iranian dissenters. Wacko. How anyone could persuade him or herself that those trucks could sneak through what amounted to an armed camp to the embassy and deliver the commandos to the right building or more likely buildings to find the hostages would be a daunting clinical question for the best of mental health professionals.

On the sad morning of April 26, 1980, America awoke to learn for the first time about both the cockamamie caper and its inevitable failure. When I arrived at the Capitol that day, I ran into my good friend and fellow Marine, Pete McCloskey, the Republican congressman from California. In addition to the Navy Cross, Pete had won the Silver Star for leading his platoon in a victorious battle to take a hill in Korea. Later, he had won something else, the 1967 special election to fill the vacancy left in California's eleventh congressional district by the very sad death of Rep. Art Younger.

The special election was special in more ways than one. Pete's opponent was, or rather Pete was the opponent of, none less than Shirley Temple Black. Mrs. Black was somewhat like Thomas E. Dewey in this situation. She and seemingly everybody else presumed she would win the election easily. She went to Washington to be photographed at the Capitol and sign autographs. Sure, she'd have to go back to California and hop through the election, but she'd be inside this edifice carrying out her duties presently.

Mrs. Black began her campaign by trashing Harry Truman, who by then had become something of an icon to most Americans, including a large number of Republicans. The target she chose for political attack brings to mind the word "gratuitous". Then there was the issue of Vietnam. Shirley and Pete divided on that one. She was for the foolishness. Pete won the Republican district and was sworn in on December 12, 1967.

I could probably count on two hands all the official Washington dinners I attended during my thirty years in Congress. I usually had better things to do, such as carrying out my pledge to read and personally answer every legislative letter from my Indianapolis constituents, but, by strange coincidence, I was seated next to Pete at such a dinner the first night he was a congressman in Washington.

Pete knew nothing about me, but I knew a great deal about him. Washington is a political town and the Washington press reports a lot of politics. Ordinarily when a U.S. House seat is up for election, hundreds of others are too. Consequently one doesn't read or hear many reports on individual districts in a general election campaign. However, a special House race is typically the only game in town and the news media are ablaze with it. Besides, he was like one of the Jerry Lewis' film titles.

Having defeated a movie star who was an American institution, Pete was a *Cinderfella*. He was a Marine officer—I had to forgive him for that—and anti-Vietnam War early enough to be classified as principled and gutsy. Someone at the table introduced us, pointing out that we were both Marines.

The ritual began. Where were you? What outfit? Did the Eleventh Marines (The division's artillery) ever drop a short round on your position? And so on. The mutual answers added up to this: The night my battalion was overrun on Hill Nine-O-Two, Pete was commanding a platoon in another regiment, but positioned no more than a thousand meters to our starboard. We were bound to be friends. I was even giving some serious thought to forgiving him for being an officer.

As our conversation continued, I asked if Pete knew that his recent opponent had once been married to an actor named John Agar. "Yes," said Pete. "Well," I asked, "did you know that John Agar was a Marine?" "Yes," said Pete, " so what?" "So what!" I exclaimed in mock surprise, "It just means you're not the first Marine who ever disappointed Shirley Temple." Pete smiled. Had he been married to his future wife, Helen, he would have laughed. Among all the other wonderful things she did for him, she loosened him up.

By the time we spoke on that spring, yet somber morning in 1980, Pete McCloskey and I had mixed a lot of political medicine together, especially in our efforts to help stop U.S. involvement in Vietnam. Pete had even run against Richard Nixon in the Republican primaries of 1972. That, by the way, proved costly. One night in New York where Pete, Rep. Les Aspen, Rep. Jerry Waldie and I were campaigning for our friend Al Lowenstein, we stayed too late to catch the last shuttle flight back to Washington and were seeking motel rooms for the night. One of Al's countless college student supporters was hauling us around in a seatless van. When he told the Holiday Inn clerk that, "Congressman McCloskey and some other congressmen are in the van, and they'd like rooms for...", he was interrupted by the clerk, who asked in a not-altogether-friendly tone, "You mean that son-of-a-bitch who's running against Nixon?" We found rooms at a much less expensive, if lumpier, hostelry.

As we stood there in the lobby of the Longworth building the morning after the failed raid in Iran, I was the first to speak. "Pete, give me a sanity check. Can you conceive of any way that maneuver last night could have worked?" "Andy, the people in the White House are the ones who should be checked for sanity." We agreed that, in the sense of the number of casualties, we were lucky the raid stopped in the desert. Had our people made it to town, as we saw it, those who were not wiped out would have been marched down the streets of Teheran in abject and ignominious humiliation of themselves and our nation.

Cyrus Vance, a man of impeccable honor, honored his pledge to give up his honored position as the United States Secretary of State. He resigned.

Just as Lyndon Johnson had paved the way for Richard Nixon to enter the White House and Nixon had for Ford and Ford for Carter, so too did Carter for Reagan.

Following the foolishness of *Desert One,* the 1980 election was just a formality, and so was Ronald Reagan's path to the Republican nomination in Chicago. However, that doesn't mean that Carter didn't struggle to catch up.

When there is a hostage-taking in a U.S. city and the police use their heads for something other than battering rams, one never hears demands from politicians for enormous new expenditures on police weapons. Yet, in the case of the American hostages in Iran and Carter's misapplication of our military, the Reagan camp found itself in *seventh heaven.* Carter's amateurish use of our superior military had delivered on a platinum platter the public misperception that our equipment, all our equipment—strategic, conventional, nukes and otherwise—was inadequate, woefully inadequate to our national security needs.

General Electric, as everybody knows, "makes good things for living." But it also makes some good and some not so good things for dying. In fact, GE was in 1980 one of the largest military contractors on Earth. Now one of their own, a former employee, was running for president and, thanks to the foolishness of President Carter, was doing rather well on a platform that claimed we were way behind the Russians in military capability. Fact: At the time and before and since we were and have been light years ahead of Russia in military capability. Still, that was an inconvenient fact for military contractors who sought more contracts with more profit.

My friend Jim Seidensticker jokes that if you're in a lawsuit where the facts aren't with you, you file a "motion to amend the facts." That, in essence, is what Carter did for Reagan and Reagan continued to do for his military contractor friends. To make money in the military equipment business, there must either be a threat of Soviet military superiority, or *seem* to be.

It was *Music Man,* "trouble in River City." The lead political role was played by a very handsome actor with a winning smile. Get out the credit card, America. "Either buy some six hundred dollar toilet seats, four hundred dollar hammers and other assorted boondoggles or the Russians will fry you alive."

Never before and no place else was so much money ever thrown at a problem so bogus. The Kennedy Administration had made the same erroneous claim about American military weakness vis-à-vis the Russians back in the early sixties. Military spending was whammed up then, but nothing to compare with the money that was borrowed and spent by the Reagan Administration with the help of a Democratic Congress, many of whose members were scared silly by Ronald Reagan's popularity.

The people who wrote things for President Reagan to say were fond of the phrase, "Democrats spend money like drunken sailors." That was true of some Democrats *and* some Republicans, but if they spent money as if they were drunken sailors, the Reagan Administration spent money as if they were inebriated admirals. It was brazen. The new Administration began speaking, not about what equipment was needed, but, putting the cart before the horse, what money needed to be spent on *something,* and by what percent that vast new expenditure needed to be automatically increased each year. For the government contractors it would be Christmas every day of the year. It would be junk at jewelry prices at this big rock candy mountain of mounting debt for our children and grandchildren to pay—with compounded interest.

While still in office, Carter struggled to escape the outrageous fortune of his outrageous raid. Noting that the public seemed to be responding to Reagan's assertion of Russian military superiority, Carter began to follow suit by borrowing and dumping vast sums into the laps of military government contractors.

In a *Washington Post* article entitled "When More Buys Less", a writer named Bill Grider reported that the more Carter spent on new military equipment, the more the unit prices went up. Because the price increases outpaced the spending increases, the increased spending in that last quarter actually bought less than the smaller expenditure had in the quarter before. Moral? Never lead with your chin *or* your wallet.

There were several ironies in the 1980 election. Here's one of them. I received a letter in the mid-seventies from my Hoosier friend, Lucille Rainey, telling me about a complaint from her east side Indianapolis neighbor who was a prison guard. Some felons in prison were receiving Social Security disability benefits. That didn't look right to the guard, Lucille or me. Social Security disability benefits were meant to put bread on the table and a roof overhead. Taxpayers were already taking care of those contingencies for prison felons. You could look at the problem two ways. Either the felons were not disabled in the financial way contemplated by the law, or they were disabled and the taxpayers were being made to pay double compensation. Clearly the oversight of sending Social Security checks to prison felons, which had gone on for two decades, should be corrected. Well, maybe not so clearly.

When I introduced the corrective legislation, my colleagues on the Ways and Means Committee did not respond, but I found co-sponsors among other Members of the House. One of them took the cause to a TV magazine show and ended up on the program pushing the proposal. Not being a publicity hound, it was never my style to seek such interviews, but the publicity in this case worked like a charm. Suddenly, my bill was thought to be urgent. It passed Congress and was signed by President Carter in rapid order. The bill became law several weeks before the debates between Carter and Reagan.

In one of those debates, Reagan cited as an example of waste, the payment of Social Security disability benefits to felons in prisons. He was right about the waste but wrong in his implication that it was solely Democratic waste. It was the inadvertent waste of both Democratic and Republican administrations over the years. It took a guard and Lucille to report it. What a put-away for the *embattled* incumbent President, a chance to return the serve right down the challenger's throat. Reagan was behind the times; Carter was way ahead of him. True, the problem had been going on for years through both Democratic and Republican administrations, but it took a Democrat, namely Carter himself, to correct the problem. Moreover, it had been in all the newspapers. Was it possible that the challenger could have missed a matter so salient in the news?

Quite possible. In fact, the President of The United States, the one who signed the corrective measure into law only weeks before, *had missed it*. And that president therefore missed a beautiful opportunity for repartee. Carter must have signed a stack of bills the way some officials sign stacks of mail, relying on others to have checked the material first. Was it just a coincidence that President Reagan named his dog, "Lucky"?

On election night when the unmistakable trend assured President Carter's dismissal by the American sovereign, it is said that he became irritable and directed his aides to arrange for him to concede immediately. "No, Mr. President," they are said to have said, "if you concede now before voting has closed on the West Coast, Democratic voters will give up and not bother to go to the polls. It will surely mean defeat for fellow Democrats running for Congress."

Would a man who was willing literally to slaughter many otherwise safe-hostages in Iran be squeamish about figuratively slaughtering some fellow party members at the polls? Nah. Two Democratic congressmen, Jim Corman of California and Al Ulman of Oregon, went down to defeat by narrow margins as discouraged Democratic voters on the West Coast stayed home that afternoon and evening. Even Speaker Tip O'Neill found deaf ears when he asked Carter not to savage their fellow Democrats. Having given the gift of a winning issue to the opposition party, why not also give it the going-away present of two more seats in Congress? If a Republican President had done the same thing the other way around, it would have been equally selfish and callous.

It is said that James Earl Carter was a better ex-president than president. With his own hands he helped build houses for poor people. My father used to say, "None is so chaste as those who have just sinned."

7

THE WIMPS OF WAR

R onald Wilson Reagan was one of the nicest people I ever met. He was sincerely every bit of "aw-shucks" friendly. There was an unrealistic side to him, though. I think he often actually believed things that were demonstratively either not quite true or altogether false.

The Army Signal Corps took motion pictures of Nazi death camps and sent the raw, in more ways than one, film to the California studio where Reagan worked during the war. The film was there to be processed and put together for the historic record and, I presume, to be used as evidence at the Nuremberg trials. Reagan saw the films in California and years later, when he was President, actually believed that he had been at the camps himself when they were being liberated. He said so.

Perhaps President Reagan's most famous fantasy was the one he recited over and over. He told it to a gathering of Congressional Medal of Honorees one evening. His story went like this.

> An American bomber took a belly hit over Europe and
> the commander gave the order to bail out. After other
> crewmen had left, the Commander was about to jump,
> himself, but he noticed that the belly gunner was too
> badly wounded to escape. The gunner was understand-
> ably distressed. So the commander removed his own
> parachute, put his arm around the shoulder of the gun-
> ner and said, 'That's alright, son, we'll ride this one down
> together.' Congressional Medal of Honor, posthumously
> awarded.

However, the incident was not in Europe; it was in the Pacific. It was not a large crew bomber; it was a two-man fighter bomber. Furthermore, it was not reality; it was a movie, entitled *Wing and a Prayer*. The President was mistaken about the circumstance. In the movie the two-man fighter was doomed to crash. The pilot told his badly wounded buddy to bail out. The latter said he was unable to move, adding, "You bail out,

111

Sir." To which the pilot responded, "Too late. We'll ride this one down together." Not only did the President's story never happen, but it was inherently incredible. Why would "the Commander" commit suicide just to comfort the doomed gunner for a few seconds? If the incident had actually happened and a pilot had actually done such a foolish thing, would he have been awarded a Congressional posthumously or would he have been sent to a mental hospital posthumously? Besides, just what witness was supposed to have lived to tell the story?

President Reagan greatly enjoyed war movies, but the thing about being president is you don't have to settle for movies if you're not squeamish about the Constitution. Over and over the President would say, "There have been four American wars in my lifetime." He was modest. True, there had been four wars in his lifetime *before* he became President, but just as the Gerald Ford ad had said he could, President Reagan, himself, added to the list by starting four more American wars, if you define "war" as combat into which a government sends military personnel to die. The greatly gifted and somewhat condescending George Will did not define war that way. In his November 21, 1983 *Newsweek* column, he defined war as:

> The intense focusing of will and material, of leadership
> and technique, to achieve clearly definable aims. War is
> a profession....

I suppose you would have to give Mr. Will this: At least he didn't adopt the Nixon theory by saying war is a professional football game.

My dad told the story of a lawyer who bragged about the greatest case he had ever tried. It took six months to put in the evidence and nine weeks to make the closing arguments. The jury was out for a month. When asked what happened to his client, the lawyer replied, "Oh, him? Well, they hanged him, but what a case."

In defining war, Will had also overlooked someone—the grunt, the dogface, the cannon fodder, the doughboy, the pikeman, if you please (Can you hear me, George?)—the guy who does the fighting, suffers the mud, rain, snow, heat or cold and dies a death of unspeakable horror. "Oh, him," the one taken for granted, the impersonal pawn in the parlor games of David Halberstam's *The Best and The Brightest*. There is yet another view, the one expressed by Bill Mauldin's dogface, Willie who shared a foxhole with his buddy, Joe, "The hell this ain't the most important hole in the world; I'm in it."

I got the impression that while the primary reason for the Reagan White House's preoccupation with martial matters was its relationship with military contractors, there was something else, the thrill of vicarious heroism. The people in the White House, beginning with the President, enjoyed war movies. I made up a mock *Abe Martin* in honor of George Will's trainee, President Reagan. "Th' thing about bein' President is ya' don't have ta' settle for a war movie."

The actual *Abe Martin* was a mythical Hoosier philosopher made up by *Indianapolis News* writer Frank McKinney Hubbard, popularly known as Kin Hubbard. In the early part of the Twentieth Century, he was the highest-paid syndicated columnist in the United States, and his column never exceeded two sentences. Example: "Nothin' will take the starch out of a great man, like meetin' some feller who don't think much of it." Another: "The Smith family who dropped out o' sight six weeks ago, wus' discovered yisterday livin' within its means." One more:

> When Lem Moon was acquitted of the murder of his wife, he wus asked by Judge Pusey if he had anything ta' say. And he said, 'I never would have shot her if I'd realized they wuz' gona' put me through so much red tape.

There was a lot of macho talk around the White House in those days and similar discourse from the Administration's strongest supporters in Congress. At the drop of a hat they, well not actually "they", were ready to take military action against anyone they decided was an international bad guy. *Indianapolis Star* writer Dan Carpenter wrote a poignant column which began with, "In this holiday season, as my President's men roam the earth in search of small nations to punish...." Those Congressmen and White House aides were the best examples yet of that quotation from the play, *Time Limit,* "...heroes on somebody else's time." They seemed to believe that if they saw a war movie without popcorn, they were entitled to veterans' benefits. To use the words of Homer, "the coward would sleep in the brave man's bed."

Every morning in the U.S. House, any member who wishes may make a one-minute speech about anything or nothing. When it came to the point where the let's-you-go-get-'um tough talk was beginning to grate, I stepped onto the Floor one day and said this:

Mr. Speaker, it's definition time. The term is *war wimp,*
noun, singular. One who is all too willing to send others,
but never gets around to going himself.

The remark was given on the spur of the moment, but somehow it hit
a nerve and caught a jet stream of national attention. The *Chicago Tribune* columnist Mike Royko called me to ask whom I had in mind. I told
him all I had in mind was making the shoe; I left it to others to see which
congressional *Cinderbellums* it would fit. Obviously he didn't need a
shoe horn to get the shoe to fit certain public officials. Mr. Royko wrote
several columns on the subject as did quite a few other news people. I
was astonished one day to receive a letter from the renowned historian
Arthur Schlesinger, Jr., thanking me for "adding the term to the historic
lexicon." Several weeks after the term was first published, an editorial
writer for the *Baltimore Sun* called about it. Whereupon I said, "If you do
a piece on it, could we just change the term a little?" "What do you
mean?" he said. "Well, my original was extemporaneous, and now that
I'm beginning to feel literary, I'd like to change it to *The Wimps of War.*
That way I could write a sequel, *War and Rewimperence.*" He was kind
enough to use the new term, but it was the old one that stuck.

In a *Washington Post* piece which examined the sudden silence from
theretofore screeching chicken hawks in Congress, the writer reported
that some members of Congress traced the change to my chance remark,
which took only one fourth of my allotted sixty seconds to make.

When Dan Quayle was tapped for vice president in 1988, Mike Royko
called me to ask if I thought Quayle was a war wimp. A question had
been raised about Quayle's military service during the Vietnam War. He
had joined the Indiana National Guard, generally thought to be a shelter
from actual service in the war.

My reply to Royko was no. I reminded him that there were two parts
to the definition of *war wimp* and that "...all too willing to send others,"
didn't fit in this case. Senator Dan Quayle had broken with President
Reagan on one of the latter's unconstitutional wars, and that took considerable political courage on Quayle's part. There was silence on the
other end of the phone connection. Then an obviously disappointed Royko
became stern and tersely terminated the conversation. I never heard
from him again. One would wonder if his column was already set in type
when he called for the answer he expected of me. Isn't it awful to have
your thinking messed up with facts?

For his Secretary of Defense, President Reagan chose Casper
Weinberger. Weinberger had been Secretary of Health, Education and

Welfare in the Nixon Administration. His nickname then was "Cap the Knife" because of his abrupt and deep cuts in social programs. This fellow didn't like government waste one bit. So now in the Reagan Administration, couldn't he be expected to institute fiscally responsible policies at the Pentagon? Dream on. Whereas he had been *Cap the Knife* at HEW, he would be *Cap the Ladle* at the Defense Department.

Enter, stage far right, the six-hundred-dollar toilet seats, the four-hundred dollar hammers, the re-commissioning of obsolete World War II battleships (re-commissioning price tag: five billion dollars), the absolutely useless MX Missiles, and the fanciful yet profitable Star Wars program. When I argued and cast votes against such prodigious waste of the taxpayers' money, many Left Wingers cheered me and many Right Wingers cursed me. When I argued and cast votes against creating the U.S. Department of Education, the Right Wingers cheered me and the Left Wingers cursed me. When Democratic presidents started their unconstitutional wars, most Republican members of Congress condemned them and most Democratic members defended them and vice versa when it was the other way around. Both sides used the Constitution and the Bible, for that matter, selectively to facilitate their shared knee-jerk philosophy that it was who, not what, was right.

Sometimes during my thirty years in Congress I felt like an orphan politically. When I arrived in 1965, my friend Sen. Birch Bayh arranged a news conference for me in his Washington office. The first question from a reporter was whether I considered myself far to the left or far to the right. My answer was that I considered myself pretty far to the middle.

As I flew from Washington to Indianapolis with a Hoosier colleague one night, I said, "Behold the airliner. It has a right wing and it has a left wing, but most of the people are in the middle." Nevertheless, because of my voting record through the years, I was often asked if I was a Conservative. My answer was, "Lord no. I wouldn't spend that much." I am not a Conservative or a Liberal. You could probably call me a *parsimonious progressive.* I definitely believed that education was more important than the boondoggle MX program, but I was not about to spend wastefully, which is to say give a blank check to education or any other government function.

Through the years I learned that for a great number of U.S. Representatives, the choice was which *way* to waste, domestic or military. The ones I liked most were the ones who chose not to waste at all—either way; no knee-jerk, subject-matter blank checks to any bureaucracy.

In a speech to the House during the Reagan Administration, I said:

Mr. Speaker, I think I've finally figured it out. In the Soviet Union, a Conservative is one who calls a Liberal soft on Capitalism. In the United States, a Conservative is one who calls a Liberal soft on Communism.

On the House Education Committee, a Liberal is one who spends liberally and a Conservative is one who spends conservatively. On the House Armed Services Committee, a Liberal is one who spends conservatively and a Conservative is one who spends liberally.

In the White House, a Conservative is one who borrows money to pay current expenses. In business, a Conservative is one who does not borrow money to pay current expenses.

So you see, *what* you are depends on *where* you are.

I'm pleased to note that, as was the case at the *San Francisco Chronicle* earlier, the Jackson, Mississippi Clarion Ledger used that statement as an editorial.v

A reporter from the *Indianapolis Star* called me one day and said my election opponent claimed I was opposed to the Trident submarine missile program. "No," I said, " I support it and have cast our district's vote for it. Missiles in the deep are the state of the dark art of warfare. Unlike Star Wars, they work and they do keep us way ahead of the Russians." A few hours later the reporter called back to tell me that the opponent had then said, "Well, maybe he's for it, but he had to be convinced." "What about that?" the reporter asked me. My reply: "He got that right. I'll always have to be convinced before I support the spending of my constituents' money—mine too."

This book is supposed to be only about U.S. military matters during my thirty years in Congress, but let me just give one example of what I mean by Far Left wasteful ways, almost always found on the domestic side of the budget, as distinguished from Far Right waste which is mostly on the military side.

In a Ways and Means Committee meeting called to consider one of the never-ending series of welfare reform bills, we took up the question of how much income would exempt in determining eligibility for public assistance. Some of the proposals seemed reasonable enough. In the case of "Workfare," an amount equal to the price of a light truck for the person's hauling business sounded okay. The idea was to help him work his way completely off welfare. In this kind of case, the start-up cost of the small business might eat up enough of the initial income to render the person and his kids unable to eat at all, a disincentive to work. Fine. How much exemption for the light truck? "Fifteen thousand dollars." No, I mean it. That is exactly what one of the committee members advocated. I was ambivalent about whether to laugh or cry or perhaps yell. Instead of any of those reactions, I calmly reported that my nephew had just bought a very strong, if not very pretty, light truck for $750. Though the idiotic proposal never became law, the folks who advocated it looked at me with something between condescension and pity. No. I wasn't a Conservative or a Liberal. I tried to be consistent. Waste is waste, wherever.

The first foreign mess the Reagan Administration got America into was Lebanon, and it didn't happen until the President's third year was nearing a close. Our involvement began innocently, though not Constitutionally, enough. The Israelis had chased the PLO in Lebanon all the way to the sea and apparently neither side was very keen about a donnybrook at that point. The U.S. would send forces to mark an unofficial line of demarcation between the hostile entities.

The Americans were welcomed by the various factions in Lebanon. All smiles—until White House aide Robert McFarlane phoned Col. Timothy J. Geraghty, who commanded the U.S. Marine garrison at the Beirut Airport. McFarlane broke the news that the Israeli/PLO mission was essentially over and the Administration had decided that as long as we were there, we'd take sides and just straighten out the Lebanese civil war between Christians and Muslims—straighten it out, of course, in favor of the Christians.

Now we were getting closer to a good-old-fashion-religious-crusade, a breather from the ideological ones. I doubt very seriously that the Administration decision-makers on this nut-cake idea even knew that the Lebanon civil war had been going on specifically for about three hundred years and generally for three thousand. Remember my dad's words, "Too many people making history who never read history." McFarlane said there would be U.S. Naval gunfire into the mountain positions of the Druse militia. The Colonel shouted back that if the U.S. did that, his Marines would be gratuitously thrust into maximum danger.

This wasn't mission creep; it was mission *leap*. The Colonel was right and McFarlane was wrong. So naturally the Colonel was officially punished for the tragic result of the absurd decision and McFarlane was promoted.

The immediate response from the Druse was artillery fire from the mountains onto the Marine position. One of the victims of the Administration's recklessness was Randy Clark, a Marine from Wisconsin. The President phoned the Marine's father to express sympathy over the death of his son. Imagine how nonplussed the President must have been when the grieving Dad gave him an earful. In essence, James Clark told the President that the President had caused his son's death for no reason remotely connected with the security or well-being of our country.

The American people were beginning seriously to question the Administration's Lebanon involvement. As the blunder became more obvious, the "Emperor's New Clothes" began fading. The Administration, therefore, was in a bad spot. It needed political cover—*bipartisan* political cover and fast.

They put President Reagan to work on no less a Democrat than Speaker of the House Tip O'Neill and Tip bought it. O'Neill, in turn persuaded one of his Democratic friends to introduce a House resolution that endorsed the Administration's Lebanon blunder. It provided Congressional cover for the Administration to keep the Marines in Lebanon for another eighteen months, but why would the Democrats sign on to so obvious a blunder committed by the opposition party? They didn't. At least a majority of the Democrats in the House didn't, but when coupled with the nearly unanimous House Republican support, votes from the Democrats who did support the resolution put it over the top.

As my friend Jud Haggerty would say, modesty forbids, or almost forbids, my reporting that I was one of the leaders among the majority of Democrats and some Republicans who opposed the resolution. Representative Lane Evans from Illinois was another. Quiet-spoken, pleasant and super bright, he, too, had served in the Marine Corps and was not anxious to send others to die in a controversy that was not ours. Together, we planned a parliamentary strategy. Here we need some orientation about U.S. House procedures.

There are some techniques, not to say tricks, of the Congressional *trade.* One tool that comes in handy occasionally is the *privileged motion.* It can be offered by any member who gains recognition from the presiding officer. Even when the time for debate on a measure is completely controlled by other members, the member who offers the privileged resolution can address the chamber for five minutes. Of course, O'Neill and his allies, including President Reagan, strongly did not want to hear any discouraging words about their plan to keep the Marines in harm's way. The leadership on both sides of the aisle controlled the debate time. They certainly were not going to give me the five minutes I wanted to debunk their scheme.

Typically toward the end of debate on a proposal pushed by the leadership, there is a quorum call for the purpose of getting up a crowd on the floor to hear the well prepared final argument in favor of passage. When the quorum call is ordered by the presiding officer, bells ring and lights flash throughout the entire House complex—offices, committee chambers, restaurants, everywhere. The movement of members toward the House Chamber reminds one of nothing so much as a fire drill. With votes or quorum answers recorded by electronic device, the exercise takes about seventeen minutes. When the members assemble, many tend to sit down and talk to one another or just rest up for the trips back to wherever they were.

In this case, I used the seventeen minutes to good advantage for those Democrats and Republicans who were not about to go along with O'Neill's favor for President Reagan.

Speaker O'Neill had appointed the venerable and extraordinarily honorable William H. Natcher of Kentucky to be speaker *pro tempore* that day. Bill Natcher and Charlie Bennett of Florida served a half century each in the U.S. House. The former left by death and the latter by retirement. Both are enshrined in the annals as towering figures of honesty and rectitude, held up as examples for others to follow, if they only would. Bill Natcher *looked* like a congressman. As was the case of General Westmoreland, who was the movie-perfect image of a general, Bill Natcher would be the logical choice to play the lead role in *The Speaker*. As speaker *pro tem*, that was his assigned role in real life that day.

Bill Natcher was most perspicacious about most things, certainly about the monumental error the House was about to embark upon with the resolution at hand.

Amid the din of noise from the chamber as it stood down, I climbed up the steps to The Speaker's Chair and told Bill that I had a plan. At the conclusion of the quorum call, I would seek recognition to offer a *privileged motion* to strike the resolving clause of the resolution, effectively defeating it. He nodded and I returned to The Well of the House.

The representative chosen by Tip to make the closing speech was going over his notes and clearing his throat as the Speaker *pro tem* announced that a quorum was present. It was more than a quorum in this case. Most of the representatives remained to hear the speech, partly out of interest, and mostly out of knowledge that the official vote would come immediately after.

Standing at the Manager's Table a few rows up the aisle from the Well, the sponsor of the resolution said, "Mr. Speaker." Standing in the Well much closer to the *pro tem*, I had said the same a nanosecond before.

In his dulcet tones, Bill Natcher said, "For what purpose does the gentleman rise?". The sponsor said, "I rise in support of the resolution." However, it was not the sponsor who had been recognized by the chair; it was I. Just as Speaker O'Neill had unwittingly been taken in by the politically anxious White House, Speaker O'Neill had unwittingly got up a crowd to hear an argument not for, but against, his pet resolution.

In response to the Speaker *pro tem's* inquiry, I intoned the magic words, "I have a privileged motion at the desk." Whereupon the *pro tem* uttered the prescribed words, "The gentleman is recognized for five minutes to speak in favor of his motion, and the House will be in order."

As I adjusted the microphone, my eyes met Tip's. There was less physical distance between us than there had been between Hubert Humphrey and me on that sad day many years before, but it was the same chamber. This is part of what I said:

> Mr. Speaker: A vicariously brave speech by a comfortable government official, and a lad lies dead. Listen again to the words of James Clark, father of the Wisconsin Marine, Randy Clark, slain in the blunder of United States involvement in Lebanon: 'This was a 19-year-old boy that is kind of...to me right now is a waste of 19 years of a boy's life. He didn't understand what he was doing there. I don't understand. And, I...think about 75 percent of our nation doesn't know what in the world we are doing over there and why we are there. We've got a hell of a lot of Marines over there in Beirut that we need home, and I, they, their parents are wondering about them....Who are we defending, the enemy or the good people? I would like for the president to answer me that question.'
>
> One of the House leaders who think the Marines should continue for 18 months as cannon fodder between the feuding war lords of Lebanon has identified the foe, with unerring accuracy, as 'the other people.' The same leader abjures having the Lebanon issue come up 'in the middle

of a presidential election.' In other words, the American people ought not have much to do with the decision.
Eighteen months? Eighteen minutes? Mr. Speaker, an incoming round can tear a person to pieces in a second. The time to stop the madness of U.S. accidental intervention in the three-centuries- old religious war in Lebanon is now. What member of Congress believes that participation in and whitewash of the Administration's blunder in Lebanon would be worth the horrible death of that member's own son? 'Theirs is not to reason why,' but as members of Congress, ours is to reason why—or why not.

A human life is precious. An American human life should be all the more precious to those of us who have been given the privilege of the sacred Congressional trust. Not one dollar and not one life should be expended by Congress for anything less than a clear national need. If necessary, I would favor ferocious combat to protect my country. To die for something is noble, but to die for nothing is reprehensible.

Who appointed us to unify Lebanon?

...Mr. Speaker, buying this (Lebanon) resolution would be like buying cancer for cash."

I'd said my piece and our side was voted down. Now, in what I presume to call an anticlimax, the sponsor said his piece, which was a prepared speech that did not respond to my arguments.

"The question now occurs on the resolution of the gentleman from...," the *pro tem* announced.

"The vote will be taken by electronic device. A majority of the Republicans voted "Aye" and a majority of Democrats voted "No." The resolution passed.

The next day a friend told me that Tip O'Neill said my remarks were the most irritating to him in the whole debate. I asked if it would be presumptuous to suggest that the truth hurts.

The resolution passed the House in September, 1983. On October 23 the shock that proved my Floor speech prophetic rocked our nation.

Just as the world will always know about the momentous drama of Dunkirk, the world will always know that the Administration's uninformed and reckless order for our military to stop being neutral in Lebanon cost the young lives of two hundred forty-one Marines. Neither side of the civil war had been hostile to the U.S. prior to our sudden change of policy, but the Muslims certainly were afterward. Our Marines suffered horrible deaths when a Muslim truck bomb was detonated at their barracks. The Reagan Administration's blunder had blown them away. The President went to the funeral and shook hands with the loved ones.

Two days after the bombing, Reagan once again validated Jerry Ford's 1976 radio ad. "President Reagan could start a war" and did, quite unconstitutionally, start yet another war, this one in tiny Grenada.

In a very emotional speech in the House Chamber shortly after the Beirut tragedy, Speaker O'Neill declared that nobody had warned him about the danger of the resolution Reagan had talked him into. Naturally I found that curious inasmuch as he had said he was irritated by my warning.

The oft-heard mantra at the White House following the humiliation over Lebanon was, "We (sic) have to win one somewhere." It didn't take long for them to pick the "somewhere". To borrow from an old *Old Blue Eyes* song, they picked "a spot that's just a dot on the map" of the Caribbean. Two days after the cataclysmic tragedy in Lebanon, The United States of America, by unconstitutional and therefore invalid Presidential order, invaded Grenada.

On that postage-stamp island there was a Communist coup against a Communist friend of Fidel Castro. The coup's leaders, therefore, had moved the country further from Cuba's influence despite the fact that there was perhaps a battalion of Cuban soldiers and quite a few Cuban laborers on the Island. Castro had publicly denounced the coup for murdering his Communist friend, Grenadian Prime Minister Maurice Bishop.

The fact that there had been some shooting and killing, albeit between Communists factions, was all the Reagan people needed to declare grave danger to this superpower from that gnat in the sea. The Administration, like so many before it, undertook a propaganda campaign to make the Presidential invasion seem reasonable. The public explanation of the invasion was laced with lies or, in more refined language, filled with fibs. It was the political equivalent of the situation in which a lawyer who knew his client was in the wrong filed what you will recall Jim Seidensticker dubbed a motion "to amend the facts."

The Administration claimed that we were invited to send in the Marines to occupy the island, but this invitation did not even rise to the level of Will Rogers' observation about sending in the Marines "to any country where we can get ten people to invite us." This invitation came from one person and the country she was in was not Grenada. She was in the Dominican Republic. In fact, she was the Prime Minister of the Dominican Republic.

The Prime Minister, Eugenia Charles, asked for the United States to "intervene"—*invade* to be exact—"to prevent the consolidation of Marxist power on Grenada..." My guess is that the Prime Minister was asked by our Administration to invite us into the internal affairs of a *third* sovereign nation. Robert McFarlane, by then promoted to the post of White House National Security Advisor, claimed that he woke President Reagan at three in the morning to tell him about the invitation from Prime Minister Charles for us to invade one of her neighbors. In his book, *Special Trust* (Cadell & Davies, New York) McFarlane quotes himself as having said to Reagan:

> The United States is seen as responsible for providing leadership in defense of Western interests wherever they might be threatened. For us to be asked to be of help and to refuse would have a very damaging effect on the credibility of the United States and your own commitment to the defense of freedom and democracy.

Those words are formal and pedantic enough for one to wonder if they were dressed up for publication or, if not, whether it was necessary to explain "apples and oranges" to the President. McFarlane writes that in response to the suggestion that we turn our foreign policy over to a foreign official, the President said, "You're dead right..." McFarlane was neither *dead* nor *right.* He was alive and wrong. Young American military men were the ones who were about to be dead precisely because McFarlane was not right.

Well, the President told the nation, the Cubans were helping build a ten thousand foot runway in Grenada. That facility could only be for the purpose of strategic military capability. Wrong. True, the Cubans, along with the Canadians, were helping build the runway, but it was being built, not to accommodate strategic bombers, but to accommodate wide-bodied passenger jet airliners. The island had three principal industries—nutmeg, tourism and one institution known in some circles as "dumbbell med school." It was the St. George Medical School. Of the three commercial activities, tourism was by far the most important no matter who was running the country, Commie or Capitalist. The big passenger jets were the tools of tourism.

After the U.S. invasion, *U.S. taxpayers* financed completion of the runway to help the island *economically*. True, the Administration did call a news conference to display hundreds of small arms, many of them machine guns, which had been found near the new runway, but the original excuse for the invasion was modern *strategic bombers*, not these aging small arms.

The next fib the Administration told was that the coup leaders had closed down the airport at St. George to prevent Americans from leaving the island. That assertion was unwittingly proved false by one the Administration's own high officials who was vacationing on the island. On the day the Administration claimed the airport was closed, he ambled on down to that airport and took a flight home, unaware of the Administration's propaganda line. Later we learned that the Administration had asked our friends in other Caribbean countries to suspend their commercial flights to Grenada, obviously to make the fib seem true.

Then there was the matter of the U.S. medical students at St. George. When first contacted by American news people by phone, the headmaster said in no uncertain terms that the faculty and students hadn't even been threatened, let alone harmed, by the coup leaders. That's when the Pentagon issued the order barring war corespondents from doing their job to cover the war.

After U.S. Forces secured the island and had a talk with him, the headmaster changed his story. Obviously, he wanted to stay in business. When the students came home, they did report they had been afraid, but that seemed to relate to shooting during the invasion. The demonstrative fact was that none was harmed or taken hostage even during the invasion. It's elementary. Whether you're a Commie or a Capitalist, if your daily bread depends on tourism, you know that murdering tourists' children is a poor way to keep your daily bread.

Most members of Congress who said anything about Grenada were supportive. They either believed the Administrations whoppers or believed their constituents did. I believed my constituents did, but I also believed it was part of my job to report facts as I knew them. On October 27, 1983, I made the following floor speech in the one minute period:

> Mr. Speaker, to use the relaxed grammar of Abraham Lincoln, don't it seem strange that of the 1000 Americans on Grenada in the cut-throat control of bloodthirsty

With mother Joyce Taylor Jacobs and sister Marjorie Jacobs. (personal file photo)

With friends Pfc. Grider and Pfc. Allen. (personal file photo)

Preparing for combat. (personal file photo)

With father. (personal file photo)

My father (far left) with 1949 Congressional delegation and seated President Harry S Truman. (Acme Newspicture photo)

1965 in front of long time workplace, Capitol Hill. (Congressional photo)

A Congressional candidate, 1962 in White House garden shaking hands
with President John F. Kennedy. (White House photo)

In happier times prior to Vietnam, shaking hands with President Lyndon Johnson in the White House. (White House photo)

Shaking hands with President Ronald Reagan in Oval Office. (White House photo)

Seated in the Oval Office under portrait of President Andrew Jackson. President Ronald Reagan and Vice President George Bush in front of fireplace. (White House photo)

White House Christmas. With (left to right), Hillary Clinton, Kim Hood Jacobs, and President Bill Clinton. (White House photo)

Pictured in 1964 with VP candidate Hubert Humphrey and, to his right, Indiana Senator Birch Bayh. (personal file photo)

Pictured with fellow Vietnam War opponent and 1968 presidential candidate, Senator Eugene McCarthy (Minnesota) (photo by Tom Hoy, Rural Electrification Magazine, 1968)

1985 speaking at breakfast meeting. Seated to my right are Senator Richard Lugar and Congressman Dan Burton, both from Indiana. (personal file photo)

October 1964 in front of Monument Circle in Indianapolis. Senator Vance Hartke (Indiana), President Lyndon Johnson. Lady Bird Johnson, Senator Birch Bayh (Indiana) and Indiana Governor Roger Branigin (left to right). (White House photo)

1965 as a freshman Congressman. (Congressional photo)

Commies for two days, not one was harmed, taken hostage or even blindfolded?

Mr. Speaker, the American lives that were in danger on Grenada were those in uniform who were sent there to die, and did die.

Aside from making the Russians look better in Afghanistan and making our Constitution look worse in the United States, what's it for? I yield back the balance of my time.

I always tried to speak for less than the full sixty seconds allotted. No sooner had I finished my thirty-second oration than I heard a chorus of chanting, "Sick, sick, sick...." I looked over to see that Rep. Jack Kemp and some of his friends were the chanters, and I got out of line somewhat myself. I ran, not walked, to the former Buffalo Bills' quarterback and demanded, "Say it on the record." To which he said "No." "Why?" I demanded. "Because I'd be out of order." "Then you are out of order," I opined. "You're out of order, Andy," shouted one of the shouters. His name was Trent Lott. He was from Mississippi. The next day I ran into Jack at the Capitol and he apologized. So did I. We became good friends, same with Trent. Emotions had run high the day before.

Nineteen American military men were killed, one hundred wounded—some permanently—and a mental hospital was accidentally bombed in this "one" the White House war wimps had to win *somewhere.* It worked for a while. The polls showed that the White House had managed to take people's minds off the outrage of Lebanon, but within a year, a Roper poll showed a majority of Americans thought the invasion of Grenada unnecessary. "Truth crushed to earth shall rise again...." Too late in this case for the young American military personnel who, buried in the earth, would never rise again.

At a news conference in which I took exception to the Grenada hoax, I was asked, "Did you ever have a good word to say about a Republican President?" I replied, "Many times, but never for an unconstitutional Republican or Democratic Presidential war."

One of the military references to the unofficial and unconstitutional American war against Grenada was—brace yourself—a *Midnight Vertical Insertion.* I didn't make that up—some one in the Pentagon did. The Nineteenth Century economist Andrew White had coined the term, *Phrase Mongers* to describe the late Eighteenth Century con artists who ran interference for the French Government's currency contamination.

I have tried to picture the poetic *Phrase Mongers* at the Pentagon—undoubtedly *War Wimps*. Bill Mauldin did a cartoon of a mean-looking soldier walking down a street past two combat veterans. One of the by-standers says to the other, "He ain't no combat man; he's lookin' fer a fight." The Pentagon poets must not be combat men either; their euphemisms about war are too glorious. A few examples:

Operation Just Cause (Panama—U.S. deaths: 23)
Desert Storm (Iraq—U.S. deaths: 293)
Police Action (Korea—U.S. deaths: 33,667)
Somewhere in the Pacific (Vietnam—U.S. deaths: 57,393)
Rolling Thunder (Vietnam Bombing deaths: number unknown)
Terminate with extreme prejudice (Plain English: murder—death)
Joint Endeavor (Bosnia—no death)
Intrinsic Action (U.S. Military exercises in Kuwait—no death)
Provide Comfort (U.S. aid to Kurdish rebels in Iraq)
Uphold Democracy (Haiti—no death)
Operation Urgent Fury (Grenada—U.S. deaths: 19)

This list was drawn from memory. Each item on it was prominent in the news when it was used, but when I called the Pentagon for the entire list, the official there said the information was *classified.* I think that, in essence, the message was, "sometimes we do things that look silly from the distance of time."

The U.S. public had been distracted from our inexplicable involvement in Lebanon. However, as American taxpayers set about the task of completing the Grenadan runway for tourist use, their thoughts began drifting back to Lebanon. The White House mantra now, though unspoken, must have been, we have *to get out of one somewhere*—Lebanon. There would, of course, have to be another *decent interval* between the Administration's obvious blunder and the order to bug out.

Referring to the barracks bombing, the President was reported to have said to his aides, "The first thing I want to do is find out who did it and go after them with everything we've got." When the CIA thought it had located the culprits, the President signed an order for the Pentagon to bomb their headquarters in the Bekaa Valley, but, according to McFarlane, Secretary of Defense Casper Weinberger refused to do so and the President accepted the refusal with a "Gosh, that's really disappointing." ("Poor Ike," Truman had said upon turning over the White House to President Eisenhower, "he thinks that when he tells someone to do something, he'll do it.") To the White House, the ordered bombing was retaliation; to Weinberger, whose IQ was probably the highest in the Administration, it was *escalation.* The Administration exchanged escalation for evacuation.

It is said that a good offense is the best defense. So the Administration passed the word to do something offensive to divert public attention as our forces quietly sailed away, except for the *New Jersey.*

The *New Jersey* was one of the ancient battleships President Reagan spent five billion dollars of tax or borrowed money to refurbish and recommission. They were World War II ships which were more like sitting ducks for Exocet missiles, as the British learned in the Falkland Islands war with Argentina. Nontheless, they did have awesome ordnance, to wit: sixteen-inch deck guns. In something of a "so-there-too," they were fired indiscriminately at Syrian held sections of Beirut as the *New Jersey* brought up the rear in the U.S. retreat. The ship became a hate object of Lebanese Muslims.

Later, when a TWA flight was hijacked in the Mideast and an American sailor aboard was brutally murdered, the hijackers made frequent references to *New Jersey.* American hostages replied that none of their number was from New Jersey. Evidently, the five-billion-dollar restoration of the old ships accomplished something: the deaths of a lot of people in Beirut plus an American sailor aboard a TWA flight. Beyond that there is no evidence that the old ships served any purpose except to drive up our national debt and provide a pleasant nostalgia for the President. Who knows? He may once have been in a movie about them. After he left office and after yet another *decent interval,* they were put aside again.

As my father said, it's tough to be the hero without a juicy villain. For a while in the eighties, Moammar Khadafy was very much in vogue for that role, a U.S. favorite. He was probably no better and no worse later than he was then, but eventually he was no longer the hate object of choice to make heroes of American politicians.

In time, Saddam Hussein eclipsed Moammar followed by Slobodan Milosevic. There is always someone. Even Charles de Gaulle had a brief run on the U.S. hate list. Franco of Spain doesn't really count. He was on the Liberal politicians' hate list, but the Conservatives rather liked him. Marcos of the Philippines was a good guy in U.S. political parlance well into the eighties when his dictatorial rule was ended by his own people and it was discovered that his wife had several more shoes than feet.

As long as there are politicians who seek cheap heroism, there will be villains, real, imagined or, much more often, just plain made up. In the novel *Lord of the Flies,* the villain was a parachute. The phenomenon is hardly unique to the United States. One recalls Big Brother in Orwell's *1984.* He was handy at inventing a dangerous adversary. Demagogues thrive where they can put their malignant roots into the tragically rich soil of ignorant fear.

For American politicians, the scary villain for all seasons was our Communist *landlord*, Fidel Castro. We rented space in Cuba from him for our naval base which remained there throughout the Cold War. The only bad thing he ever managed to do to us, aside from briefly turning off the water he supplied to our sailors, was send to the welcome arms of the publicity-seeking Carter Administration a flotilla of felons and others who were giving grief to the bearded cigar salesman.

Villain Khadafy served nicely for the Reagan Administration. He no doubt did some abominable things. He wasn't likely to do them to us, however, for a very secure reason. He couldn't. Unless, of course, we delivered American military air personnel to him for slaughter. Which is what the Reagan Administration did on the heels of a terrorist bombing which killed American soldiers in a German discotheque. The Israelis were reported to be of the opinion that the cowardly act was sponsored by the Syrians, but the Syrians wouldn't do as villains because by then the Administration was beginning to cozy up to them. So, if someone had to be punished, why not Khadafy? The Administration sent pilots to rocket-bomb Libya, thus enabling Khadafy to do something to us; kill one of our pilots with anti-aircraft fire. Of course, we handed Khadafy the perfect excuse, self-defense.

I have asserted that, in validation of Jerry Ford's 1976 radio ad, President Reagan did start four wars in addition to the four to which he often referred as having taken place in his lifetime. His were Lebanon, Granada, Libya, and Nicaragua. The first two are obvious. The third cost the life of one American military man. Nicaragua, the fourth war, was somewhat clandestine. One might question whether the military attack on Libya was a war since it was brief and one American died. For that one American, his family and all the Libyans who died, it was not only war, but *total* war. As George Will said in his definition of war, American materiel was expended. War.

American personnel and an enormous amount of American "material" were expended in the Reagan Administration's Nicaraguan war. One villain, who, according to domestic politics was an OK villain, was Anastasio Somoza, whose father the U.S. installed as the dictator of Nicaragua. Our country also trained the army he used to stay on top of the political heap. He was very definitely our SOB. The United States was no stranger to Nicaragua. Somoza's predecessors divided into two categories, those militarily installed by the U.S. and those who took power by violent internal processes.

Shortly before our civil war, a Tennessean named William Walker organized a small army, proceeded to Nicaragua and declared himself President of the country, without even so many as "ten" Nicaraguans inviting him. The U.S. quickly recognized the U.S. citizen as President of this foreign and supposed sovereign country. Eventually, in the manner of the Vietnamese, the Nicaraguans, themselves, threw their American master out. In 1909, again without Will Rogers' ten people to invite them, a couple or three companies of U.S. Marines were sent to Nicaragua to overthrow the native government and install the U.S. Government's choice to run the country, one Adolfo Diaz. Three years later, the Marines went back to shore up the shaky Diaz regime. The Marines stayed for twenty years until the Nicaraguans had enough of it. Under the leadership of Cesar Augusto Sandino, considerably more than ten Nicaraguans got together, showed their teeth and invited us out. At which the U.S. ordered its forces to come home, but not before training a local force they called the "National Guard." Of course, the thing the Nicaraguan National Guard was to guard was the budding Somoza dictatorship.

Somoza immediately murdered Sandino and three hundred other popular Nicaraguans in order to solidify his power—and wealth. Once in secure power, Somoza proceeded to plunder his own people. They became the poorest in the world and he became one of the wealthiest. Now he was not only our SOB, but our very rich SOB.

By the time Cadillacs had grown tail fins, the elder Somoza was assassinated. In tandem, his relatively good son, Luis and his relatively bad son, Anastasio, took over.

During the first year of JFK's presidency, a native pro-democracy and therefore anti-Somoza organization was formed. They named themselves after the murdered Cesar Sandino, hence the Sandinistas. Their protests were initially peaceful, but were violently quelled by Somoza's National Guard. The road to peace is paved with justice. The road to war, then, is paved with injustice, and that was the road Nicaragua embarked upon.

As if to underscore the regime's foul stench, when international earthquake disaster aid arrived in devastated Nicaragua, Somoza and his henchpeople swiped the money for themselves.

With that, Nicaraguans from more and more walks of life, including businesspeople, began supporting the Sandinista revolution.

In the summer of 1979, Somoza and his agents fled from the country and the Sandinistas took over. At first they were widely celebrated both within and without the country, but in time, as they themselves demonstrated little enthusiasm for democracy, their popularity diminished not to the level of the misanthropic Somozans, but enough to encourage remnants of Somoza's National Guard to creep back into the country, calling themselves Contras. Either because the Reagan Administration had not read history or because it chose to disregard it, the Contras became *Freedom Fighters* in White House propaganda parlance.

A lot of people, including one of the most popular movie stars ever, John Wayne, took strong exception to the Administration's sending U.S. tax dollars and some personnel to support the Contras. The U.S. domestic opposition took place despite the fact that, by then, the Sandinistas had, in effect, declared themselves Communist Russia's SOB's.

On June 3,1985, Senator William Proxmire placed something about Nicaragua and me on page seven thousand two hundred fifty-five of the Senate part of Congressional Record. Relaxed modesty permits me to quote it here:

> Mr. Proxmire: Mr. President, one of the brightest and most articulate Members of the U.S. Congress is the Representative from the Tenth District of Indiana, Andrew Jacobs. On May 27, the *New York Times* published a letter from Mr. Jacobs vigorously protesting the attempt by the Administration to sell aid to Nicaraguan rebels as aid to freedom fighters.

Jacobs smacks that sales job right on the nose. He writes:

> The so-called freedom fighters in Nicaragua are in fact commanded by remnants of the reign of the dictator Anastasio Somoza Debayle. Forty-six of the forty-eight *Contra* commanders are former Somoza national guardsmen. And the anemic civilian front for the *Contras* is constantly complaining that the military is running their show.

> The *Contras* are right-wing dictators.

> The *Sandinistas* are left-wing dictators.

> So where did anybody get the idea that either side in Nicaragua is for freedom? From the Reagan Administration, that's where.

President Reagan sent over to wardrobe for some sheep suits.

In other words, the *Contras* are wolves in sheep's clothing and the *Sandinistas* are wolves in wolves' clothing. 'Whose side should we be on? Neither.

Mr. President, this letter by Andrew Jacobs is a masterpiece. It is so directly relevant to the issue of aid to the Contras, which this body will take up on Wednesday, that I ask unanimous consent that the letter be printed in the Record.

A congressional colleague and good friend of mine differed with me on Nicaragua. He was in the habit of arguing that the U.S. was militarily vulnerable to this little impoverished country the U.S. had, through the years, pushed around so often. His poetic approach was, "Nicaragua is pointed directly at the soft underbelly of the United States." One day when he and I were engaged in a formal debate on the subject and he used his metaphor, I gently asked, "Have you spoken to the Texans about that?"

Congress and the Reagan Administration arm-wrestled over the President's fantasy definition of the Contras as "Freedom Fighters." At one point he signed a bill which forbade further military aid. The White House's grudging acceptance of the publicly popular measure was voiced by one of the President's speech writers. (Wouldn't it be refreshing to have more presidents who could write their own speeches?) The word-weaver who expressed White House indignation about the bill was the pleasantly pugnacious Pat Buchanan. Speaking, I presume, for the President and himself, he said, "We have not yet begun to fight."

Even though the Reagan White House had told a few fibs about Iran, Libya, Grenada and the Contras generally, they certainly told the truth about at least two things. They said the Contras were Freedom Fighters. That was true. The Somoza gang had been fighting freedom for decades. It was certainly true that the President and Buchanan had not yet begun to fight. President Reagan, though sometimes confused about it, spent World War II in California making training films for the government and regular ones (with pretty ladies) for himself.

Buchanan, on the other hand, or *foot*, had a bad leg which made him ineligible for the war of his generation. He hadn't done any fighting either. The good news: the leg miraculously recovered. During the Reagan years, Buchanan was a regular participant in the annual Washington running marathon.

In the 1996 Republican primaries, Buchanan competed with an authentic and severely disabled infantry combat veteran. In that contest, the former Reagan spokesman did his best to speak in military terms again. His favorite that season was one used on stateside firing ranges, "Lock and Load." Such discourse by such a person brings to mind writer Phillip Wiley's "doctrine of the opposites."

I do not regard the Iran/Contra scandal as so much a foreign policy malfeasance as a domestic one. Details about it, except for the fact that President Reagan prevaricated to the American public about his sending sophisticated and lethal weapons to terrorists as ransom for American hostages, are not very relevant to this part of our book. Besides, there is a wealth of literature already published on the subject. Yet one aspect of the caper has never been reported, and we might as well see it here.

When the joint Congressional hearings on Iran/Contra were cranking up, Col. Oliver North, who had already taken the Fifth Amendment during another congressional hearing, refused to testify before the House/Senate panel unless its members granted him *use immunity*. That means prosecutors could not use things he said before Congress in a criminal proceeding against him. In other words, the more incriminating evidence he could get into the hearing record, the less the prosecutors could use against him in court. With strong political allies among the congresspeople questioning him, getting such material into the immunized record was no trick at all.

The prosecutors urged the committee members not to grant the immunity. In the case of one of those joint committee members, I did some urging myself. In retrospect, the conversation almost seems funny. I saw that member in the House gym one morning and did my urging thus: "If you give North immunity, you cut him loose from criminal responsibility. Anything you don't know, he'd fib about. Anything you do know, he'd grandstand about." The response: "Well, Andy, the public has a right to know." To which I said, "The last time I heard, the courts were still open to the public, including the news media. I think people like you guys are whom Jimmy Durante had in mind when he said, 'Everybody wants to get into the act.'"

Later a federal petit jury convicted Oliver North of crimes involved in the scandal, but he never went to prison. The appeals court found, in essence, that Congress had indeed cut him loose. And loose he went, taking his usual chutzpah with him. With a straight face, he declared himself "exonerated". This spectacle had at least one positive result, though. My nephew, Andrew Martin Landwerlen, did a dandy cartoon showing North holding up a newspaper. The headline read, "North off on Technicality." In the drawing, North was repeating, "I'm exonerated!" Marty's caption: *Oliver's Twist.*

There was another amusing thing about North. Once turned loose by my gym friend and his committee colleagues, North adopted the style of TV evangelists and set up a mail order operation, of which he declared himself president.

The trick to such mail order money raising schemes is to scare each addressee into mailing a check. The old *villain* trick. The villain North made up was veteran—both military and congressional—United States Representative Ronald Dellums of California who had just been appointed to the U.S. House Intelligence Committee. North urged his targeted donors to believe that somehow—he didn't say exactly how—the appointment of Dellems posed grave danger to our Republic. According to North, it was essential to our national security for North's targeted contributors to send money to him immediately.

Apparently, the money rolled in. Sitting on this easily acquired stash, Col. North undertook the task of sparing the country the horrific fate he had made up about Congressman Dellums. He spent a few dollars on a form letter to every member of Congress demanding to know what each was going to do to rescind the terrible appointment. This was my answer to the letter he sent me:

> Dear President North:
>
> To the best of my knowledge Rep. Ron Dellums has never compromised U.S. Government classified material. He has on occasion taken sharp exception with the foreign policies of both Democratic and Republican administrations. Thomas Jefferson would call this an act of freedom. Marx, Lenin and Stalin would call it treason.
>
> Congressman Dellums served as a Sergeant in the Marine Corps until honorably discharged. You will recall that the motto of the Marines is *Always Faithful.*
>
> If you ever obtain information that Mr. Dellums has engaged in the un-American act of supplying arms to

terrorists, please notify me immediately. That would constitute a serious security threat to our country.

Sincerely,
Andy.

Congressman Dellums had never supplied arms to terrorists; on behalf of the Reagan Administration, North had.

As the Reagan Defense Department's $600 toilet seats and $400
hammers began to pound their way into public consciousness, the President undertook the challenging task of proving his administration was
not squandering the taxpayers' money on unnecessary purchases which
happened to be profitable to his old employer, General Electric, and
other contractor friends of his. He said that most of his military spending
was for things like a soldier's "wardrobe". Oops.

A few days latter, Jesse Jackson appeared on *Saturday Night Live*
and showed a videotape of the President's statement. Jackson stopped
the tape immediately after the President said the word, "wardrobe," and
said, "Now, a uniform is worn in a war; wardrobe is worn in a *war movie.*"

Though advertised as an inexpensive method of generating electric-
ity, nuclear reactors were in fact enormously expensive when government
subsidies to the industry were taken into account. That was sufficient
reason for many members of Congress, including me, to cast votes against
the related appropriations, and with the scary nuclear accident at Three
Mile Island, the American market for the technology evaporated. Not so
good for General Electric profits. The company needed new customers,
and China, *Communist* China, that is, was not the least bit squeamish
about buying the reactors. Mind you, it was against the law for G.E. to
sell the stuff to a Communist country. Julius and Ethel Rosenberg were
put to death for just giving information about such technology to the
Reds.

Well, let's see. Before he entered politics and after he left the movies, President Reagan had been given a good job at General Electric.
Now, lo and behold, President Reagan, thought to be *holier than Mao,*
proposed an amendment to allow G.E. to sell the fearsome technology to
Communist China. The proposal did not even so much as include a requirement that the Chinese refrain from using the by-product uranium
for military purposes. As far as the White House was concerned, China's
vague word that it would not divert the by-product, the word of this participant in the "evil empire" of Communism, would be sufficient.

The bill got to the House floor strangely rapidly. I cast the Indianapolis Congressional vote against it after asking the committee chairman, "Does this mean the Rosenbergs are forgiven?" Later the President met with Chinese leaders and declared, "Well, I don't agree with their politics, but they are nice fellows."

There was a funny footnote to the affair. On Independence Day, 1997, George Will, the man who doubled as Reagan campaign worker and independent political columnist, pontificated that the United States should re-establish the "Reagan-era seriousness about exports of technologies with ominous military uses..." to Communist China.

It was funny, but I'm not kidding; he really wrote it.

I never stopped liking President Reagan personally, but I believe that no other president since Warren Harding, including Richard Nixon, was so extensively ill-served and misused by trusted aides and cabinet members. As a consequence, both he and our country, which he truly loved, were harmed. He had one very good and decent advisor, though. Her name was Nancy Reagan, who did constant battle with the flat-earth *War Wimps* in the White House.

8

THE UNREAL WORLD

Early each December, the President hosts a White House Christmas party for members of Congress. It is always charming, even dreamlike. The decorations remind one of the most fabulous of old Hollywood musicals. As you enter on the basement level, you immediately encounter a U.S. Marine Corps string and woodwind quartet. Most guests walk on by. I never could; it was too beautiful. Much more awaits.

You climb the stairs to the first floor where the pungent perfume of freshly cut flowers is benignly intoxicating. Christmas trees, wreaths and holly are everywhere. The trees tower to the enormously high ceilings. Buffets are set up both in the foyer and the West Room where the immortal Abraham Lincoln looks down wanly from the huge painting which dominates the west wall.

Dressed in black tie and formal frock finery, members of Congress and their spouses or significant others, even an occasional gay other, line up to shake hands and be photographed with the President and First Spouse.

It is a mellow evening of refreshing civility, even kindness. With scant exception, political adversaries put aside their adversities and become kindly with one another. "'Tis the season."

George and Barbara Bush hosted their last White House Christmas party in 1992 about a month before Bill Clinton's inauguration. The President seemed unusually relaxed that evening, and he did something unusual.

The holiday East Room is always the most resplendent. Here, where President John F. Kennedy's casket rested for private devotion; here, where the ancient concert grand piano can always be found, a charming chamber orchestra plays the songs of the season, and here, George Herbert Walker Bush broke with the tradition I had known. Halfway through the evening, he mounted the band stand and, as the Christmas music and congressional dancers paused, the forty-first President of the United States gave a little, which is to say informal, farewell address.

149

The President noted that he was not the only lame duck in the room. Incumbent members who had lost their bids for re-election or who had chosen to retire were among the President's guests. He went on to reminisce about the friendships he had made with many in his audience, friendships which ranged all the way back to his own days as a U.S. Representative. I served with him in the House. Of the seven presidents who occupied the White House during my service in Congress, he was my second favorite. I was very fond of him. An elected term in federal office is for two, four or six years; friendship is forever. Toward the end of his amiable talk, the President gave a summary of his political life. Upon leaving the White House, Jefferson had said, "I go forth to accept a promotion, from servant to master." Bush now smiled as he said something similar, "I'm going back to the real world." Now he could be the master of his own opinions. It would not be long before he would freely break with the National Rifle Association over a vicious verbal attack it made on federal law enforcement officers.

George Bush was a political moderate and a very nice guy. He was a political moderate, that is, when he wasn't in Republican presidential politics where Right Wingedness tends to dominate.

At the other end of the political spectrum was another Texan, Jim Hightower, a sometime elected officeholder himself. Like the attitude of the Far Right, he didn't care much for the middle. Of that location he said, "There's nothing in the middle of the road but yellow lines and dead armadillos." Considering the American automobile traffic pattern, the logical conclusion to his metaphor would be that politicians should keep to the Right. I never saw a lot of difference between the Far Right and the Far Left. In my father's words, they are "feuding blood brothers." Both placed ideological locks on their steering wheels and plunged straight ahead. We all know why that doesn't work; the road does turn. Those who cannot turn with it end up in some kind of ditch, usually taking others with them.

George Bush, as do most people in the real world, had common sense. However, as was the case with Hubert Humphrey, he didn't always have the fortitude to apply that common sense when he was in his *unreal* world of presidential politics. True, he had shunned tergiversation in the 1980 nomination contest. He had called one of Ronald Reagan's grander fantasies, "Voodoo Economics". That was pretty much on the money considering the explosion of national debt at the behest of Reagan and the acquiescence of some scaredy-cat Democrats in Congress who feared Reagan's fame. However, when Bush's presidential ambition became more viable, he began to ride the back of the Right Wing tiger. As vice president he swallowed Reaganomics and when it came time for him to run for president in his own rite, despite being a high-born Episcopalian, he let one of the TV profits of prayer send him back to the womb for another exit. Suddenly he was some kind of Southern Baptist. That was supposed to help Bush in the Republican primaries where, before the cock crowed thrice, the evangelist Pat Robertson had defrocked himself and denied he had ever been an evangelist in order to run for president.

There was one thing George Bush was not; he very definitely wasn't a *war wimp*. He was among the first and youngest in World War II to "get around to going himself." The fighter plane he flew was shot down by the Japanese. His inability as president sometimes to speak and act on his best judgements, therefore, underscored those words of Chesterton, "Sometimes it takes less courage to die for one's country than to tell her the truth."

During Bush's first year in office, there was some official native hostility and violence toward our military people in Panama. At a Panamanian military check point, one of our Army officers was shot to death by Panamanian soldiers. Unlike the case of Grenada, this time there was provocation, albeit an on-the-spot incident. Still, the presidential order to invade without a Congressional declaration of war was quite unconstitutional. Besides, there probably was a better way to work it out, anyhow. For example, when I worked my way through night law school as a police officer in the Marion County (Indianapolis) Sheriff's Department, I received a coded signal from the dispatcher one Saturday morning as I patrolled the east side of the city. In essence, the message meant "meet a person" at a filling station. There could scarcely be a more innocuous assignment. It usually meant someone from out of town in need of directions, but this time it meant something entirely else. The lieutenant on the desk, Bill Chance, had a sense of humor, and in his zeal for a practical joke that day, he forgot an important part of the procedure for assigning runs. He forgot to request my "ten-twenty," meaning my location. For some reason he thought I was miles from the assigned filling station; I was less than a minute away.

Normally the inquiring citizen would be standing on the filling station driveway and would identify himself or herself. That didn't happen on this occasion. In fact, no one was on the driveway. I proceeded to the filling station office and no one approached me there, either. So I addressed the attendant: "Is somebody looking for me?" He hesitated, then stammered, "Those guys are going to beat me up." "Those guys" were four in number and *big*—and standing behind me.

In a singular act of bravado, I intoned, "Well, they're leaving now." Turning to the four subjects themselves, I simply said, "Let's go." Fortunately, they did.

Outside, as I faced them, I asked, "What's this about?" A pause. Then, in reference to the attendant, one of the men blurted out, "That son-of-a-bitch has been going out with my lady." To which I said, "Do you have a picture of her?" Puzzled, he asked, "Why?" "Because," I replied, "if you're willing to be arrested today, locked up in the county jail until Monday, go to court all rumpled and crumpled and icky and sticky, and then be convicted of assault and battery" (I pointed out to him that I was a law student and therefore knew how to gather, preserve and present evidence—freshmen law students usually know everything) " and spend the rest of your natural life on this earth with an indelible official record that shows that you are a violent person, if you're willing to do all that for her, I'd just like to see her picture. She must be right up there with Helen of Troy, the 'face that launched a thousand ships.'"

All four men began to smile. I went further, "Let me ask you: do you ever get out of town?"

Yes, he did. "And do you ever go out with other women?" Well, yes he did. "Are the rules different for this lady?" To that, he replied, "Well, officer, you just don't know how mad a woman can get a man." My response: "I don't? What makes you think I'm exempt?" Clearly no arrest was necessary in this situation. The imminent explosion had been completely defused through diplomacy. The same human nature and possibility of peaceful resolution of conflicts can be found in international relations.

A few minutes after the four men left, having changed their moods to civility, four sheriff cruisers, with red lights blazing and sirens wailing, thundered into the station. The officers dismounted with truncheons at the ready. The desk lieutenant had assumed I would arrive after heads were cracked and the bad guys were headed for jail, but on that sunny Saturday the fellow with the dating problem did not acquire a police record for violence. Instead, he went on to become a prominent businessman in Indianapolis, the proverbial pillar in the community—much better result.

I applied the same logic when I sponsored a bill brought to me by Marian Franz, executive director of the Peace Tax Foundation. Simply stated, the bill provided a peaceful and effective result for both the IRS and conscientious objectors, some of the latter of whom were withholding the parts of their income taxes which they figured were allocable to the government's military spending. The idea was to let such conscientious objectors pay their full tax obligations with an assurance from the government that the payments would be applied to any function of the government except military. The provision would not reduce military spending, the government would get its money, not having to spend any of it on related prosecution and prison costs, and the objectors would get to meet their tax obligations with clear consciences.

"Win-win" was the way Marian liked to put it. Alas, no, something mindlessly macho in many of the members of Congress meant the easy way would not be adopted. "Jail the tax dodgers," was their answer. Yet, it cost the government a ton to do so—usually much more than the amount the objectors would not object to paying if allowed to do so in good conscience. Furthermore, there were many cases where conscientious objectors quite legally avoided taxes. Some who were professional and could earn large incomes simply chose jobs that paid below the threshold for federal taxation. Under the regular conscientious objector law that had applied to military service since Washington's time—with Washington's support—the government lost a particular kind of service it would otherwise have obtained from the objector. Under this proposal, the government would have only gained in its taxing program. However, like my buddies with the billy clubs, my courageous colleagues elected to continue the lose-lose approach. As indicated in chapter one, I am not a conscientious objector, but, with all due modesty, I don't think I'm stupid either.

Despite the fact that the soldier son of good friends of mine was severely wounded and permanently disabled in the invasion, I remained silent on the Bush invasion of Panama except for the constitutional issue. I can't be absolutely sure that subconsciously my friendship with Bush did not play a role in my restraint. The same might be true of my refusal to join other Democrats in assailing the new president on Iran/Contra. In the latter case, though, I saw no clear evidence that he was culpably involved.

The second Bush war was probably not unconstitutional for the simple reason that the Congress, while not following the language of Article I, Section 8, did vote essentially to send our military to Americanize the Gulf war at the beginning of the '90s.

As everybody knows, Iraq invaded its neighbor Kuwait in the late summer of 1990. However, some may have forgotten that prior to the invasion, our government cheered Iraq's invasion of Iran. Our country even supplied arms to facilitate that invasion, and when the government of Iraq approached our ambassador concerning possible military action by Iraq against Kuwait (There is some controversy about exactly what she said) it seems that she at least mumbled something to the effect that Middle East border clashes were of no concern to the U.S. In the context of the answer, it could very well have looked like an American green light for the Iraqis to go after Kuwait. Shortly before the 1950 North Korean offensive against the South, our Secretary of State, Dean Gooderham ACHESON had declared Korea not to be within our "defense perimeter." That traffic light had the distinct tint of gree n as well.

With some supporting evidence, the Iraqis claimed the Kuwaitis were drilling for oil diagonally at the border into Iraqi territory, but there was reason to believe it was happening both ways.

When I spoke during the House debate on Iraq, I said:

> Let's face it, we have a checkered past when it comes to invading small countries, the most recent being Grenada. As for invasions by other countries, this proposed rescue mission certainly represents selective morality. Where was the U.S. Cavalry-to-the-rescue when China hammered Tibet into submission?

At this point, Representative Sid Yates of Illinois asked me to yield the floor, which I did:

> Mr. Speaker, Hafiz al-Asad of Syria is doing the same thing in Lebanon today. He is taking over Lebanon without our protest.

I responded:

> I thank the gentleman from Illinois for making that point.

> Mr. Speaker, it isn't indignation; it's oil. And it may not be oil so much as a quest for points in the polls which this Administration has been losing rapidly.

The Administration's slide in the polls apparently was a result of a forensic attack launched by Speaker of the House Thomas Foley against the Administration. The issue was the Administration's proposal to reduce the tax on capital gains. Foley made political hay with charges that the Administration's tax policy favored high-income citizens over those with middle and low incomes. To some extent this was true, but not to the extent that it was true of the Reagan Administration, in which favoritism for those whom fate had already favored, was blatant. In any case, Bush had announced that the U.S. would respond to the invasion of Kuwait with economic sanctions against Iraq, adding that the sanctions would, in his opinion, take about a year to work. Still, as his poll numbers began to fall, he decided that a couple of months were enough of a trial period for the sanctions. At that point, he began using American tax money and, in the case of Egypt, cancelation of an eight billion dollar debt owed us, to persuade key countries to support a United Nations resolution authorizing a mainly American war against Iraq. Then, despite his party's bellicose hostility to the UN and its supposed threat to our sovereignty, the President told Congress it had to vote authorization for military action because of a UN mandate. Go figure.

The Americans were to do most of the fighting and dying while some other countries in the alliance were to contribute money. One prominent news columnist dubbed this arrangement, "renting out our armed forces." Good line, but somewhat wide of the mark. The death of a young American is not a temporary lease; it is *fee simple absolute* forever. There were more than 293 American deaths in this one. At the outset, I penned a poem for the Congressional Record:

> Though we send your kin to foreign soil,
> We'll not spill a drop of American oil.

Even that was a bit too generous with the Administration. Most of the Kuwaiti oil was shipped, not to the U.S., but to Japan. The Japanese did contribute some money to the American military operation, but no KIA's, not even a drop of blood.

The Administration's rhetoric on its reasons for thrusting us into the Gulf War was like something out of a Marx brothers' movie. At first it was moral indignation at the invasion of a small nation by a bully neighbor. When people began to see the inconsistency of that argument with U.S. indifference to similar invasions including a recent one of our own in Grenada, our Secretary of State, Jim Baker, told us that the purpose of the military invasion was to *save American jobs*. It pretty much added up to just one job, a snow one. Well, maybe another one, too. The one at the vortex of the U.S. government was to be saved.

At about the time the Administration and Congress struck the match of American war in the Gulf, a Martin Luther King, Jr. celebration was held in Indianapolis at the Light of the World Baptist Church. The pastor, T. Garrott Benjamin, is one of the most dynamic in the country. The most venerable of Hoosier ministers was Andrew Brown who, as King's chief

lieutenant in Indiana, was the guest of honor. By tradition, various officeholders were invited to speak. The speakers were in varying degrees
supportive of the war until my turn came. I said this:

> I have three questions. Would Andrew Brown have started
> an American war in the Persian Gulf? Would Martin
> Luther King have started an American war in the Per-
> sian Gulf? Would Jesus Christ have started an American
> war in the Persian Gulf?

> John Quincy Adams said it: 'America does not go abroad
> in search of monsters to destroy; she is the vindicator of
> her own people.'

> All this American blood in the name of Jesus Christ.
> One more question—What is blasphemy?

The response from the enormous audience surprised me: It *shocked*
my fellow officeholders. The applause was both thunderous and sustained, reminiscent of that long ago day in the Indiana House of
Representatives when I dared to declare the Vietnam policy wrong.

All those young *Desert Storm* Americans died while rich Kuwaiti young
men partied in Egyptian nightclubs. Of course, the American lives were
lost most specifically in order to put a lecherous monarch back on the
decadent Kuwaiti throne. By "lecherous" I mean the man was allowed by
his laws to have three wives, two regular and one new teenager each
weekend.

The leader at the Branch Dividians in Waco also indulged his appetite for sex with under-aged girls. Interesting how the Far Right can find
favor with men who under U.S. law are statutory rapists.

The Administration and a majority in Congress ordered these young
Americans to fight for everything we did *not* believe in and one thing we
and the Japanese *wanted*, oil.

What if our supply of oil from Mideast suppliers were cut off altogether? How bad would that be? It would certainly change things in our
country—for the better. The U.S. supply of natural gas is sufficient literally to keep us going for a very long time, easily long enough to develop
inexpensive methods for processing hydrogen from water. Motor vehicles
which now use gasoline can be easily converted to use natural gas or
hydrogen. Many have already been converted to natural gas use, and

these fuels are better because, by quantums, they are cleaner. Good news, or at least there could be good news, for Los Angeles.

With our inevitable victory in the Gulf War, the expected political phenomenon came to pass. Tax policy was, for a time, forgotten and the President's new poll numbers were prodigious—for a while. Had the presidential election been held in the wake of the war, George Bush probably would have remained in his unreal world for another four years, when the 1992 election rolled around, the rosy poll numbers had wilted. By then, other matters mattered more, and a nice guy with a little less fortitude than would have been nice on occasion, re-entered the "real world."

9

NEW HOPE

I sent a letter to William Jefferson Clinton. It was timed to arrive on January 20, 1993, the day he became President of The United States. A copy of that letter later went to Senator Ernest (Fritz) Hollings of South Carolina. I heard from the Senator first:

Hon. Andy Jacobs
2313 Rayburn Building   May 5, 1993
Washington, D.C. 20515

Dear Andy:

You are very thoughtful....and this letter to President Clinton is a masterpiece. I noted the January date; it's even more timely now. Please re-send this to the President immediately—if you are at all hesitant, give me permission to do so and I will make sure he reads it because I doubt if he had much time to read it in January.

Many thanks.

Warm regards,

Ernest F. Hollings
United States Senator

My answer to the Senator was one of gratitude and hope that he would make sure the president saw the original letter, which read:

Dear Mr. President:

At any given time there are thirty or forty wars raging around the world. And if a U.S. President wants to get us into one of them, he can always find a reason. But, to paraphrase Shakespeare, while presidents can 'rhyme' the people into enthusiasm for such military insinuation, the people, on reflection, 'do always reason themselves out again' when fireworks have stopped and young bodies are buried.

It is impossible to be a hero without the cooperation of a villain. The Chinese were villains when they marched into Tibet. They are still there. The Syrians were villains when they marched into Lebanon. They are still there. In musical terms, has anybody seen our old friend, Gaddafi? Mr. Bush's erstwhile friend Hussein is the current billboard villain. Before you took office, I had served with six U.S. Presidents. And I believe that each of them sought vicarious, which is to say *pseudo* heroism by sacrificing the lives of young Americans in foreign military action unrelated to our national security or international obligations. In other words, they borrowed money to borrow trouble in other people's wars.

You could do the same. On behalf of your standing in history and in the next presidential election, I urge you not to. You have already shown enormous strength of character. You do not have to prove anything.

Lord Chesterton said it: 'Sometimes it takes less courage to die for one's country than to tell her the truth.'

In the campaign last year you suffered and survived primitive, cynical and absurd attacks on your courageous opposition to an American military involvement most Americans now see as foolish, just as polls show they retrospectively tend to see most modern presidential wars.

The courage you showed as a young man by publicly calling on our government to come to its senses over Vietnam, was the sort of Christ-like courage displayed by Gandhi, King and Sadat—the ultimate courage, the courage to *appear* to be a coward when one is just the opposite.

Hubert Humphrey said, 'It takes courage to be a peace-maker.' But sadly he was unable to summon that courage when icy stares from Lyndon Johnson demanded the Vice President's tergiversation in order to appease boisterous war hawks in the long years of Vietnam. Johnson, who had advised Eisenhower to stay out of Vietnam, later said, 'I'm not going to let them do to me over Indochina what they did to Harry Truman over China.'

I was there. I heard him say it. And what did it profit him?

Richard Nixon, who had said of World War II that he 'was there when the bombs were falling' and was not, chose to be a 'hero on somebody else's time' by continuing our Vietnam involvement, calling it 'our finest hour.' And what did it profit him?

Gerald Ford sent forty-two young Marines to their unnecessary deaths on Tang Island *after* his Secretary of State was informed that the Mayaguez had been released. Ford saw the raid as an opportunity to show that he was as tough as the war movie make-believe hero he faced at the Kansas City convention. And what did it profit him?

Despite knowing that between one-third and one-half of the otherwise physically safe American hostages in Iran would be slaughtered by a tactically illogical and unnecessary raid into Tehran, Jimmy Carter ordered the misadventure anyway in the hope that it would halt his slide in the polls. His Secretary of State honorably resigned over the moral lapse. And what did the reckless scheme profit Mr. Carter?

President Reagan 'stood tall' while young Marines lay dead in Lebanon. Then he sought to obscure the blunder by sending more young Americans to die in Grenada, the White House mantra at the time being, 'We have to win one somewhere.' Eighteen months later a Roper Poll showed that the American public considered the invasion of Grenada a mistake. So ultimately, what did it profit Mr. Reagan?

George Bush temporarily improved his sagging poll numbers by changing *Desert Shield* into *Desert Storm* which snuffed out 292 innocent American lives and put a lecherous despot back on a decadent throne. And what did it profit President Bush?

John Adams and Dwight Eisenhower had the political courage to avoid unnecessary war. Adams in the case of war with France in 1798 and Eisenhower in the cases of Dien Bien Phu, the 1956 Mideast war and Hungary. Eisenhower's wise decisions prompted the John Birch Society to declare this authentic hero of the war in which our security *was* involved, 'a conscious and dedicated agent of the Communist conspiracy.' Instead of the carnage and additional debt, Ike built an interstate highway system which is self-financing.

If our country ever goes to war it should be because we have to, not just because we have a chance to.

'Courage,' my mother says, 'is fear that has said its prayers.' The maxim applies to political courage as well as physical courage. In praying for you, which we do, my wife and I also pray for our two little boys and every other American's children, too.

There is nothing conservative about squandering American lives and money.

Sincerely,

Andy Jacobs, Jr.

In other words, what did the unconstitutionally rogue presidential wars profit the presidents and what did they cost the country?

On May 7, 1993 the president wrote a gracious reply. Without his permission, which I did not seek, I would not presume to publish it. However, I can say it indicated that, at the time, he cognized the contents of Barbara Tuchman's masterful volume, *The March of Folly*. There seemed to be hope for common sense from the new administration. The American tragedy in Somalia, in which U.S. soldiers were killed and some of their bodies dragged through the streets of Mogadishu in pagan procession, happened on Clinton's watch, but President Bush had initiated the military mission as a humanitarian one. U.N. food aid was not reaching hunger victims in Somalia because of hijacking. The U.S. forces were there to act as escorts. The mission seemed to have the tacit acceptance of Somalia's various warlords, until a ding-a-ling American admiral decided to punish one of them. The Americans he sent to do it were caught in an ambush. The admiral was a mission *creep* himself. Even though the mission was a holdover from the Bush Administration and the additional borrowed trouble in the incident seemed like a bureaucratic blunder, it was still under the Clinton Administration. There is no evidence, however, to suggest a presidential display of vicarious macho.

The president did order an invasion of Haiti, but it is unclear whether it was a bluff or a willingness to snuff out Americans lives to solve an immigration problem. The fact that the dictators in that unhappy and impoverished land backed down and personally bugged out, probably means that they, we and perhaps the president, himself, will never know if the president would have gone forward with carnage in the absence of capitulation. On the record, the intervention was bloodless—and unconstitutional.

Bosnia was much to the president's credit, at least in terms of sending troops into combat. He did not. His decision against sending them to die is all the more impressive when you consider the demands to do so from some very prominent Americans, including his own Secretary of State—none volunteering to participate him or herself.

One day during the free-for-all morning speeches on the House floor, a chicken hawk war wimp made a particularly abusive speech criticizing the president over his refusal to send U.S. troops into Bosnian combat. I rose on the occasion, was recognized by the Speaker to say:

> Mr. Speaker, one hears it said that President Clinton is breaking with the bipartisan tradition in American foreign policy. Considering the fact that the *tradition*

consists of politicians killing our kids for points in the
polls, good for President Clinton.

In the matter of unconstitutional pseudo-macho presidential wars,
there was cause for new hope on Thanksgiving Day, 1997. However,
after the heinous bombing of two U.S. embassies in Africa in 1998,
President Clinton went beyond an extensive FBI investigation which resulted in arrests and indictments. He ordered cruise missile attacks on
suspected terrorist sites in Afghanistan. There were no American casualties in the attacks. However, because of them, Afghanistan released from
its custody two prime suspects in the embassy bombings. The Afghan
government had planned to extradite them to the U.S. Then, in late
December, 1998, Bill Clinton ordered the bombing of Iraq following its
refusal to allow the full inspection of Iraqi weapons ordered by the U.N.
It was a foolish and deadly decision—Iraqis were killed. There were two
stated objectives: to force Iraqi dictator Saddam Hussein from power
and to destroy Iraqi weapons of mass destruction. The second objective
was impossible. If the U.N. inspectors could not find those weapons on
the ground, the U.S. military certainly wasn't going to find them at the
safe distance from which the air strikes were launched. As for forcing
Hussein from power, we might as well have sent PAC campaign contribu-
tions to him. Does anyone suppose that, had things been the other way
around and Iraq had bombed us, President Clinton would have become
less popular?

Still, up until 1999, among the seven presidents with whom I served,
Clinton had the best record on the subject of *killing our kids for points in
the polls.* However, even during those first six years of his presidency, his
record was not devoid of foolish military misadventure. Anyone could
know that our enmity toward Iraq would come to a close at some point,
just as it had in the case of other fusses we had with other countries
where nothing had changed but *our* attitude. The question was, how
much hatred on the part of the Iraqi public would be engendered against
us in the meantime? We had got along just fine with the same Saddam
Hussein when he was conducting aggression against Iran. Indeed, we
had helped finance that aggression.

It was at least ironic that, at the same time we were telling the
Israelis and Palestinians that they ought to be able to lay aside their age-
old hostilities and seek a compromise, we seemed not to practice that
preachment with Iraq. True, Saddam had vicious weapons—probably not
yet including nuclear devices. True, in a few cases he seemed to have
used the gas ordnance, but we had the same gas and biological weapons

and so did several other countries. True, we had never used them on an enemy, but we were a major member of the world's nuclear bomb club. Only one of those members had ever used those weapons of mass destruction on the civilian population. *We.*

During those first six years, with the sad exception of Iraq, Clinton racked up a pretty impressive foreign policy record. The president refused the ill-considered urgings of congressional and administration war hawks and sent no American to die in Bosnian combat. Instead, he skillfully facilitated a settlement of sorts in Dayton, Ohio. It was a settlement that could not have been achieved by U.S. belligerence. Moreover, he managed to get rid of a military dictator and an illegal immigration headache without firing a shot in Haiti. With the wise choice of former Senator George Mitchell as his envoy, Clinton engineered a peace agreement which had eluded many others on many other occasions over many bloody decades in Northern Ireland. Despite partisan carping at home, Clinton was one of the most respected of U.S. presidents around the world at the time.

That carping did little to diminish his standing in this country either. A Gallup poll taken in November and December, 1998, showed that a majority of Americans thought Clinton was the best foreign policy president of the ten who had served since World War II. In commenting on the poll, a Washington D.C. think tank thinker said the American people were mistaken, adding that Clinton had missed several foreign policy opportunities. Probably true, but those opportunities were mostly opportunities for unnecessary war. Had the Clinton foreign policy story ended there, it would have been a relatively happy ending. It didn't.

Frank Sinatra and his daughter Nancy recorded a song which told the tale of a budding love affair cooled by overstepping its development. The chorus was, "And then I go and spoil it all by saying something stupid like I love you." On the eve of spring, 1999, President Clinton spoiled his otherwise commonsense foreign policy record. He elected to violate the Constitution by borrowing money to borrow trouble in one of those 40 wars I had mentioned in the letter I wrote to him six years before. For years war wimps, including Clinton's *she-hawk* Secretary of State, Madeleine Albright, had clamored over and over for American armed intervention and, therefore, American blood in a variety of other countries. Despite all the importuning, the president had done pretty well at emulating the example of Eisenhower by resisting their entreaties for illegal, reckless and lethal action. Because of the public disclosure of his extra-marital affair, however, and all that his political enemies had tried to make of it, 1998 had been excruciating year for Clinton. Publicly he seemed to bear-up remarkably well, but the whole affair took its toll. By the early months of `99, his resistance was down. Because that last year of partisan punishment of the president seems to have been an influential factor in changing the course of his theretofore carefully thought-out foreign policy, it might be useful here to take some time to examine that surreal series of events.

Through the years, clearly factual information was brought to me about the extramarital affairs of more than one of my congressional opponents. In each case I said nothing about it to anyone else, not even my closest friends. It was none of my business and none of the business of anyone else, except the people directly involved and God. My father-like friend Congressman Bill Bray was shown similar evidence about one of his opponents and rejected use of it out of hand. Historians tell us that political enemies of Alexander Hamilton happened upon a tryst between him and a married woman—not his wife. They hated him, but drew the line on human sexual misconduct. Then and there, his sworn enemies tipped their hats and withdrew, saying nothing about it in their political efforts against him. There came a time, though, when a more personal and vicious brand of politics emerged in America. Political discourse no longer ended at the bedroom's edge.

In the second half of the Twentieth Century, our nation's progress toward incivility and savagery seemed to be "pretty rapid." By the 80s, the non-criminal sex lives of public officials became fair political game for some politicians and most of the news media, most of the time. During the 1996 presidential election campaign, *The Washington Post* quite rightly declined to publish an embarrassing aspect of Senator Bob Dole's private life. When it was President Bill Clinton's turn in 1998, however, it was different. According to the president's severest critics, it was the scandal of the century, one more president with one more extra-marital affair. *Washington Post* columnist David Broder wrote that the president's private marital infidelity—unlike King David, Clinton had not sent an extra lover's husband into combat to be killed—was worse than President Nixon's *Watergate*. That would be the *Watergate* that, though unsuccessful, threatened the institutions of American freedom. Mr. Broder's reasoning was that "however neurotic and criminal" Nixon's actions were, they were motivated by and connected to the exercise of presidential power. He knew the place he occupied and he was deter-mined not to give it up to those he regarded as 'enemies.'

Yes, David Broder, not Newt Gingerich, wrote that. Some translation is useful here. By "presidential power," Mr. Broder meant the public office to which Mr. Nixon had been elected to serve, not wield, for four years. Those whom President Nixon "regarded as 'enemies'" were the Democrats who, by law and tradition, nominated a candidate for the office Nixon sought again in the upcoming election. Broder was saying that a hugely precedented presidential peccadillo was "worse" than extreme and criminal abuse of presidential authority to manipulate the American electoral process. Shame on that dirty ol' liberal *Washington Post;* favoring the Democrats again.

A guest columnist in *The Wall Street Journal* detected a difference between Clinton's extra-marital affair and that of another prominent figure in American politics, Dwight David Eisenhower, who is lofty on my list of good presidents. According to the writer, Ike's affair with his lady-driver was "discreet." Not very; all the people around them, including the news media, knew about it. The affair wasn't discreet; the press was.

With Clinton, we had one more case where the same faults that prove friends are only human prove adversaries are inhuman. "But," the Clinton critics insisted, "Clinton lied; he lied to the American people." So did five of the six other presidents with whom I served. They lied to the American people about the American people's business, not their own private monkey business. The exception to the fibbing, I think, was George Bush. There were accusations against him of falsehoods in connection with the Iran/Contra malfeasance, but, to the best of my knowledge, no real proof.

Bush's predecessor specifically lied to the American people about using their tax money illegally to send sophisticated and lethal weapons to terrorists. One of Clinton's congressional critics undertook to justify that predecessor president's prevarication by invoking the vague mumbo-jumbo of "national security". Just how surrendering such awesome ordinance to conscienceless killers—which is to say mass murderers—could make any nation more secure, the mumbo-jumbo member failed to explain. In any case, if I could choose between having a president lie to me about his sex life and having a president lie to me about using my taxes to arm terrorists, I'd choose the former. My first choice would be no lies at all. Still, I've always thought that when it isn't anyone else's business, lying doesn't count. Besides, lies about sex are not unusual, except that lies from men about sex tend to be claims rather than denials.

There's no telling how many million certain and conclusive words of criminality were spoken and written by Clinton's attackers on the subject of that household word, *Whitewater.* Nobody ever said just what Mr. and Ms. Clinton were supposed to have done wrong—except lose money—on the Arkansas land deal. No wrongdoing was ever found despite the expensive and emotionally-fueled efforts of sworn and sworn-in enemies.

Yet, Clinton's strident detractors surely made it sound sinister. A Republican *Special Prosecutor*, widely respected for his objectivity, was appointed to investigate the vague charges. However, for the President's enemies, that Republican's impartiality wouldn't do, and, by chance, they were in a position to do something about it.

One of the president's bitter critics, Senator Lauch Faircloth of North Carolina had, in effect, appointed one of the three judges on the Federal panel named by the Chief Justice to exercise jurisdiction over the investigation. That judge was Republican David Sentelle who lunched with his senatorial benefactor and immediately thereafter managed to bring about the removal of the fair-minded Republican Special Prosecutor and replace him with one of Clinton's implacable foes.

The replacement prosecutor, Kenneth Starr, was a Right Wing ideologue who had more than that reason to be biased against Clinton. Starr made a lot of money as a lawyer for the tobacco interests that were faring badly—as they should—under Clinton's Administration. The "investigation" dragged on for years and for forty million of the taxpayer's dollars. In the end, the best the critics could do was the bedroom. They "had labored mightily and brought forth a mouse." The critics settled on *sex* just as the Polish Communists had done in an effort to discredit Poland's modern-day George Washington, Lech Walesa. At the other end of the spectrum, strange J. Edgar Hoover had used the machinery of the Federal Bureau of Investigation to spy on an extra-marital affair of another national leader, Martin Luther King, Jr.

Phillip Wiley wrote in his *Generation of Vipers*, "I have seen captains of industry melt like water at the appearance of a female piece of candy." And for such "pottage", President Clinton committed adultery. That is a sin, *im*pure and simple. It's right there in the Ten Commandments, but it is not right there in the Constitution under the subject of impeachment. In Robert Bolt's *A Man for all Seasons,* Thomas More is urged to arrest a betrayer and More asks what law the villain has broken. "God's law," comes the answer. "Then God can arrest him," says Thomas. Fair enough, the Clinton critics allowed, but the investigation of the president was not about sex. It was about lying and doing so under oath. Of course, it *was* about sex; *lying* about sex is about sex. The gifted American writer John Weaver told me that a friend of his said, "It's not about sex; it's about hate."

Did evasiveness under unwarranted oath about adult *consensual* sex in a meritless sexual *harassment* case constitute perjury? "Yes," said Clinton's bitter enemies. They said Clinton was splitting a legal hair about whether he had committed perjury; that he was relying on a technical definition of "sexual relations"—albeit the definition approved by the judge—when he testified he hadn't had *those* relations with the lady in question. His accusers said he intended to mislead.

In another scene from Bolt's *A Man for all Seasons*, Thomas More remains silent when asked to take an oath that the king is "The Supreme Head of the Church in England." At the trial in which More is accused of criminally denying that the king holds that title, Cromwell, the prosecutor, says More's silence amounted to denial of the title. Whereupon, More efficaciously splits a legal hair himself. "Not so, Master Secretary," More replies:

> The maxim is *Qui tacet consentire.* The maxim of the law is, 'Silence gives consent.' If, therefore, you wish to construe what my silence 'betokened', you must construe that I consented, not denied.

Now Cromwell trumpets:

> Is that what the world in fact construes from it? Do you pretend that is what you *wish* the world to construe from it?

More calmly replies:

> The world can construe according to its wits; this court must construe according to the law.

Ironically, the outside counsel hired to work for the Republican members of the House Judiciary Committee, during the Clinton impeachment deliberations, cited Thomas More in a comment before the Committee. What a choice, inasmuch as both the Clinton case and the More case rested essentially on trumped-up charges..

Did telling the American public lies that resulted in the deaths of tens of thousands of them in Vietnam deserve impeachment? Did telling lies that resulted in the deaths of forty-two U.S. Marines on a Cambodian island deserve impeachment? Did telling lies that resulted in hostage-taking and a few American deaths in Iran deserve impeachment? Did telling lies that resulted in American deaths in Lebanon and Grenada, and telling lies about sending weapons to terrorists deserve impeachment? "Okay," it was said by Clinton's critics, "the lies about abuse of authority and fatally illegal misuse of our military and diplomatic personnel and our military equipment, may have been worse than lies about a president's sex life, but were the other presidential lies told under oath?" Well, yes, they were told under oath. They were told under the *presidential oath of office.*

> I do solemnly swear (or affirm) that I will faithfully execute the Office of President of the United States......

It is an oath which has much more to do with the subject of impeachment than an oath that probably wasn't violated in a fake civil suit. However, according to the Clinton critics, those other presidents were different. All they did was just wrongfully thrust thousands of their unsuspecting fellow Americans into that cruel cauldron of brutal, terrifying and torture-drenched death—the sort depicted in the movies *war wimps* enjoy.

The presidential oath does not say "wrongfully execute" a president's fellow Americans. It says, "...faithfully execute the Office of President of the United States."

On a gloomy Saturday late in December of 1998, goaded by the Right Wing of their party, the Republicans in the U.S. House, with scant exception, voted to impeach President Clinton. Having the greater number of representatives at the time, they prevailed. There were also scant exceptions to the Democratic vote against impeachment. The handful of exceptions in both parties were members who were generally considered members of their parties in name only.

Only a few months earlier, the champion of the Right Wing in the House had been Speaker Newt Gingrich. Just before the '98 election he had taken a fatal political step by arranging for heavy-handed TV ads about Clinton's affair. The ads backfired and he was fired by the very House members who had been his myrmidons only days before. At that point a remarkable irony occurred.

Having got rid of Gingrich because he wallowed politically in the presidential peccadillo, the congressional Right Wing Clinton-haters proceeded to get rid of *themselves* by doing the same thing. Through the storm of public opposition to it, they raged on to impale themselves with the impeachment of Clinton, dragging their party down to a 32 percent approval in the national polls. They drove Clinton *up* to 80 percent, quite possibly not so much because of public support for the president as public opposition to the excesses of his enemies.

It is my considered judgement that had the congressional haters of Clinton simply let his affair speak for itself, his public approval in the polls, despite the cornucopia of a robust economy, probably would have hovered just below 50 percent as the new year of 1999 arrived. However, immersed in blind hatred, the President's congressional critics could not see the damage they were doing to themselves as they bestowed upon him the "briar patch" he so badly needed. "None is so blind as those who will not see."—Mathew Henry

Thus, in the new year of '99, there would be a Senate trial on the two articles of impeachment adopted by the majority party in the House. It's a good rule of thumb that if they have the votes and want to impeach you, they can always find a reason. The impeachment vote told more about hatred in the U.S. House than sin in the White House.

The first article of impeachment alleged perjury by the president when he was asked about his mutually-consenting sex life before a grand jury. The second alleged obstruction of justice by him in the same matter. Thus, the presidential impeachment of 1999 was the third ever in the United States and the first ever not to allege misconduct in the discharge of official presidential duties. Moreover, the charges the impeachment did allege were quite flimsy.

Lincoln said, "I shall do nothing out of malice. What I deal in is too vast for malice." However, Clinton was impeached by his political enemies in the House. When the president was tried on the trumped-up charges before the 55-45 Republican majority Senate, he was acquitted. Neither of the articles achieved even so much as a 51 percent majority in the more objective and less Right-Wing-fearing "upper body". Conviction required 67 votes.

Just before the House vote, one more of the president's oppressors acknowledged, not just one, but several extra-marital affairs. He was the newly-designated GOP Speaker of the House. When he told his party colleagues in their party conference about his repeated adultery, they gave him a standing ovation. Then, despite public statements to the contrary, they made it clear to him that it would be best if he stepped down—and he did. The oppressors, however, insisted their infidelities were different; they only lied about them under the oath—"before God and all these present"—of their marriage vows. How far off base were adulterers' when any marriage counselor worth salt will say, "Amend your life and go on from there. Spare your spouse the pain of learning about it?"

One might wonder, by the way, just how the Clinton-haters were able to get him under oath in court to talk about his sex life in the first place. Having gobs of money, they filed that sham *sexual harassment* lawsuit—the court threw it out—against him and subpoenaed him to give a deposition about his *consensual* sex life, which was immaterial to the subject of the fake case, anyway. When he was compelled to do so, he did his best to shield his private life without committing perjury. In other words, someone who has some extra money and doesn't like you can file a meritless lawsuit, alleging sexual harassment, against you and force you to navigate between the Scylla of perjury and the Charybdis of telling the world about your most private non-criminal sex life that has nothing to do with sexual harassment. Perjury is not just lying under oath; it requires lying about a fact *material* to the issue or issues in the case. Do we need better rules governing the filing of such suits? Obviously. If it can be done to a president, to whom can it not be done?

During the political pillorying of Clinton for his extra-marital affair, one of the high officials in the Republican Party who acknowledged having had such affairs was a very good friend of mine and I hurt for his hurt. Just as some Republicans had been attacking Clinton, some Democrats began attacking my Republican friend, moving Kin Hubbard's worthy *Indianapolis News* successor Wendell Trogdon to write in his *QUIPS* column of Sep.5, 1998:

> Sexual affairs are personal—except when they happen
> to someone in the other political party.

In an interview by lawyer-entertainer-host Mark Shaw on Indianapolis radio station *WMYS*, I was asked about the so-called public scandals of the two officials and gave this response:

> They are both friends of mine and my heart goes out to them and their families in their embarrassments. It's been years since I've heard anyone recite that 'to err is human; to forgive is divine.' As for these Democratic and Republican friends of mine, I think they have had enough trouble without having to put up with pious pronouncements by the self-seeking and sanctimonious politicians who are 'piling on.' My father said, 'Some people's hearts are so filled with virtue that there is no room left for charity.' And, by the way, here's another American family value: MYOB, *Mind your own business.*

Mark asked about the book I was writing and if he would be in it—and here he is. Way to go, Mark.

When asked on another radio call-in program if I was just "carrying water for Clinton," I reminded the caller that I had also condemned unfair partisan attacks on Dan Quayle, adding, "I'm not carrying water for anyone; I'm pouring water on the fires of the hypocritical sanctimony that inspired the song, *Harper Valley PTA.*"

Franklin D. Roosevelt, whose extra-marital affair was also a matter of *press discretion,* said:

> Governments can err, presidents do make mistakes, but the immortal Dante tells us that the sins of the warm-hearted and the sins of the cold-blooded are weighed in different scales. Better the occasional faults of a government that lives in a spirit of charity, than the consistent omissions of a government frozen in the ice of its own indifference.

Somehow, the extremists who hated Clinton seemed to do so more viscerally than even the extremists who hated Truman, Lincoln and Adams, the elder. With Clinton, the hatred seemed laced with an intense and vicious voyeurism and recklessness never before paraded in the case of presidential peccadilloes. Their clumsy attacks on Clinton's personal life reminded one of the immortal words of '*Brer Bear,* "I'm gona git a big club and knock your head clean off." As for the cruel exposure of Clinton's inappropriate sex lapse, I saw such sadism a few times in my police work. When I ran across undressed people coupling in parked cars, I looked away while they dressed and stayed around only to warn them about what physically dangerous places they had chosen in terms of murderous maniacs. In a few—and very few—similar situations, I saw the outrage of sadistic so-called police officers ordering the unclothed couples into bright headlights in order to accommodate sadists' (what else?) perniciously pornographic voyeurism. Clinton's critics didn't go that far; they couldn't. These latter-day American ayatollahs were kindred spirits of those completely contemptible cops.

William Bennett was appointed by President Reagan to be our drug czar. Whereupon, Mr. Bennett proceeded to squander a large sum of tax money in his fanciful and failed project to make Washington, D.C. drug-free—drug use went up there. Later, he appointed *himself* keeper of everyone else's morals. As with Santa, he knew when you'd "been good or bad." In frustration over another failure, that of the voyeur special prosecutor to oust Clinton from office, Bennett wrote a book entitled, *The Death of Outrage...,* denouncing Americans for failure to join Kenneth Starr in peeking through keyholes. In Bennett's own case, the *birth* of outrage was a little slow in arriving. One can find no record of his being the least bit outraged over President Reagan's lying to the public about slipping those weapons to the terrorists at taxpayers' expense a few years before.

A friend of mine was outraged over the Clinton affair and told me so in no uncertain terms. I asked him if, while married, he had ever been tempted to make love to another woman. He bristled at the suggestion, saying, "Certainly not. I love Mary and I'll never be tempted to be unfaithful." "Then," said I, "you really don't get any credit for resisting temptation, do you? Perhaps rather than concerning yourself with other people's sins, you should be thanking God for the blessing of your own good marriage." I said much the same thing in an interview at the television station where my wife, Kim, was an on-the-air talent:

> Benjamin Franklin said, 'Where there is marriage without love, there will be love without marriage.' Some of us find it easier than others to be faithful to our wives. But, let's face it: Not everyone can be married to Kim Hood.

That was my wife Kim's maiden name and her professional one as well and I figured the Channel Thirteen audience could understand what I meant. This was a good *promo* for Kim, too.

In this book, though clearly I have expressed strong beliefs and consequent views, I have done my best to apply those beliefs and views evenhandedly without regard to party affiliation. Keeping faith with that approach, it is my considered opinion that when Clinton's critics gave up on finding wrongdoing by him in the *Whitewater* ballyhoo and, in desperation, stooped to the use of prosecuting authority to delve into his sex life, they hit him below the belt—so to speak—and did the same to our legal system.

An old joke about unsavory prosecutors had them charging political adversaries with spitting on the sidewalk. Two of my good friends in the House, one a Republican and the other a Democrat, were indicted on trumped-up charges by their respective political adversaries who had managed to become United States Attorneys. When the respective cases at long last went to juries, acquittals snapped back like rubber bands. The personal prejudices of those prosecutors, by a sufficient standard of decency, should have disqualified them from participation in the decision of whether prosecution was warranted.

The transmogrification of American blind justice into twenty-twenty telescopic targeting of political foes had been the sadistic fun essentially of one faction by the late 90s, but it could backfire. In the *Merchant of Venice,* Portia warns, "....'twill be recorded for a precedent and many an error, by its example, will rush into the state." Once the evil genie of official injustice slips the seal of the bottle, an entire society is in jeopardy.

It is well known how Hitler's splinter party was the laughing stock of Germany and yet gradually positioned itself to take over by murdering the leaders of its opposition. Less familiar is how the Nazis got away with those murders *before* they took over. Not complicated. While the World War I allies were busy taking foolishly vengeful and cruel reprisals against Germany at Versailles, they overlooked the German judiciary which was left intact. That judiciary was right up Hitler's cutthroat alley. When his thugs murdered opposition political leaders on public streets in broad daylight, they were arrested and taken to those courts. However, in the manner of American Southern juries during the civil rights struggle, the courts routinely turned the cold-blooded killers loose so that Hitler's "grizzly gang" could continue to "work his wicked will."—Churchill

The hijacking of the American judicial system for use as a political weapon was a straw in the wind that blew far beyond any particular political adversary and could become a tornado, even a holocaust. No one should be so foolish as to believe it couldn't happen here. Remember Secretary John Hay's amazement at, "....public acceptance of a concise impropriety." The most permissive authority in our society is the general public which, because of hapless neglect, can be made " playthings in an hour and victims forever." A fair and independent American judiciary broke down during the scourge of *Reconstruction,* but administered in its intended form, it is by far our strongest bulwark of freedom. In the late 1990s, we were heading down a dangerous road winding through Puritan Salem, *The Harper Valley PTA* and the cruel, sexist Taliban government in Afghanistan. Be careful, America, be very careful.

In the spring of 1999, Independent Counsel Kenneth Starr testified before Congress that he favored discontinuation of the Independent Counsel law. Many commentators were surprised. Not I.. The Far Right could very well have envisioned a time when, as mentioned above, the tables could be turned, when there might be a Republican president and a Democratic congress with a Democratic independent counsel to scratch out a premise for impeachment. From the Right's point of view, to be on the safe side, it would be wise to preclude a future use of their misused tool for the purpose of retaliation. Some say that "turn about is fair play." Not always. Turn about is not fair play when the act involved was not fair in the first place. Two wrongs don't make a right. If the tables ever were turned, we should hope that Democrats will heed the Biblical command to "render not violence for violence done." If, under reversed circumstances, Democrats decline retaliation, they will be serving their country well.

By March of '99, no doubt weary from the battle of the sex and dashing the *New Hope* that titled this chapter, President Clinton succumbed and plunged us illegally into the cauldron of war. This time it was Yugoslavia. Once more an American president had elected to violate the American Constitution by borrowing money to borrow trouble in somebody else's war. I was sadly disappointed in him.

Was it or was it not war? In the manner of the downtown property owner who, in evaluating his property, says one thing to his banker and another thing to Center Township Assessor Jim Maley, when it came to how our Yugoslav-captured American soldiers were to be treated, the Administration insisted we were at war. When it came to Article One, Section Eight of the Constitution, which requires a declaration by Congress to go to war, the Administration insisted we were not at war.

American history was repeating. In 1954, as senate majority leader, Lyndon Johnson had understood and advised Eisenhower to stay out of Vietnam. Later, however, as president, himself, Johnson forgot history's lessons—and his own, for that matter, caved-in to please American chicken hawks and brought about the tragedy of *Vietnam* for his nation and himself. Now it was President Bill Clinton who, as a college student, had understood about Vietnam and, as president, had understood about Bosnia and showed restraint, but chose to satisfy the firebrands by ordering Air Force bombing of Yugoslavia.

The phrasemongers of our federal government dubbed it *Operation Allied Force* as distinguished from *reason*. The more accurate name would have been *Operation Briar Patch.* As was the case with Iraqi leader Saddam Hussein, the Vietnamese leader Ho Chi Mien and the British leader Winston Churchill, massive bombing could only have been expected to make the Yugoslav leader Slobodan Milosevic more popular inside most of his country. Hitler's bombing of London didn't cause British subjects to be angry with Churchill. When it comes to bombing, from the bomb-ee's point of view, "what you see is what you get" mad at. And what you see is the nationality of the aircraft dropping the bombs.

"Always," Franklin Roosevelt declared, "will we remember the onslaught against us." He was talking about the only air raid ever carried out against the United States. We didn't like it. Still don't: "Remember Pearl Harbor."

Because of European circumstances peculiar to the time, the assassination of Archduke Francis Ferdinand in Sarajevo triggered World War I. On the limp logic that all cottage cheese is made in cottages and that nothing about Europe had changed in three quarters of a century, President Clinton triggered the first air war ever by NATO against the central government of a sovereign European nation. He argued that not to do so would result in a conflagration that would spread all across Europe. Of course, in order to believe that masterpiece of superficial logic, one would have to believe that U.S. failure to bomb Yugoslavia would mean that a modern and democratic Germany would invade France and other countries in the neighborhood.

Conceding that Yugoslavia had committed no aggression against another country—unlike Hitler's Germany, there was almost no chance it would or could—the president pointed out that Yugoslavia had moved brutally to put down a rebellion by those of Albanian descent within the Yugoslav borders in the province of Kosovo, the Yugoslav army torching villages along the way. The president implied that we were entitled to a high moral tone with Yugoslavia because we'd never do a thing like that, if you didn't count General William T. Sherman's picnic at the seashore— "getting there is half the fun." "Okay," the president would tell us, "but the Yugoslavs are committing genocide." God knows we'd never do a thing like that; just ask any native American.

The implication the Administration gave was that, in their rebellion, the Kosovo rebels didn't murder innocent civilians and commit other acts of terrorism. That implication was false. Both sides in that civil war had been ruthless. The Serbs were wolves in wolves' clothing and Kosovo rebels were wolves in Clinton Administration-tailored sheep's clothing. The principal difference between the two was that, like Lincoln's North in our civil war, Belgrade was the stronger. Also, there was one other thing. One of the constantly changing reasons Secretary of State James Baker gave for our war against Iraq was oil. It was a cynical and selfish reason for bringing about the deaths of more than two hundred young Americans who could no longer even walk to the grocery in lieu of gasoline for there cars. Not even a selfish economic factor was involved in the Balkan bailiwick of this newest enemy we chose. If human rights was the reason for picking that new enemy, why had our government shirked the Turks? Turkey's suppression of the Kurdish rebels made Kosovo seem almost mild. Turkey, however, was *our* son-of-a-bitch. Had we bombed there, we would have been bombing some of our own air bases. Selective morality is contrived morality, usually used for justification.

Beyond the arrogance of borrowing money to borrow trouble in other people's wars, was the question of military effectiveness. The president's misuse of authority only added to the agony. In the process, NATO bombs killed three Chinese officials when, because of the use of an outdated map, a pilot was ordered to bomb an unintended taget, the Chinese embassy in Belgrade which he hit with deadly accuracy. The Chinese and Russians had already voiced their strong opposition to the NATO raids. Killing an archduke in Sarajevo in 1999 was not likely to start a world war, but slaughtering three officials from the largest nation on Earth at the hands of NATO might knock some dust off the dove.

Some military varieties endure despite progress in the dark art of what my grandfather called "machines of terror." If you don't count the apocalyptic nuking of an already mostly exhausted Japan, terror from high in the air was hard-pressed to stop land armies, especially one like Yugoslavia's, extensively deployed in mountains and forests with a lot of bad weather to boot. The horrible and painful way you defeat such armies is to get on what my Marine combat infantry commander called "Nick and Charley" and march across the objective, suffering and dying along the way. Hundreds of civilian human beings in Yugoslavia were killed or frightfully injured by our bombs. In one instance, an accidental bombing blew up 47 Yugoslav civilians on a passenger train. The next morning, amid scrambled eggs, French toast and coffee, eerily echoing the words of Rudyard Kipling quoted on the title page of this book, the NATO ministers said they "regretted the loss of life."

It was troubling and soul-searching to contemplate essentially one-way killing and destruction from the air. One could not help wondering about a day of reckoning some day. The tactic of the technologically weak belligerent is terrorism, bombs furtively delivered by car or truck. The tactic of the technologically strong belligerent is terror from thousands of feet up. Call it *airrorism.*

On another occasion when the *War Wimps* were after him to pull the lanyard of unnecessary war, I wrote to the president, "Those who are urging this foolishness on you would be the first to criticize you if the things they advocate would go badly." And sure enough, the prediction proved painfully prophetic in the case of Kosovo during that first blush of spring, 1999. The criticism from the amateur agitators was as zany as their initial advice—"the president should have acted (bombed?) sooner. Well, he should send in ground troops," throwing good resources after bad in the manner of Las Vegas. Since the president had acceded to the ill-conceived advice about bombing, Yugoslavs could not be certain he would not do the same when it came to sending U.S. infantry personnel which held the potential of being disastrous for both sides.

Well worth the cost, the Administration's stately hawk, Ms. Albright, insisted. She said we were bombing Yugoslavia into democracy. Not so. In fact, just the opposite. Before the NATO attacks, Milosevic had plenty of *Serb* opposition, replete with public demonstrations and a local election victory for his opponents. Then NATO became the villain. Did this advance Yugoslav democracy? On the contrary, NATO bombing—90% U.S. financed and done—managed to set democracy back a long way in that brutal and hard to understand land..

At the beginning of the summer as the dust settled NATO had managed only to exacerbate the Kosovo suffering and extend it throughout Yugoslavia. Milosevic had pretty much achieved his dastardly goals on the ground in Kosovo. The diplomats seemed headed toward a settlement of the war, pretty much along the lines of the settlement NATO was offered by the Yugoslavs but rejected as insufficient before the bombing ever started. Hundreds of Yugoslav civilians, including Kosovars had been blown away by NATO's increasingly reckless and merciless bombing. In frustration over their failure quickly to vanquish the Yugoslavs, our fearless NATO leaders began expanding their defintion of "military targets" to include television stations, urban bridges and even the electric and water supplies to the civilian population. Most of those NATO ministers were heirs to the Allied bombing of the strictly civilian city of Dresden in World War II. Then, as in 1999, there was only one purpose in such savagery from the side that claimed to be civilized, to demoralize the civilian population. In the midst of the rubble and the broken, lifeless bodies of babies at the long-distant hands of NATO and the consequent hatred of NATO by Yugoslavs, it seemed likely that Milosevic would be politically stronger than ever and more easily able to crack down on dissent. All this was paid for with money borrowed from Social Security. The Administration had managed to use our country's nest egg to lay an egg.

It was easy to predict that once the settlement was in place, both sides would begin spinning their yarns of victory. The truth—always the first casualty of war—was that in the manner the song, *Nobody Wins in the Game of Broken Hearts*, neither side had won. That is always the case with a compromise settlement. Using the logic of Bill Mauldin's little boy catoon character who said, "Wars is impossible unless both sides is right [sic]," compromise settlements of wars are impossible unless both sides can say they won.

Were the Kosovo rebels villains? Yes. Was Milosevic a villain? Absolutely. It's a shame that we became the same. On NATO's part, where selective morality had looked the other way when it came to intense cruelty by the Turks, the decision to rain devastation on the civilians of Yugoslavia involved a lot of ego. "Pride goeth before destruction, and an [sic] haughty spirit goeth before a fall (of bombs)."—Proverbs.

It is interesting to note how Democrats think Democratic presidents do God's work when they order people slaughtered and Republicans tend to think the same when Republican presidents do it while each political side discovers the Constitution, common sense and morality when presidents of the other party deal in death. Call it Pavlovian politics.

I liked President Clinton and for a long time gloried in his political courage when it came to rejecting unconstitutional and unnecessary war. I think he deserved credit for all those other displays of wise restraint, but there is no way around his responsibility for the decision to bomb Yugoslavia. His desire to do something about Kosovo should not have led to his willingness to try anything. In terms of his foreign policy record, the bombing didn't "spoil it all," but it spoiled a lot of it. And what did it profit him?

10

THE GREATEST WASTE

The witness has just testified that he went to "witness school." Attorney Jud Haggerty cross-examines:

> What did they teach you there?
> They *taught* me to tell the truth!
> How long did it take?

If an adult has to be taught to tell the truth, he probably won't learn it. The same goes for frugality. Truth and frugality should be innate.

Government frugality is a way of thinking, or rather a way of not having to think about it much at all. It should be second nature, a way of sensing the unnecessary, the waste in small things as well as large. It is a sense of not imposing on people with whose tax money government officials are entrusted. "There are two kinds of people," said *The Manchurian Candidate,* "those who upon entering a room automatically turn a television set on and those who automatically turn it off."

If you want to know about waste at the Department of Health and Human Services, best not ask a "Liberal". If you want to know about waste at the Pentagon, don't waste time with a "Conservative".

When I first went to Washington to serve Indianapolis in the United States House of Representatives, I craned my neck every time a chauffeured government automobile went by. I wanted to see which important official was in the back seat with the bed lamp over his shoulder, frowning in what often turned out to be feigned lucubration. Later I learned that, nine times out of ten, the rider was nobody but a sub-cabinet-level bureaucrat, who, when he arrived at the office would put aside his urgent reading and take a coffee break. When I offered an amendment to delete from an appropriation bill limousines for U.S. House leaders, Representative Chet Holifield from California took exception. This is the American Bankers Association account of the House Floor debate:

Holifield: I am just amazed at the statement the gentleman just
             made...Every bureaucrat downtown has a car and he has a
             driver, if he is in any kind of position of importance in the
             executive bureau...Here we are, the greatest legislative body
             in the world, advised to deny our leadership an automobile
             and a driver. How penny-pinching can you get?
Jacobs: The gentleman asked the question—how penny-pinching can
             you get?
Holifield: That is exactly what I asked.
Jacobs: I do not know, but I do not have many constituents who
             regard limousines and chauffeurs as being in the penny-pinch-
             ing category.
Holifield: I doubt if your constituents have the dignity and leadership
             and responsibility of the leaders of the House of Representa-
             tives.
Jacobs: I thank the gentleman very much for his compliment to my
             people. A man is dignified, not according to his car and ser-
             vant, but according to how he behaves—not according to
             what he has—at taxpayers' expense—but according to what
             he is.
Holifield: (silence)

Representative Adam Clayton Powell was severely punished for con-
verting to his personal use airline tickets supplied by the taxpayers, but
in the so-called reform One Hundred Fourth Congress, U.S. House Members were the only ones in the Legislative or Executive branch who
arrogated to themselves the personal use of frequent flier airline tickets
issued as volume discounts for tax-paid official air travel. The chief House
reformer, who said his wife used the bonus tickets accrued from his
official travel, called challenges to the inexcusable practice a "Mickey
Mouse" issue. I, on the other hand, smelled a rat. Had I swiped the
frequent flier tickets issued by the airlines in consequence of my travel
back and forth between Indianapolis and Washington, the practice would
have cost the taxpayers one thousand two hundred dollars a year. Some
mouse. Lots of waste.

Star Wars™ might be a great movie, but it has been a wasteful program for the taxpayers. A while back, the profit-making contractors and
the Pentagon tested the antimissile systems over the Pacific and brought
back dramatically successful results. That's great—except for one thing:
the tests were faked. According to a *New York Times* article by Flora
Lewis, one of the scientists directly involved said after the so-called test,

"Instead of a weapon, we have a toy." But the incumbent President was a believer and the program plowed on through the pocketbooks of America. In the entire tragic history of this earth's dark art of war, from the longbow to the French Maginot Line, the shield has almost never kept pace with the sword, but the profiting weavers are still hard at work on this version of *The Emperor's New Clothes.*

One could argue that in the federal budget scheme of things, cars and airline tickets don't make much of an impact, but in terms of examples, they speak libraries about what is or is not seriously expected of employees farther down the pecking order of government service. Former Representative Chuck Brownson of Indiana said the 1969 Congressional pay grab (41% increase when the five-year cumulative inflation had been only 14%) was one of the most expensive things the government did that year, not because of the specific amount directly involved, but because of the example. Sometimes little things really do mean a lot.

A president can make radical changes in this high-end welfare for high-level Washington workers, but probably only if that president is willing to start with him or herself. Mark Twain said, "To do good is noble; to advise others to do good is also noble—and much less trouble." But cutting waste at the White House would be an insufficient example if only symbolic. Lyndon Johnson turned out unused lights at the Executive Mansion and Jimmy Carter carried his own suitcase, but those gestures didn't have much effect.

If you wish to lead by example, it must be substantive example. How about White House employees? "Max, you're dangerously overstaffed," said the Chief in TV's *Get Smart* series. Funny line; compelling concept.

My father was parsimonious without pretense. He taught us that showering could be thriftier and *easier* if we would turn off the flow of water before soaping and back on to rinse. The soaping is handier if one is not standing in a downpour. You waste money and shower less efficiently if you are *overshowered.* And so it is with being overstaffed.

Overstaffing doesn't just waste money; it also wastes the time of an official. And what is worse, it distracts; it interrupts the official's train of thought and hinders effective decision making. Surplus staffers become bored and find or invent useless projects. And when they pelt the official with their foolishness, rejection of their respective proposals requires time and tender diplomacy.

In 1940, 984 people were employed in the executive office of the President. By 1944, with World War II raging and our effort pretty much being managed by the White House, the number was down to 707. (Were some staffers drafted?) In 1980 it was 2,013. In 1992 there were 1,869 and in 1996 the number was 1,559. The Reagan Administration was billed, of course, as more frugal than either the Clinton or Bush Administration, but by 1983, President Reagan had more than doubled the number of highest-paid White House jobs. The Bush Administration ended up with 144 fewer White House Jobs than existed when Reagan entered office. And by the end of the first Clinton term, the number had been reduced by another 310. Good for the Bush and Clinton Administrations, but not good enough. In the early part of the twentieth century, Mr. Eli Lilly was asked how many people worked in his pharmaceutical company. "About half of them," he replied. Does the Executive Office of the President today really need twice the staff F.D.R. used to govern this country and run World War II? Doubtful. Here is a good place for a president to prove she or he is not kidding about cutting waste throughout the government.

Being overstaffed isn't the only pitfall for a president. Watch out for crises. More often than not, they cry wolf and cry out for healthy skepticism. Like Kipling's "triumph and disaster," crises are often imposters. Not tornadoes, floods, or earthquakes; they are real and require real public concern and effort. The fiscal danger lies in the monumental, the monstrous crises; the ones too vast, too abstract, too arcane for mere taxpayers to comprehend.

How could an ordinary mortal citizen understand a crisis that is not war, but the "moral equivalent" of it? That's what Jimmy Carter said about the so-called Energy Crisis. Most people over forty know about a *personal* energy crisis, but the other kind, the big picture energy crisis of the seventies made it easy for government contractors and officials to scare more than a few bucks out of the taxpayers' pockets.

A century and a half ago, Alex DeTouqueville told how, in the government bureaucracies of post-revolutionary France, each department expected its own separate identity and "edifice." And he warned that in the fullness of time, the same could happen to our republic.

Sure enough, like clockwork in 1977, armed with an "Energy Crisis" most people thought was real, but was not, Congress and the White House slipped in a brand-new Department of *Energy*, much of whose energy in the early nineties was devoted to sending its Secretary off on luxurious globe-trotting junkets.

For those amused by Anderson's tale of *The Emperor's New Clothes* and anything but amused by rip-off profit-making government boondoggles, it's hard to beat the governments' Synfuels Corporation, which began picking American pockets on July 30, 1980. The scheme, not to say "scam", gave huge sums of tax money to contractors who in turn were supposed to beat oil out of rocks. Dave Stockman, then a U.S. Representative and later budget chief in the Reagan Administration, pointed out that improving the gas mileage of the American fleet of motor vehicles by just one and one half miles per gallon would equal the tax-paid annual output of ten multi-billion-dollar synthetic fuels operations.

It took about five and a half years for the public to realize that the energy crisis was pretty much synthetic itself and that in this latter-day version of the famous fairy tale, the emperor was once again a streaker. After squandering more than six billion of the taxpayers' dollars, the rip-off was repealed on December 19, 1985. Merry Christmas.

In 1979, it was the Department of *Education* without which we could not do. Ten years after that, big government got bigger when the politicians proved their love for veterans by saddling the public, veterans and non-veterans alike, with a Department of *Veterans Affairs*. Alex DeTouqueville, I salute you. I am prepared to believe that if, in some future year, more people than usual catch the flu, some fool will want to show concern for the beloved voters by creating a Department of the *Common Cold*, insisting that the crisis is nothing to sneeze at—just something to go deeper in debt over.

Elected officials seem to sense that no matter what the crisis, real, imagined or contrived, they must, in the paraphrased words of Shepherd Mead, "either do something or seem to do something." And drive up the debt.

Two missile gaps, neither of which ever existed, resulted in our borrowing enormous sums to catch up with the Russians who were never able to keep up with our normal pace in the first place.

Although the budget for Congress itself, the money used to run the legislative branch, is only 0.13% of the entire federal budget, that thirteen hundredths can include some real whoppers.

Behold the case of the "Bugtusle Building" which, because of God's mercy, was never actually built. In 1975, there was wide bipartisan agreement, both in the House and in some newspapers, that taxpayers should put up the money and put up with a fourth U.S. House office building to be named for the former Speaker, Carl Albert. It was to be named the *Carl Albert Building,* but we can call it the Bugtusle one because that's where he was born in Oklahoma.

The magnificent structure was to be situated on New Jersey Avenue just south of the old Congressional hotel. Price tag? Fully equipped including a Tunerville Trolley tunnel to the U.S. Capitol so deep that it would pass under the regular full sized railroad tunnel which goes beneath the Cannon office building: five hundred million 1975 dollars.

A congressional hearing was conducted to obtain expert advice about how the building should be built and how the offices and committee chambers should be laid out. The experts, of course, were members of Congress, but the experts did not agree on how the project should be done. With only two exceptions, however, all the Congressional witnesses agreed that the project *should* be done.

Staffers were inhumanely crowded into the existing three office buildings according to one newspaper editorial. Here we have what I call the Parkinson's Law of Architecture: first the unnecessary expansion of staff, then the unnecessary expansion of facilities to house the additional staff together with thousands of additional square feet of expanded grandeur.

Despite a thirteen percent increase in House membership from 1906 to 1932, the House got along pretty well with just one office building. In 1932, the Longworth Building with 251 additional offices was constructed. A thirteen percent increase in the number of representatives and a seventy-five percent increase in the number of offices. There was no increase at all in the House membership between 1932 and 1965 when the Rayburn Building was erected with its additional 169 offices. Waste, there is thy sting.

Representative Robert Bauman of Maryland and I were the only witnesses at the 1975 congressional hearing who had the temerity to suggest that the representatives could get along all right with the three office buildings they already had. And the pocketbooks of the people they represented could get along even better.

Did the government need that fourth office building as much as the taxpayers needed the price of it? A quarter of a century later, with no Albert Building on the horizon, the answer is fairly obviously no.

During a television interview in the late Eighties, a prominent member of Congress proposed a brand-new program whose price tag was forty billion dollars' worth of *pork* for a couple of companies whose Political Action Committees happened to be campaign contributors. The interviewer asked if the congressman was willing to introduce a tax increase of forty billion dollars to cover the new spending. This is the answer the interviewer got: " We spend forty billion dollars a year in this country just on dog food." Unfortunately, the interviewer failed to ask the next logical question: "Who's going to ask those dogs if they'll give up their food?" The congressman smiled at the omission.

The same congressman declared that the relatively small amount in the 1994 crime legislation for the purpose of beckoning kids away from lives of crime was "pork". One might conclude from this that his definition of "pork" was any government spending from which a campaign contributor could not derive a profit.

One caveat. We should take care not to condemn as waste that which most people, given the facts, would agree is *not* waste. Sometimes a fully worthy government project can, on the surface, sound silly. A while back, the *Washington Star* editorially denounced a government grant for mosquito research. Sounded silly, but a short time later, the paper ran a second editorial apologizing for the first. With that grant, Dr. Walter Reed had discovered the cure for malaria.

Malaria, unfed children, flood, famine and earthquake are crises. Trumped-up troubles to "make government machinery hit the jackpot" for contractors are not.

Another kind of waste is worth mentioning, wasted opportunity. In 1997 there were about eighteen million U.S. children between birth and kindergarten growing like weeds in dirt ignorance. Deprived of sufficient tutelage to develop auditory skills, they would be unable to learn to read efficiently and, therefore they would not learn job-qualifying skills and many of them would likely lack the most basic requirement of civilization, self-control. If you know how many such children are growing without civilizing influence today, you also know what the impersonal street crime rate will be fifteen years hence. This disaster could be averted at a small cost to the taxpayers. The kind of appeal that attracted volunteers to the Peace Corps and Vista could staff an effective, cognitive preschool program for educationally disadvantaged children, to "shape the twigs so the trees grow straight."

Of course the "great-granddaddy" of all government waste is borrowing money to borrow trouble in other countries' wars. If a Congress chooses to do this, it is ill-advised; if a President chooses to do so, it is illegal.

11

MAD MATH

There will be wars and rumors of wars. Not being a cynic, I'm not so sure about that. I am, however, quite sure about this: The apocalyptic prophecy is more likely to be validated when those we suppose to be educated and intelligent declare that war is a reasonable means by which "to acheive clearly definable aims."

Have you ever seen two grown men in a bare-knuckle fist fight on a public sidewalk? Probably not. If you ever did, what would your reaction be? Shock? Disgust? Insecurity? Probably all three. Most people would consider such behavior a primitive, even psychotic way to deal with dispute. Yet, multiply those two men by tens of thousands, and intensify the violence by tons of dynamite, steel and gunpowder with the resultant quantums of blood, viscera, stone-cold rigor mortis and corresponding broken hearts back home, and frail wise men like writer George Will will vicariously celebrate such madness, itself, as "a profession."*

Go figure.

* see Chapter 7, page 112

EPILOGUE

ROLE CALL

Travelers are often asked, "Did you meet any interesting people?" My geographical travel was by air and, in another sense, it was mostly *pedestrian*. It was between Indianapolis and Washington and there's not a lot to report about looking down on cloud formations from 33,000 feet. I can't help you with foreign and exotic places because I never took a junket—if you don't count that one trip I took to Korea at public expense when I was a frightened and sparsely-fed teenage Marine.

On the other hand, I found my philosophical travel through a third of a century of public life was fascinating. I met people who were interesting, warm and wonderful. They played noble and significant roles in our country's progress and my congressional duties.

Belgian poet Maurice Maeterlinck wrote:

> At every crossway on the road that leads to the future, each progressive spirit is opposed by a thousand men appointed to guard the past. Let us have no fear lest the fair towers of former days be sufficiently defended. The least that the most timid among us can do is not to add to the immense dead weight which nature drags along.
>
> Let us not say to ourselves that the best truth lies in moderation, in the decent average. This would perhaps be so if the majority of (people) did not think on a much lower plane than is needful. That is why it behooves others to think on a higher plane than seems needful. The average, the decent moderation of today, will be the least human of things tomorrow. At the time of the Spanish Inquisition, the opinion of good sense and of the good medium was certainly that people ought not to burn too large a number of heretics; extreme and

unreasonable opinion obviously demanded that they should burn none at all....

We have read in this book about extraordinary people who played major roles in the political struggle for common sense in U.S. foreign policy. There were others who played various roles in the effort toward peace, too. In the following pages, I'd like to take you for a walk through my personal hall of acclaim and briefly introduce some of them to you. In the process, perhaps we can sing some unsung heroes.

This is George Grider. I met him in 1965 as he and I were sworn in as freshmen in the 89th Congress. He was from Tennessee, but you might find his look-alike seated on a cane chair in a Hoosier general store, unwittingly endangering his life by smoking a down-home pipe. He had the aura of a wise and kindly father. You might not guess that he was an authentic American hero of World War II. He was. A graduate of the United States Naval Academy, he commanded two of our submarines, Flasher and Cubera and won the Navy Cross for heroism in the Pacific. Many times he and his crew narrowly escaped watery graves. He spoke quietly, but with complete self-assurance. He joined with others to give our country Medicare which, though not without some small problems, has solved momentous problems for tens of millions of Americans and their working children. No member of Congress was more greatly respected, nor deserved it more. He added his prestige to the struggle for common sense regarding Vietnam.

By remarkable coincidence another new congressman from Tennessee in '65 had also been a submarine commander. In his naval service, he had a *first* as well. Freshman Representative Bill Anderson of Tennessee was also highly decorated as a World War II naval officer and was an Annapolis graduate. He commanded the nuclear submarine *Nautilus* on its historic voyage beneath the polar icecap. Sandburg called the ship, "that marvel of the sea." Pre-nuclear subs were properly called boats, but the "marvel" rated the title, *ship*. As we have seen, during the Nixon Administration Bill discovered the tiger cages operated as torture chambers by our regime in the south of Vietnam. He was remarkably like his seafaring congressional colleague from the landlocked state of Tennessee. Quiet-spoken, modest to a fault, he was the picture of political courage and spoke out quietly and effectively against the foolishness of sending U.S. expeditionary forces to make war in that third world nation.

Let's stay in the same time warp and go to an Indianapolis Methodist Church on the banks of Fall Creek. The pastor was a handsome young man with the gift of spellbinding discourse. His voice was sonorous and his conscience was clear. He was headed for trouble because he was an apostle of peace, one of God's special own. Though his talents made everyone believe he would be the next Methodist bishop of Washington, D.C., he was sent to the Dakotas where his arresting words against Lyndon Johnson's and Richard Nixon's unconstitutional Vietnam War were less likely to embarrass his Christian church nationally. Obviously, his witness for peace is no embarrassment to Jesus Christ, the *Prince of Peace*. We saw Jim Armstrong during the Nixon Administration, standing with quiet Quakers on the steps of the U.S. House to remind congresspeople that the young Americans they so casually condemned to Southeast Asian graves, had names and mothers and fathers and siblings and wives and sweethearts. In the end Jim Armstrong paid an awful price for preaching the Gospel of peace in specific terms. His reward, a celestial mansion, will await completion of his earthly scourge.

Allard Lowenstein spoke soft words and spread the joy of humor with a bright twinkle in his eyes. He gave his life to, and, by assassination, lost his life for our country. Because of his "Dump Johnson" movement in 1968, he, more than any other, deserves credit for beginning the process that ended the madness of America's unnecessary expedition to Vietnam. He was a civil saint who was there for all the demands of social justice and governmental frugality, especially with the lives of young citizens. He was among the first of the college professors to lead student civil rights workers into the racially segregated cauldron of the old Confederacy. He and Martin Luther King were close. Al led a UN sanctioned and dangerous investigation in Namibia and gave a persuasive report to the world body, eventually expanding that report into a book, *Brutal Mandate*. He brought good counsel to many other third world countries. He sacrificed wealth, comfort and a happy home for the cause of justice. The number of lives he saved can never be exactly calculated—but that number is vast. On Friday, March 14, 1980, the last day of the workweek, Al did his last earthly work. He was assassinated in the city of New York by a demented follower who believed Al arranged to install radio equipment in the assassin's teeth. In Allard Lowenstein, the world has another martyr together with memories of him and copies of his wisely written words.

Back home again in Indiana was the immortal Andrew Brown, long the pastor of St. John's Missionary Baptist Church. He was the Martin Luther King of Indiana. In fact, as an ally of King's, he headed the Southern Christian Leadership chapter of Indiana. In World War II, he served his country as a soldier and then came home to ingratitude and further oppression because of the pigmentation in which God clothed him. In helping to lead the struggle against the national hypocrisy of racism and the national blunder of Vietnam, he never lost his gentle ways, nor his sense of humor which was scintillating. There was that cherub-like face, always on the verge of a puckish smile. When he headed for heaven, he not only left his examples and wise words, but also Rosalie, his delightful widow and his brilliant minister-son Tommy Brown, both of whom continued the work for social justice, examples of excellence in education and peace on earth.

This one is not Fredric Douglas, but you could be pardoned for thinking so. Father Boniface Harden was the living and stunning image of the immortal leader. Father Boniface had some of the same kind of trouble the Rev. Jim Armstrong suffered. Boniface was very early with his outspoken opposition to the U.S. policy in Vietnam. It meant trouble for him from his church. Yet he regrouped and established a significant institution of higher learning, Martin University of Indiana.

Interesting—is it not?—that all these wonderful people had one thing in common, that Christian humility and gentleness without a trace of arrogance. It has been said that "Absolute positiveness is uncertainty at the top of its voice." Absolute positiveness is arrogance and, of course, arrogance and stupidity usually produce the same result.

Now let's welcome Tony and Phyllis Coelho. They happily met in 1965 when they were, respectively, congressional staffers from California and Indiana. Phyllis was my co-worker and had been for several years in the law office back home. She graduated from Shawswick High in Bedford, Indiana, took the bus to Indianapolis, checked-in to stay with her Aunt Lottie and called on the Indiana Employment Security Division. She was job-hunting and our office turned out to be the hunted. We had registered for a stenographer and Phyllis, in Nixonian terms, "was the one." She was seventeen, sweet, pretty, ten times bright and little, probably not even weighing 90 pounds soaking wet. One day my dad forgot her name—Ms. Butler at the time—and referred to her as "...oh, Miss Muffet." It stuck. During her congressional career she was known as either Muff or Muffi. She was known to be kind, compassionate and efficient. Tony fell in love with her partly because of her Harry Truman style of plain talk and she fell in love with him partly because of his charm and downright brilliance. One evening during their courtship, her Volkswagen stopped dead as they were en route to the movies. Without the slightest sign of distress or even frustration, Tony exalted, Muff hopped out, lifted the engine bonnet, pulled out a hairpin—or some such thing—made a deft connection and they were on their way to the pleasures of popcorn.

Tony worried about something as they headed toward marriage. He had epilepsy and, though it was completely under medical control, well, what would she think? Before he could pop the question, he had to summon the fortitude to drop the bombshell. With commensurate apprehension, he took a deep breath one day and told her, "I have epilepsy." Without hesitation, she replied, "So what?" They will be in love forever—and married. Eventually, Tony ran for Congress, himself, and was successful. One of his opponents tried to make the epilepsy an issue, saying, "Think how embarrassed our district would be if my opponent had a fit at the White House." Tony had a response: "Many people have fits at the White House. At least, I'd have an excuse." Tony rose quickly in the U.S. House, becoming his party's chief whip. His success was a consequence of the fact that, once Phyllis scoffed at his essentially unimportant health anomaly, the possibility of failure never even entered his mind. Columnist James J. Kilpatrick, generally not in sympathy with Tony's political philosophy, was so taken with Tony that he wrote *two* laudatory national columns in a row about this brainy and eternal optimist. Both Phyllis and Tony did their parts in helping to bring about an end of the Vietnam War.

Look at these two ladies, Nancy Land and Marky Scott of Indianapolis. They were, among other things, letter writers—letter writers "to the editor." Their use of English, irony and humor was devastating. Thank God it was always used on the side of a sensible U.S. foreign policy..

Over here is Sally Crow whose face is the proverbial map of Ireland, framed so beautifully by such lovely red hair. She was from the old sod, sounded it and told members of congress where to go, that is, if they wanted to eat. Ms. Crow ran the U.S. House restaurant. She always had a cheerful word of wise philosophy and words of praise for everyone—if you don't count the tyrant representative, Wayne Hays of Ohio. ("He's a dreadful man.") She, too, saw the foolishness of Vietnam and wasn't afraid to say so.

Now we come to another World War II hero. Jim Corman was a Marine Corps infantryman who fought on Iwo Jima and came home to become one of our nation's best public servants. First, he served as a city councilman in Los Angeles, then it was on to Congress. He arrived a couple of years before I did and was about the only "upperclassman" who greeted me warmly without the slightest hint of an *old salt's* condescension. If ever the extremely poor, the one's without PAC's (political action committees) had a voice in Congress, it was his. Our friend Bill Archer who chaired the House Ways and Means Committee, said to me, "There is almost nothing Jim Corman and I agree about politically, but he is one of my favorite people." That was because of Jim's friendly disposition and kindly attitude for everyone, even the presidents against whose unconstitutional wars he so tirelessly worked as a member of Congress.

The man standing next to the barber chair with comb and scissors in hand had the appearance of a barber. He was, at least for the purpose of making a living, but he was something else, too. M.C. Hansburough was an encyclopedic historian, albeit without portfolio. If it's Twentieth Century American history, especially the political side of it, M.C. could tell you about it, at the drop of a lock of hair. In the early days of the American war in Vietnam, he sometimes was too candid about his opposition to the policy for his own wellbeing as an employee of the U.S. House. However, that wasn't the only reason he was resented by some of his bosses, the members of Congress who were blowhard supporters of the Vietnam policy and knew little about history. Many were the times when I'd be seated in the House barber shop awaiting M.C.'s professional service, when one of the stuffed shirts would make a dead-wrong assertion about American history. M.C. would never correct such backward members' ignorance about America's background, but once in a while they would catch the wink of amusement he would flash to others present. Eventually, the tin horns managed to force him out of his job. They were not, however, able to force him out of his U.S. Capitol. He spent a lot of time there to the even greater consternation of those officials who presume to make history without ever reading history. If you had the time, he would also tell you anything you wanted to know about American jazz music. Tall and most distinguished-looking he was a delight to know and devoted to ending the Vietnam War.

Look at this handsome fellow. He's an Adonis, fair-haired with classic features and a slender athletic form. You might think Don Edwards hailed from the sunny lotus land of California and you'd be right. A former FBI agent, he brought to Congress a soothing civility which melted the hearts of even those who disagreed strongly with his polite but firm opposition to the presidential wars. He also melted the heart of a tall, statuesque beauty. I played a small role in their romance and marriage. She was Edie Wilkie from the Brahmin end of New York. Brainy, progressive and principled, she was the executive director of the Capitol Hill organization, *Members of Congress for Peace Through Law,* whose purpose was to do research and suggest conflict resolutions that did not require death or dismemberment.

One evening at about nine when the House was still in session, Congressman Don Edwards turned to me and, indicating a woman in the gallery, said, "I think she is as perfect as God allows." To which I replied, "Why tell me? Tell her." "Oh no, Andy," Don the Adonis too modestly said, "She'd never be interested in me." I shrugged and called on Cervantes: "Well, 'Faint heart ne'er won fair lady'." About a half hour later, having become painfully bored by the repetitious House debate, I wandered down to the House Restaurant where Sally Crow said in her lovely lilt, "Take any table you wish, Congressman." The table I wished was the one at which Edie Wilkie and her friend Debbie happened to be seated. I was acquainted with them both and as I approached, I asked Edie what she thought of Don Edwards. "He's wonderful," she effused with dreamy eyes. "Please don't go away," I said, "I'll be right back." Whereupon, I climbed the steps to the second floor, entered the House chamber and found Don with eyes that were also dreamy, but in a different way from Edie's. The so-called debate was putting him to sleep. I rousted him and said he looked as if he could use a cup of coffee. Whereupon, he accompanied me to the restaurant where I declared the almost empty room to be crowded. "Why don't we sit here?" I suggested. "Here", of course, was at Edie's table. As we sat down, an engaging grin crept across Don's face. That was about all there was to it. They left the Capitol together that night and never parted. Close friends of Al Lowenstein, they were an enormously important team in the effort to bring our country to its senses about Vietnam.

Here is another handsome man. Many years my junior was Representative Lane Evans of Illinois. He was Marine and, in Congress, he worked tirelessly for peace, playing a major role in delivering a majority of his party's votes against that resolution endorsing the Reagan Administration's foolish intervention in the Lebanese civil war. He softly spoke powerfully persuasive words in congressional debates. Then one day he fell ill. Yet, despite his bout with Parkinson's, he bravely continued the "good fight" against fighting.

Ah, this handsome lady was my successor in office. She was elected to the Congress in 1996 and re-elected in 1998, receiving 58 percent of the vote. U.S. Representative Julia Carson, my co-worker, was against war right from our congressional beginning in 1965. She was later *twice* voted *Woman of the Year* by readers of the *Indianapolis Star,* having had an illustrious career in public service before entering Congress. For years she was a member of the Indiana State Legislature, first as a representative, then as a state senator. Later she showed them how it's done as Indianapolis Center Township Trustee. She entered that office to find a staggering debt, and she instituted efficiencies which swiftly wiped it out. Moreover, she put into effect the first and most effective *and humane* welfare reform in the country. Bellicose politicians from the Atlantic to the Pacific made the speeches and some political hay, but she made the difference; she made the reform. She was one of the most intelligent people I ever knew. Julia was very much family to my wife, Kim, and me. Eventually my father became to Julia the father figure she never had.

Now look at this erudite fellow. He was the first administrative assistant in our Washington congressional office. Enormously well read, Dick Franzen was also something of a disciplinarian, believing that a place of work is a place where everyone *should* work. In time, he mellowed and began to brook a little fun which lubricated the work machinery and enhanced the product. He was steadfast at my side in the work against unnecessary war. I learned a great deal from Dick. He was a valued friend.

This next lady will surely go to Heaven. She is surely a saint and will do much to make her surroundings Heaven on earth for others. She is U.S. Representative Elizabeth Furse from the state of Washington. A female Allard Lowenstein, she was born in Nairobi, Kenya to American parents who were working there. Her life since the beginning has been devoted to giving American life to the *Sermon on the Mount.* What a delight to be her friend.

Here are two laid-back lanky and enormously likable fellows. One, Lou Maiden, is a whiz at maintenance at the U.S. Capitol and the other is the already towering figure of U.S. history, Morris K. Udall of Arizona. Both played their strong roles in the peace movement. Lou not only had the wisdom both hardships and superior intellect produce, he was my fellow Great Dane fancier. Mo Udall was a natural leader. He ran for president in 1976 and, but for labor rejection in Michigan, almost certainly would have been nominated and elected. The public would have seen him as a second Abe Lincoln because of his wise words and self-deprecating humor and, well, that "Lincoln something" even Carl Sandburg confessed he couldn't quite get into words. I think Mo would have gone on to be re-elected in 1980—and the national debt would not suddenly have tripled.

Dan McGinn is that exceptionally quiet-spoken fellow over there. We became close friends despite the fact that I initially perceived him to be aloof. He was a staffer for John Slack, a representative from West Virginia. John suddenly died in office and Dan needed a job in which, thank God, I was in a position (chairman of the Medicare Sub-committee) to place him. It was one of the nicest things I ever did for our country. Behind his refreshing stillness, ran very deep water. He was one of the most intelligent people it has ever been my privilege to know. His suggestions to me concerning foreign policy debates were invaluable. Eventually, his wife Deb joined us as a co-worker in the Washington congressional office. Following his Capitol Hill career, he became the owner of his own private business and became wealthy because of it. Deb went to work in the White House social office and dazzled official visitors. Her friend Theresa Guise was a staffer in our congressional office, too, and did some dazzling, herself. She dazzled all of us because whoever came to the office was someone she already knew and knew well. Eventually, she played a role in promoting the romance that joined Kim and I in marriage. To borrow from the Sarah Lee cake people, "Nobody didn't like Theresa."

Here is a man of letters whom I met at the scintillating dinner table of Florence Mahoney whom we shall meet in a moment. John Gardner founded *Common Cause,* the Ralph Nader-like citizens lobbying organization. John calls to mind the *iffy* words of Kipling, "If you can keep your head when all about you are losing theirs..." In the midst of the too often disorderly public protests against the American war in Vietnam and the corresponding bullheadedness of many in seats of authority, John wrote that if the American experiment ever fails, it will be because, "those who criticized its institutions did so without love and those who loved its institutions did so without criticism." He was a man of reason and, therefore, a man of peace.

Here is Florence Mahoney, heir to the vast Cox communication company. For decades, she was the den-mother for Democrats. Her beautiful home in Georgetown was a getaway for Margaret Truman when the latter's father worked down the street at the White House. Florence actually traveled the world with Margaret Higgins Sanger and was an effective advocate for women's good health. I met Florence one evening in the home of Senator Birch Bayh. The Senator's wife Marvella, who fell fatal victim to cancer a few years later, told me that the lady at the other end of the room liked the toast I had given during dinner and wanted to meet me. After Florence and I spoke for a while, she asked if I might be able to drive her to her home. That didn't seem like much of a chore, so I agreed, still not knowing just who she was. I began to believe she was pretty prominent, however, as we walked out into the night. Three limousines were parked at the curb and the owners of each implored Florence to let them give her a lift. No, she preferred to go with this young man she said. So we proceeded to my elderly Oldsmobile in which my Great Dane *C-5* regularly rode. Not to worry, she told me, "At the ranch in Idaho, we haul calves in the car all the time." Ranch in Idaho, yet! The fact that she strongly disagreed on foreign policy with the man who owned the Johnson Ranch on the Pedernales River in Texas meant she was a tower of strength for me.

People tend to believe that this fellow is humorless—not so. Meet Ralph Nader, another civil saint who literally dedicated his being to the safety of his fellow Americans, including those wrongfully sent by their government to unnecessary war. We had a brief fuss of sorts over a piece of legislation. Still, I never stopped admiring him and I am more than happy to report that he and I worked together on a very large number of public issues. He remains, of course, an American institution, a conscience for our country. His vast fame began with the Corvair automobile. His book about it, *Unsafe at Any Speed,* so disturbed the manufacturer that the corporation engaged a private detective firm to dig up some dirt on him. Since there was no dirt to be dug, the caper was a failure. The only thing the manufacturer got out of it was the detective bill and a lawsuit which forced the company to pay damages to its noble nemesis. In fairness, it should be added that by the 1964 model year, the bugs had been ironed out. My dad had one and loved it—my mom, too. Nevertheless, Ralph Nader was accurate in his criticism of the original models. I not only admired Ralph, I liked him.

Here's Barney Frank, the openly gay member of Congress. He is also the openly brilliant member of Congress. One of the most effective in the anti-unnecessary war movement. In some ways, I consider him the wittiest person ever to serve in the U.S. House. He was an ally of the great Al Lowenstein, whom we met earlier, and Barney was a voice for sensible priorities with the public purse.

It's nice that we have run across Sam here. You'd really like him. He was among the first American soldiers to enter France for the history-altering Normandy invasion. In fact he got there before the invasion—by parachute. An authentic American war hero, himself, tall affable Sam Gibbons became a U.S. Representative from Florida and eventually he chaired the Ways and Means Committee. Sam was my good friend and no friend at all of those illegal presidential wars. He was a champion for progress in our country. It is he who said in a meeting with President Bush's Secretary of Treasury, "Read my lips, no more *borrowing.*"

This next fellow will always have critics because he will almost always be right and not afraid to say what he is right about. He was one of the earliest opponents of the Vietnam foolishness. He was also the one who insisted on tracing the Watergate cash through Mexico at a time when even his fellow party members of the House Banking and Currency Committee thought the suggestion too brash. As usual, though, Texas U.S. Representative Henry B. Gonzalez was later celebrated for his perception. Henry was a delight, always pleasant, even jovial and always on the trail of the wrongdoers. Many of his colleagues scoffed at his early warnings of trouble in the savings and loan industry (not the S&L's in Indiana, by the way) and he was right again. Eventually, he became chairman of the House Banking and Currency Committee and continued to serve in the way that made his title more than poetry; he was, indeed, honorable.

That lanky fellow with the wry smile was an American prisoner of war after his bomber was shot down by the Nazis in World War II. He was a freshman with me in the 89th Congress. He was a strong opponent of the abuse of military power by presidents. He was elected U.S. Senator from Maine in 1972. When Bill Hathaway and Senator Bob Dole of Kansas served together on the Senate Finance Committee, they saved my life more that once. Without them, I would have died from boredom in the interminable series of House-Senate conferences on tax legislation. Each of them rivaled Barney Frank for wit and neither of them takes himself seriously.

You're about to have a real treat. This polite man is another scholar and gentleman. My co-workers and I had been in Washington for several years when along came a new co-worker. He was bright and affable Joe Romer, who not only had great suggestions to further the effort for sense in U.S. foreign policy, but went on to become two things, a high official in the Easter Seals organization and, together with his wife Theresa, among Kim's and my very best friends. His quiet idealism, blazing intellect, imaginative sense of humor and refreshing modesty are among the reasons we are so fortunate to be his friends.

This tall lady is among the most distinguished of the Hoosier state. She stood tall as one of my strongest supporters in the early days of my outspoken opposition to the Vietnam War. She was a reader and sharer of what she read, literally. Pat Ulen would go to great expense—which is to say voluminous photocopies—to share relevant and important information on public issues. Because of her voracious appetite for the printed word, she could find the objective truth no matter how hard unworthy people might work to obscure it. She reminds one of the late I.F. Stone. She had a great sense of humor, but in another sense she would brook no nonsense. Having her in my corner politically was my very good fortune.

This friendly fellow is another saint. He was born and reared in Tennessee at a time when civil rights for all citizens wasn't even considered. He went to Indianapolis in the late forties, joined the United Auto Workers, become an officer of the union and spent a career, not only advocating for its members, but insisting that God knew what God was doing when God varied the skin pigmentation of his children, all of whom God loved equally. Buford Holt who was of European descent was very early on the right side of history in the civil rights and anti-Vietnam movements. Buford reminded me of the TV character *Colombo,* modest—even self-effacing—with the gift of brilliance for problem solving and reconciliation between parties at odds. He was one of my heroes.

David Wildes and I operated especially well as co-workers and eventually he became the top staffer in our Washington office. As you might assume, he, too, was soft-spoken and bright. He was refreshingly empathetic. He was a natural at working well with such people as Marion Franz, the pretty and blazingly bright director of the Peace Tax Fund Foundation, an organization that advocated the perfect way for the government to get all that is due from conscientious objectors who withhold the part of their income taxes allocable to military matters. The fellow David often spoke with on the phone was back in the Indianapolis end of our hall. He was Steve Barnett and he was like the internet when it came to quickly-needed information. He had an uncanny capacity to know exactly what data to save in his files and could produce it immediately five years later to fill a need. A lot of his files were in the most personal of PCs, his head. Both of these friends would volunteer to work overtime when it came to preparing material to slow down a presidential plunge into wasteful war.

In 1968 at the Chicago Democratic Convention, we briefly met Bob McKinney, prominent Indianapolis attorney and businessman. Then and after, he gave me words of reassurance about my then controversial stand on the Vietnam War. His father and mine and his mother and mine were good friends and my mother told me that Bob would have to be a very nice person because of his "wonderful mother." My mother wasn't wrong. Bob McKinney achieved enormous success in a number of building-related businesses, including one of the state's most respected banks, *First Indiana*. He was also the pride of the Indianapolis law firm Bose, McKinney and Evans, but more than that, he was a public spirited pillar of our community. He was an Indiana leader in John F. Kennedy's 1960 campaign and when Kennedy came to Indianapolis to campaign, he was so taken with Bob, he invited the latter to join him for the rest of that week's campaign swing around the country.

Bob McKinney served on the Indiana University Board of Trustees and, in the seventies, he went to Washington to serve as chairman of the Federal Home Loan Bank. His presidential appointment was confirmed by the Senate. Once in office, he ran the Federal Home Loan Bank the way he ran his own bank, with skill, compassion and without a breath of impropriety. It's unfortunate for the country that he couldn't have continued to head the Federal Home Loan Bank. If he had, there would not have been a breath of impropriety in that institution. Under subsequent leadership, there was worse than just a breath of impropriety; there was outright scandal. Back in private life after my service in Washington, it was my privilege to serve on his First Indiana Bank's board of directors. There I saw up close his admirable character. He made wise and careful business decisions that profited his depositors and investors, but those decisions and those profits were specifically and intentionally never contrary to the public interest.

Here's another Indianapolis businessman you'd enjoy knowing. This is Jim Morris, once an aide to then-Mayor Richard Lugar. His talents were so superlative that from his association with Dick, he went on to fill a number of important posts in the private business sector, culminating in his becoming president of the Indianapolis Water Company. He, too, served as an Indiana University Trustee. Jim was an especially deeply religious man, not the unctuous sort, one of whom would be too many, but the sort who chose to follow the word of the Lord as expressed in the book of Mathew. He did his praying quietly and lived his religion constantly in his daily life—without fanfare. He was another of my fellow Hoosiers who encouraged me in my legislative battles against unnecessary wars.

While we're at it, let's meet two more Indianapolis businessmen, small businessmen, but significant businessmen because they, too, were ever mindful of the public good and well informed about it. This is Jim Warrum, earth grading, conduit and masonry contractor. I served with his brother Dick on the Marion County, Indiana Sheriff's force in my law school days. Jim helped Kim and me immensely with the building of our home. Grading and masonry were things we did not care to tackle ourselves. A major Hoosier weightlifter, he was runner-up to be Mr. Indiana in that category one year. He was gentle in discourse and in demeanor as well. He had the concern a citizen should, not only about the expenditure of the taxpayers' money, but of their sons' lives as well. He was always in my corner, also, when it came to unnecessary war.

The other Indianapolis small businessman we should greet is Jim Snyder. He and his associate Gil Wheeler installed and kept in good repair geothermal as well as conventional heating and cooling systems for Indianapolis. Jim Snyder was a scholar, gentleman and philosopher, who could cut through the confusion and shower his friends with insights that showed the way from war to peace.

Here are State Senators Glen Howard and Louie Mahern and Representatives Bill Crawford, Vanessa Summers, John Day and Candy Marendt. If you wanted honest officeholders with heartfelt devotion to the public betterment, you had to look no farther. While their official duties did not involve issues of foreign policy, their straight thinking was helpful to me when I discharged my duties in that arena.

Let's meet a couple of cops here. One can rightly be called a police officer's police officer. He served as a state trooper in both Florida and Alaska. He served in another uniform capacity; he was a combat infantry Marine who fought in Vietnam and later gave me encouragement in my efforts to curb violations of the Constitution in the war area by presidents. He became a small businessman, himself, and the small business was a big deal. His private company trained police officers all over our nation. His headquarters was in—brace yourself— Santa Claus, Indiana. He had a contract with the Indiana State Police to improve their already outstanding policing. Bill Westfall was one more modest and quiet-spoken child of God—who did God's work to help our society along toward gentler and safer ways.

This other police officer may have missed his calling to some extent. He should have been a television comedian. Instead, Indianapolis city police Lieutenant Don Burkert spent a career protecting and amusing his fellow citizens, and cheering me up when the war wimp chicken hawks were on the war path against me. A spoiled son turned on his father one night and beat the elder. Don and his partner Walt Thickston had the run. When the officers entered the home, the offender grabbed Don's winter uniform coat and pulled a button off. Without any expression of anger, Don simply made the wayward offspring sit down, then and there, and sew the button back. After that the miscreant became a guest of the taxpayers for a while. Borrowing from scriptures, a good police officer is worth her or his weight in rubies—although, in Big Don Burkert's case, that could be expensive.

That matinee idol standing over there, the one with the abundant blond hair, chiseled features and athletic build, was possibly the fastest wit in the Midwest. Attorney Jud Haggerty was an activist, political and civic. He once explained his humble and character-building Depression era origins to an assemblage of voters by saying, "I won't say I was born in a log cabin, but we moved into one as soon as we could afford it." Jud was fairly fearless in stating and acting on his political beliefs. His son, a Marine, was wounded in Vietnam. The father, however, was an outspoken opponent of President Johnson's policy of perfidy on Vietnam long before that. He was a natural leader who served in various public offices, including the Indiana State House of Representatives, the Marion County (Indianapolis) Prosecutor's Office and on the Marion County Election Board. His very presence was theater and he died much too soon.

This is Loretta Raikes. We worked together in the congressional office over three decades. Her thirst for justice and compassion for those *least of the little ones* the Lord called his brethren, was stunning to behold. She was bright, articulate and ready to see what was funny in the human comedy. Public life would have been much more difficult for me and my efforts against the policies of those 1600 killers much more of a burden without her.

This is Indianapolis Center Township Assessor Jim Maley, a man of encyclopedic knowledge about the civics of our society, current and historical, local and national. I could always count on him for good counsel on the deadly foreign policy of some federal officials. If you wanted to know the margin by which a given president was elected, you didn't bother with the internet; you just asked Jim. Compassionate to a fault, it's a wonder he ever managed to be fully clothed. Every day he tended to give someone the proverbial shirt off his back. He was willing to risk his own political success to help a friend who was running for office. He certainly did that for me. Civics was not the only area where his knowledge was vast; Bob Hope would have done well to have bought Jim Maley's list of memorized jokes. Jim Maley did well not to sell them. He continued to use them himself to the delight of everyone around him.

Look at this distinguished woman, my political ally on the Vietnam issue from the very start. Hers was Herculean discipline and literary excellence, truly a scholar and a lady. Patty Welch not only managed to earn her Ph.D. in enormously effective child development, she also had to her credit a stint as an editor at Bobbs-Merrill, the fine old Indiana firm that, among other more significant books such as *The Joy of Cooking,* published my first book, *The Powell Affair: Freedom Minus One.* She found time over the years to be an important political activist. St. Mary's Child Center of Indianapolis was most fortunate to have her as its director.

See the fellow over there beside the bicycle? (That's typical of him, but not the most significant thing about him.) This is Colman McCarthy, one of the most gifted writers God ever put on earth. Let's get the former managing editor of the *Washington Post* and, before that, of the *Atlanta Constitution,* Gene (Red) Patterson to tell us about Coleman's entry into the world of professional journalism. Red told this to us at that fabled Florence Mahoney table in Georgetown:

> This disheveled fellow walked into my office at the *Atlanta Constitution* and stuttered, 'I want to b-be a wr-writer.' My reaction was bewildered and charitable. I

asked if he had any samples of his work and he handed me a portfolio. I opened it, prepared for the worst, but that's not what I found. It was golden paintings and silver pears. Containing my surprise, I asked what he wanted to write about and he said, 'Sp-sports.' Later, when he was working for a wire service in New York, rounding up the week-end athletic scores, he was heard to say, 'Wh-what the hell are the D-Dodgers doing in Los Angeles?' Before Colman came to the *Constitution* he had been cloistered in Thomas Merton's *Seven Story Mountain* studying to be a Trappist monk which he had decided against. It was while he was there that the Brooklyn Dodgers moved to Los Angeles.

Colman's speech impediment was not unique among journalists, even broadcast journalists. Of course, by the time the ones in broadcasting got into broadcasting, they had managed to correct the problem. Along the way of a brilliant journalism career, Colman slipped out of his speaking handicap. He also slipped out of the stereotypical mold of hard-nosed journalism. He became one of the nations leading advocates for peaceful resolution of conflicts, even going so far as to establish a high school and post-secondary academic course on the ways of peace. This gentle man has been one of my greatest inspirations and most admired friends.

Look over here and see another super handsome man. He was one of the most articulate speakers you could ever hope to hear. His education was largely from that most comprehensive of institutions, the school of hard knocks. He was immaculately groomed, soft spoken and polite to a fault—God's gift, not only to women, but to all God's children. Meet U.S. Representative Kweisi Mfume—and try to pronounce his name on the first try (Kwy-see M- Fume-may). He represented a district in Maryland and his words of wisdom changed more than a few congressional minds for the better ways of peace. Later, he resigned from Congress to become head of the NAACP where he continued to dazzle all who saw and heard him.

Jim Beatty, my close friend, is the one sitting over there, taking it all in. He reminded me of my mother's favorite poem:

A wise old owl sat in an oak
The more he saw, the less he spoke
The less he spoke, the more he heard
Why can't we be like that wise old bird

Well, maybe *we're* not, but Jim Beatty was. God gave him something very special, the ability to think clearly on a lofty philosophical level and to do the same in the minutia of life's nuts and bolts. That made him one of the most talented and effective political county chairpeople in the history of Indiana. When he shifted into the detail gear of nuts and bolts, he produced organization that harnessed political energy and maximized the best possibilities for his party. When he shifted into the high gear of political philosophy, his carefully thought-out thoughts were lofty and altruistic. His friendship and very early political support are among my most cherished treasures. His wife Phyllis was my philologist; if I groped for a word and she was there, she always had it for me immediately. Both she and he were among my strongest backers on those many and controversial war issues.

If you don't look closely, you might miss her, but here is Bessie Gasaway, who, though tiny in physical stature, is a giant of principles in a sometimes unprincipled political world. She was a tower of strength in efforts toward a world of peace through the political process. As in the case of Jim Beatty, she was one of my earliest supporters, especially in matters of war and peace, and her memory continues to warm my heart.

You'd be impressed just by seeing this woman. Who wouldn't be? She is plainly, or rather beautifully, Cynthia McKinney. She was the embodiment of "those bright eyes and sweet smile" immortalized in the *Red River Valley.* Cynthia McKinney could have been a Hollywood goddess; she could have got by on her looks alone. She had two more things: brains and, more important, the discipline to use those brains to achieve a distinguished college record including a Ph.D. That was remarkable because she was pursuing the Ph.D. while working in a much more than full time job in Washington. Meet U.S. Representative Cynthia McKinney of Georgia. She had another outstanding quality; courage, the courage to call them as she saw them and she saw them with common sense, especially in the area of unnecessary and unconstitutional presidential wars. When she was first elected to the House, the district in which she ran was easy for her to win. The second time out, however, the geography and demography had been changed by the Georgia authorities. The new district was drawn in the form of a political gas chamber for her. It was assumed by pundits that she didn't have a chance. Perhaps she didn't, but the voters didn't know it. They saw the qualities I have described and sent her back to Washington.

We met James Porter Seidensticker in the acknowledgements of this volume—an old friend and early supporter. Standing next to Jim here is Gary Taylor, also an early supporter of mine, eventually becoming my campaign chairman. Gary was a lawyer for the American United Insurance company which, of course, would place him in the yuppie category. The fact that he was a faithful member of the Methodist church meant there could be little doubt that he fit into the group described by Eric Sevareid as "cultivating the proper friends, thinking the proper thoughts and, as Thomas Wolf described them, 'men of measured merriment and of measured tears.'" Looking at Gary's face, plain glasses and even plainer expression, you would conclude that there was no merriment to be measured, but you'd conclude at your peril. Behind all those establishment credentials, behind that placid countenance and those small-town bookkeeper's eye glasses, lay a blazing mind cooking up the most delightful of mischievous pranks. One of his long-running put-ons made him the toast of the Indianapolis service club circuit as a lunch speaker. It would be unfair of me to tell you about the continuing practical joke he is so deftly playing at the expense of people who make their money in a less than admirable old fashioned way. At this writing, he is writing a book about it and should, that is *should* finish soon. Illustrative of his sneaking shticks, however, is the fax he sent to our Washington congressional office immediately after I was obliged to cast an enormously controversial vote. It read as follows:

> I hope you're satisfied. You've made enemies for me of
> half my friends whom I assured you'd never do anything
> this asinine. Get yourself a new campaign chairman.

Gary Gene Taylor

The co-worker who brought the message to my desk, was all but trembling with concern. He knew the National Rifle Association would be less than enchanted with the vote to restrict the size of ammunition magazines, but here was Gary Taylor, a close through-thick-and-thin friend expressing terminal words about our association. I asked a direct question of my co-worker: "Don't you know Gary by now?" Gary managed to stay on as chairman, taking pride in the fact that he had at least fooled my co-worker. When it came to his support of my foreign policy efforts, there was no fooling at all. He was squarely in my corner.

Did you ever see anyone more dapper than this next fellow? Look at the perfect-fitting tweed suit, the elegant white shirt and, of course, the bow tie as befits a thoughtful journalist of the old school. He is none less than John V. Wilson who went to Washington as correspondent for the *Indianapolis Times* about one year before I first arrived to serve in the Congress. John and I were already good friends from my days in the sheriff's office when he was a city-side reporter for the *Times.* By the time I first ran for Congress and lost, he was assigned to cover both my opponent's and my campaigns, tagging along with the opponent one day and with me the next. As we rode in my car from one stop to the next, John casually mentioned something "Don" had said the day before. "Don" was my opponent and, being young and callow, I expressed displeasure at the friendly-sounding reference my friend John made to him. "Don!", I exclaimed to John. "Well, we'd better just talk about it after the election," my somewhat older and much wiser and bemused friend said. John went from journalism to the public relations office of the Department of Justice and had a distinguished career there. He figured prominently in my opposition of the Johnson-Nixon unconstitutional war.

Speaking of dapper, this is Bud Myers. He spent the night with as yet uncounted absentee ballots to ensure their security when I was first elected to Congress. "Greater love…" He became one of my co-workers in the Washington congressional office and, by the time Bud retired in the 1990s, he had been the top assistant to four different members of the U.S. House—quite likely a record. His quiet demeanor and wise judgements were prized by all who worked with him. He was shoulder-to-shoulder with me in opposing those game-board wars of the various presidents with whom we served. When I decided that it would be improper to accept an inordinate congressional pay raise in 1969, he volunteered to turn down a pay raise that applied to him.

Here is another colorful person who has participated mightily in my political efforts. She is fabulously well-read, has the fastest wit of any of my associates and was kind enough to give me four wise and witty nephews, Tom, Mart, Dan and Greg. Meet my sister Marge Landwerlen, whose husband Tom is more brother than brother-in-law to me. Kin Hubbard's Abe Martin character said, "Nothin 'ul take the starch out of a great man like meetin' a feller who don't think much of it." I've tried not to be a stuffed starched shirt, but when Marge found even so much as a suggestion of it in me, she was always able to wring it out in an appropriate and pithy phrase. For example, when I became a police officer at a relatively tender—certainly callow—age, I told Marge I might just get an "AR" license plate. For some reason which I have long since forgotten, such a plate was supposed to indicate importance. Marge had a response: "AR plate, big deal." To which I said, "Well, it's not just anybody who can get one." Back came her reply in mock agreement, "No, you have to have a car." In my loneliest moments of early opposition to the Vietnam War, it was Marge who always seemed able to cheer me most.

Of course, other members of my family helped keep me humble along the way and especially in the case of those nephews, were squarely in my corner during each election campaign and my peace efforts. My wife Kim managed to keep me on an even keel and well-supplied with witticisms for those campaigns as have our young sons Andy and Steve. My dad and mother were constantly helpful to me in those efforts, too. They, more than any others on earth brought me along in the ways of justice and peace. They reared me to understand that savage *March of Folly* about which Barbara Tuchman so wisely wrote.

Dad said, "Nobody ever got anywhere without a lot of help from a lot of other people." My experience in the. world of politics and government has been a long-standing example of that variety. The number of people who, through the years, have helped me would boggle a fairly proficient computer. Even if they read this book, they will never know how much they comforted and sustained me during my thirty-year official journey through American history. They will never know because I will never know how to put it all into words. Many of those friends are not mentioned here, but still loom large in my debt of gratitude. If you are one of them, I give you my heart-felt thanks.

INDEX

A

Acheson, Dean G. 154
Adams, John 39, 162, 173
Adams, John Quincy 156
Agnew, Spiro 96, 97
airrorism 178
al-Asad, Hafiz 154
Albert, Carl 185
Albright, Madeline 165
American Bankers Association 181
Amos 'N Andy 28
Anderson, Bill 192
Anderson, John B. 82
Armstrong, James 87, 193, 194
Aspen, Les 106

B

Baker, Jim 155
Barnett, Steve 202
Bauman, Robert 186
Baxter, Oscar F. 80
Bayh, Birch 47, 115, 199
Beatty, Jim 61, 206
Belafonte, Harry 53
Bennett, William 173
Bishop, Maurice 122
Black, Shirley Temple 105
Bolt, Robert 62, 169
Bradley, Omar Nelson 53
Bray, Bill 60
Broder, David 166
Brown, Andrew 155, 193
Brown, Rosalie 194
Brown, Tommy 194
Browning, Charles 59
Brownson, Chuck 183
Buchanan, Pat 143
Burkert, Don 204

COMING SOON

SLANDER AND SWEET JUDGEMENT

by Andy Jacobs, Jr.

"You can't throw dirt without losing ground."
—Adlai Ewing Stevenson

"Apples to sweeten my judgement."
—Jurist Thomas Moore (to litigant who offered candied fruit)

"Never watch sausage or laws being made."
—Otto Von Bismarck